# Adobe®
# PHOTOSHOP® CS6
## INTRODUCTORY

Joy L. Starks

COURSE TECHNOLOGY
CENGAGE Learning®

SHELLY
CASHMAN
SERIES®

Australia • Brazil • Japan • Korea • Mexico • Singapore • Spain • United Kingdom • United States

**COURSE TECHNOLOGY**
CENGAGE Learning·

**Adobe® Photoshop® CS6: Introductory**
Joy L. Starks

Editor-in-Chief: Marie Lee

Executive Editor: Kathleen McMahon

Senior Product Manager: Emma Newsom

Associate Product Manager: Caitlin Womersley

Editorial Assistant: Sarah Ryan

Director of Marketing: Cheryl Costantini

Marketing Manager: Adrienne Fung

Marketing Coordinator: Michael Saver

Print Buyer: Julio Esperas

Director of Production: Patty Stephan

Content Project Manager: Jennifer Feltri-George

Developmental Editor: Amanda Brodkin

QA Manuscript Reviewers: Danielle Shaw

Copyeditor: Foxxe Editorial

Proofreader: Kim Kosmatka

Indexer: Rich Carlson

Art Director: Jackie Bates, GEX Publishing Services

Cover and Text Design: Lisa Kuhn, Curio Press, LLC

Cover Photo: Tom Kates Photography

Compositor: PreMediaGlobal

For product information and technology assistance, contact us at
**Cengage Learning Customer & Sales Support, 1-800-354-9706**

For permission to use material from this text or product, submit all requests online at **cengage.com/permissions**
Further permissions questions can be emailed to
**permissionrequest@cengage.com**

Library of Congress Control Number: 2012939209
ISBN-13: 978-1-133-52591-2
ISBN-10: 1-133-52591-1

**Course Technology**
20 Channel Center Street
Boston, Massachusetts 02210
USA

Adobe, the Adobe logos, and Photoshop are either registered trademarks or trademarks of Adobe Systems Incorporated in the United States and/or other countries. THIS PRODUCT IS NOT ENDORSED OR SPONSORED BY ADOBE SYSTEMS INCORPORATED, PUBLISHER OF PHOTOSHOP.

Cengage Learning is a leading provider of customized learning solutions with office locations around the globe, including Singapore, the United Kingdom, Australia, Mexico, Brazil, and Japan. Locate your local office at:
**international.cengage.com/region**

Cengage Learning products are represented in Canada by Nelson Education, Ltd.

For your course and learning solutions, visit **www.cengage.com**

To learn more about Course Technology,
visit **www.cengage.com/coursetechnology**

Purchase any of our products at your local college bookstore or at our preferred online store **www.cengagebrain.com**

Printed in the United States of America
1 2 3 4 5 6 7 18 17 16 15 14 13 12

# Adobe® PHOTOSHOP® CS6
## INTRODUCTORY

# Contents

iii

# Appendices

# Preface

The Shelly Cashman Series® offers the finest textbooks in computer education. We are proud of the fact that our previous Photoshop® books have been so well received. With each new edition of our Photoshop® books, we have made significant improvements based on the comments made by instructors and students. The Adobe® Photoshop® CS6 books continue with the innovation, quality, and reliability you have come to expect from the Shelly Cashman Series®.

For this Photoshop® CS6 text, the Shelly Cashman Series® development team carefully reviewed our pedagogy and analyzed its effectiveness in teaching today's student. Students today read less, but need to retain more. They not only need to be able to perform skills, but to retain those skills and know how to apply them to different settings. Today's students need to be continually engaged and challenged to retain what they're learning.

With this Photoshop® CS6 text, we continue our commitment to focusing on the user and how they learn best.

## Objectives of This Textbook

*Adobe® Photoshop® CS6: Introductory* is intended for a course that offers an introduction to Photoshop® and image editing. No previous experience with Adobe® Photoshop® CS6 is assumed, and no mathematics beyond the high school freshman level is required.

The objectives of this book are:

- To teach the fundamentals and more advanced features of Adobe® Photoshop® CS6 using student-focused exercises

- To expose students to image editing and graphic design fundamentals

- To develop an exercise-oriented approach that promotes learning by doing

- To encourage independent study and to help those who are working alone

## The Shelly Cashman Approach

### A Proven Pedagogy with an Emphasis on Project Planning

Each chapter presents a practical problem to be solved, within a project planning framework. The project orientation is strengthened by the use of Plan Ahead boxes, that encourage critical thinking about how to proceed at various points in the project. Step-by-step instructions with supporting screens guide students through the steps. Instructional steps are supported by the Q&A, Experimental Step, and BTW features.

### A Visually Engaging Book that Maintains Student Interest

The step-by-step tasks, with supporting figures, provide a rich visual experience for the student. Call-outs on the screens that present both explanatory and navigational information provide students with information they need, when they need to know it. Each chapter presents a real-world, photo scenario with current topics and new CS6 features.

### Supporting Reference Materials (Quick Reference, Appendices)

The appendices provide additional information about the application at hand, such as the Help Feature and customizing the application, as well as a new appendix, For Mac Users. With the Quick Reference, students can quickly look up information about a single task, such as keyboard shortcuts, and find page references of where in the book the task is illustrated.

### Integration of the World Wide Web

The World Wide Web is integrated into the Photoshop CS6 learning experience by (1) BTW annotations; and (2) a Quick Reference Summary Web page.

### End-of-Chapter Student Activities

Extensive end of chapter activities provide a variety of reinforcement opportunities for students where they can apply and expand their skills through individual and group work. To complete some of these assignments, you will be required to use the Data Files for Students. Visit http://www.cengage.com/ct/studentdownload for detailed access instructions or contact your instructor for information about accessing the required files.

## New To This Edition

### Completely Updated for CS6 Features

This edition reflect all of the new CS6 features, including the new Content-Aware Patch and Move, the new Crop Tool, the new Blur gallery and others!

### Mac User Support

A new appendix, For Mac Users, provides information and details for students on a Mac where instructions may differ.

### Publishing to a Web Server

A new appendix discusses considerations and instructions for publishing to a web server.

### New Images

Updated photos in chapter project reflect topics of interest and are geared towards today's students.

## Instructor Resources

The Instructor Resources include both teaching and testing aids that can be accessed via the Instructor Resouce CD or at www.cengage.com/login.

**Instructor's Manual** Includes lecture notes summarizing the chapter sections, figures and boxed elements found in every chapter, teacher tips, classroom activities, lab activities, and quick quizzes in Microsoft Word files.

**Syllabus** Easily customizable sample syllabi that cover policies, assignments, exams, and other course information.

**Data Files for Students** Illustrations for every figure in the textbook in electronic form. Visit www.cengage.com/ct/studentdownload for detailed instructions.

**PowerPoint Presentations** A multimedia lecture presentation system that provides slides for each chapter. Presentations are based on chapter objectives.

**Solutions to Exercises** Includes solutions for all end-of-chapter and chapter reinforcement exercises.

**Test Bank & Test Engine** Test Bank includes 112 questions for every chapter, featuring objective-based and critical thinking question types, including page number references and figure references, when appropriate. Also included is the test engine, ExamView, the ultimate tool for your objective-based testing needs.

| BOOK RESOURCES |
| --- |
| 🔒 Blackboard Testbank |
| 🔒 Instructor's Manual |
| 🔒 Lecture Success System |
| 🔒 PowerPoint Presentations |
| 🔒 Solutions to Exercises (Windows) |
| 🔒 Syllabus |
| 🔒 Test Bank and Test Engine |
| 🔒 WebCT Testbank |

**Additional Activities for Students** Consists of Chapter Reinforcement Exercises, which are true/false, multiple-choice, and short answer questions that help students gain confidence in the material learned.

## Learn Online

CengageBrain.com is the premier destination for purchasing or renting Cengage Learning textbooks, ebooks, eChapters and study tools, at a significant discount (eBooks up to 50% off Print). In addition, CengageBrain.com provides direct access to all digital products including eBooks, eChapters and digital solutions (i.e. CourseMate, SAM) regardless of where purchased. The following are some examples of what is available for this product on www.cengagebrain.com.

**Student Companion Site** Quizzing, learning games and activities are available for no additional cost at www.cenagebrain.com to help reinforce chapter terms and concepts.

**Adobe Photoshop CS6 CourseMate** CourseMate with ebook for Adobe Photoshop CS6 keeps today's students engaged and involved in the learning experience. Adobe Photoshop CS6 CourseMate includes an integrated, multi-media rich and eBook, and a variety of interactive learning tools, including quizzes, activities, videos, and other resources that specifically reinforce and build on the concepts presented in the chapter. These interactive activities are tracked within CourseMate's Engagement Tracker, making it easy to assess students' retention of concepts. All of these resources enable students to get more comfortable using technology and help prepare students to use the Internet as a tool to enrich their lives. Available at the Comprehensive level in Spring 2013.

## CourseNotes

Course Technology's CourseNotes are six-panel quick reference cards that reinforce the most important and widely used features of a software application in a visual and user-friendly format. CourseNotes serve as a great reference tool during and after the course. CourseNotes are available for software applications, such as Microsoft Office 2010, Word 2010, PowerPoint 2010, Excel 2010, Access 2010, and Windows 7. There are also topic-based CourseNotes available for Best Practices in Social Networking, Hot Topics in Technology, and Web 2.0. Visit www.cengage.com/ct/coursenotes to learn more!

**course|notes™**
quick reference guide

## About Our Covers

The Shelly Cashman Series is continually updating our approach and content to reflect the way today's students learn and experience new technology. This focus on student success is reflected on our covers, which feature real students from Naugatuck Valley Community College using the Shelly Cashman Series in their courses, and reflect the varied ages and backgrounds of the students learning with our books. When you use the Shelly Cashman Series, you can be assured that you are learning computer skills using the most effective courseware available.

# Textbook Walk-Through

**Plan Ahead** boxes prepare students to create successful projects by encouraging them to think strategically about what they are trying to accomplish before they begin working.

**Step-by-step** instructions now provide a context beyond the point-and-click. Each step provides information on why students are performing each task, or what will occur as a result.

**2**
- Click Reset All Tools to display a confirmation dialog box (Figure 1–9).

**3**
- Click the OK button to restore the tools to their default settings.

Fig...

---

**BTW**
**Screen Resolution**
If your system has a high-resolution monitor with a screen resolution of 1280 × 800 or higher, lowering that resolution to 1024 × 768 might cause some images to be distorted because of a difference in the aspect ratio. If you want to keep your high-resolution setting, be aware that the location of on-screen tools might vary slightly from the book.

## Overview

As you read this chapter, you will learn how to edit the photo shown in Figure 1–1a on the previous page by performing these general tasks:

- Customize the workspace.
- Display and navigate a photo at various magnifications.
- Crop a photo effectively.
- Create and modify a border.
- Stroke a selection.
- Resize and print a photo.
- Save, close, and then reopen a photo.
- Add stroked text to the photo.
- Save a photo for the Web.
- Use Photoshop Help.

**Plan Ahead**

**General Project Guidelines**
When editing a photo, the actions you perform and decisions you make will affect the appearance and characteristics of the finished product. As you edit a photo, such as the one shown in Figure 1–1a, you should follow these general guidelines:

1. **Find an appropriate image or photo.** Keep in mind the purpose and the graphic needs of the project when choosing an image or photo. Decide ahead of time on the file type and decide if the image will be used on the Web. An eye-catching graphic image should convey a theme that is understood universally. The photo should grab the attention of viewers and draw them into the picture, whether in print or on the Web.

2. **Determine how to edit the photo to highlight the theme.** As you edit, use standard design principles, and keep in mind your subject, your audience, the required size and shape of the graphic, color decisions, the rule of thirds, the golden rectangle, and other design principles. Decide which parts of the photo portray your message and which parts are visual clutter. Crop the photo as needed.

3. **Identify finishing touches that will further enhance the photo.** The overall appearance of a photo significantly affects its ability to communicate clearly. You might want to add text or a border.

4. **Prepare for publication.** Resize the photo as needed to fit the allotted space. Save the photo on a storage medium, such as a hard drive, USB flash drive, or CD. Print the photo or publish it to the Web.

When necessary, more specific details concerning the above guidelines are presented at appropriate points in the chapter. The chapter also will identify the actions performed and decisions made regarding these guidelines during the creation of the edited photo shown in Figure 1–1b on the previous page.

**BTW**
**By The Way Boxes**
For a complete list of the BTWs found in the margins of this book, visit the BTW chapter resource on the student companion site located at www .cengagebrain.com.

## Starting Photoshop

If you are using a computer to step through the project in this chapter, and you want your screen to match the figures in this book, you should change your screen's resolution to 1024 × 768. For information about how to change a screen's resolution, read Appendix F, the Changing Screen Resolution appendix.

### To Start Photoshop

The following steps, which assume Windows 7 is running, start Photoshop, based on a typical installation. You may need to ask your instructor how to start Photoshop for your computer.

---

### To Reset the Interface Color

Photoshop CS6 allows the user to choose from among four different color schemes for the interface: Black, Dark Gray, Medium Gray, and Light Gray. The color scheme you choose depends upon your personal preferences for contrast, focus, and readability.

The following steps reset the interface color to Medium Gray, which displays the work area in dark gray and the panels in medium gray.

**1**
- Click Edit on the Application bar, and then point to Preferences to display the Preferences submenu (Figure 1–10).

Edit menu command

Edit menu

Preferences submenu

Preferences command

Interface command

**Explanatory** callouts summarize what is happening on screen.

**Navigational** callouts in red show students where to click.

**Figure 1–10**

# Textbook Walk-Through

**Q&A** boxes offer questions students may have when working through the steps and provide additional information about what they are doing right where they need it.

## To Select the Default Tool

The following step selects the Rectangular Marquee Tool, which is the default tool for a new installation of Photoshop. When you select a tool on the Tools panel, the options bar reflects the settings of that tool.

**1**

- If the tools on the Tools panel appear in two columns, click the double arrow at the top of the Tools panel.

- If necessary, click the second button from the top on the Tools panel to select it (Figure 1–7).

- If the button does not display a square icon, right-click the button and then click Rectangular Marquee Tool on the context menu.

**Q&A**
What appears when I point to the button?

When you point to many objects in the Photoshop workspace, such as a tool or button, Photoshop displays a tool tip. A **tool tip** is a short, on-screen note associated with the object to which you are pointing, which helps you identify the object. This button's name is the Rectangular Marquee Tool.

Figure 1–7

**Other Ways**
1. Press M

## To Reset the Options Bar

As you work through the chapters, editing and creating images, you will find that the options bar is **context sensitive**, which means it changes as you select different tools. In addition, the options and settings are retained for the next time you use Photoshop. To match the figures in this book, you should reset the options ... oshop. A **context menu**, or **shortcut menu**, appears when ... space. The menu displays commands representing the active

... the options bar using a context menu.

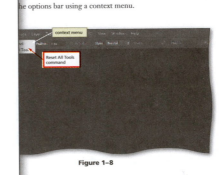

Figure 1–8

---

**BTW**

**Q&A**
For a complete list of the Q&As found in many of the step-by-step sequences in this book, visit the Q&A chapter resource on the student companion site located at www.cengagebrain.com.

## Customizing the Photoshop Workspace

The screen in Figure 1–3 on the previous page shows how the Photoshop workspace looks the first time you start Photoshop after installation on most computers. Photoshop does not open a blank or default photo automatically; rather, the Application bar and the options bar appear across the top of the screen with a work area below the options bar. The Tools panel is displayed on the left; other panels are displayed on the right and across the bottom. The work area and panels are referred to collectively as the **workspace**.

As you work in Photoshop, the panels, the selected tool, and the options bar settings might change. Therefore, if you want your screen to match the figures in this book, you should restore the default workspace, select the default tool, and reset the options bar. In addition, users might change the default color for the workspace. For more information about how to change other advanced Photoshop settings, see the Changing Screen Resolution appendix.

Because of a default preference setting, each time you start Photoshop, the Photoshop workspace is displayed the same way it was the last time you used Photoshop. If you (or another user) move the panels while working in Photoshop, they will appear in their new locations the next time you start Photoshop. You can create and save your own workspaces, or use Photoshop's saved workspaces that show groups of panels used for certain tasks. For example, the Painting workspace displays the Brush panel, the Brush presets panel, and the Swatches panel, among others — all of which you would need when painting. You will learn more about panels later in this chapter. Similarly, if values on the options bar are changed or a different tool is selected, they will remain changed the next time you start Photoshop. If you want to return the workspace to its default settings, follow these steps each time you start Photoshop.

## To Select the Essentials Workspace

The default workspace, called Essentials, displays commonly used panels. The following steps select the Essentials workspace and reset its default values.

**1**

- Click Window on the Application bar to display the Window menu.

- Point to Workspace on the Window menu to display the Workspace submenu (Figure 1–4).

**Experiment**

- Click each of the workspaces that are displayed in the list to view the different panel configurations. Notice that Photoshop displays a check mark on the menu, next to the chosen workspace. When you are finished, click Window on the Application bar and then point to Workspace again to display the submenu.

Figure 1–4

**Experiment Steps** within our step-by-step instructions, encourage students to explore, experiment, and take advantage of the features of the Photoshop CS6 user interface. These steps are not necessary to complete the projects, but are designed to increase the confidence with the software and build problem-solving skills.

### To Select the Default Tool

The following step selects the Rectangular Marquee Tool, which is the default tool for a new installation of Photoshop. When you select a tool on the Tools panel, the options bar reflects the settings of that tool.

**1**
- If the tools on the Tools panel appear in two columns, click the double arrow at the top of the Tools panel.

- If necessary, click the second button from the top on the Tools panel to select it (Figure 1–7).

- If the button does not display a square icon, right-click the button and then click Rectangular Marquee Tool on the context menu.

**Q&A** What appears when I point to the button?

When you point to many objects in the Photoshop workspace, such as a tool or button, Photoshop displays a tool tip. A **tool tip** is a short, on-screen note associated with the object to which you are pointing, which helps you identify the object. This button's name is the Rectangular Marquee Tool.

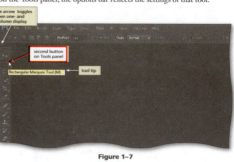

**Figure 1–7**

**Other Ways**
1. Press M

### To Reset the Options Bar

As you work through the chapters, editing and creating images, you will find that the options bar is **context sensitive**, which means it changes as you select different tools. In addition, the options and settings are retained for the next time you use Photoshop. To match the figures in this book, you should reset the options bar, using a context menu, each time you start Photoshop. A **context menu**, or **shortcut menu**, appears when you right-click some objects in the Photoshop workspace. The menu displays commands representing the active ... the options bar using a context menu.

**Figure 1–8**

**Photoshop Chapter 1**

## Chapter Summary

In this chapter, you gained a broad knowledge of Photoshop. First, you learned how to start Photoshop. You were introduced to the Photoshop workspace. You learned how to open a photo, change the magnification, zoom, and display rulers. You learned about design issues related to the placement of visual points of interest. You then learned how to crop a photo to eliminate extraneous background. After you added a blended border, you resized the image and added text. Once you saved the photo, you learned how to print it. You used the Save for Web command to optimize and save a Web version. You learned how to use Adobe Help to research specific help topics. Finally, you learned how to quit Photoshop.

The items listed below include all the new Photoshop skills you have learned in this chapter:

1. Start Photoshop (PS 4)
2. Select the Essentials Workspace (PS 6)
3. Select the Default Tool (PS 8)
4. Reset the Options Bar (PS 8)
5. Reset the Interface Color (PS 9)
6. Open a File (PS 11)
7. Save a File in the PSD Format (PS 20)
8. Use the Zoom Tool (PS 24)
9. Use the Navigator Panel (PS 26)
10. Minimize the Navigator Panel (PS 27)
11. Use the Hand Tool (PS 28)
12. Change the Magnification (PS 29)
13. Display Rulers (PS 30)
14. Crop a Photo (PS 33)
15. Create a Selection (PS 35)
16. Stroke a Selection (PS 36)
17. Modify a Selection (PS 39)
18. Switch Foreground and Background Colors (PS 40)
19. Deselect (PS 41)
20. Save a File with the Same File Name (PS 42)
21. Close a File (PS 42)
22. Open a Recent File (PS 43)
23. Resize the Image (PS 45)
24. Select the Horizontal Type Tool (PS 47)
25. Set Font Options (PS 47)
26. Insert Text (PS 48)
27. Stroke Text (PS 50)
28. Save a File with a Different Name (PS 51)
29. Print a Photo (PS 52)
30. Preview using the Save for Web Dialog Box (PS 53)
31. Choose a Download Speed (PS 54)
32. Preview the Photo on the Web (PS 55)
33. Save the Photo for the Web (PS 56)
34. Access Photoshop Help (PS 58)
35. Use the Help Search Box (PS 58)
36. Quit Photoshop (PS 60)

### Apply Your Knowledge

Reinforce the skills and apply the concepts you learned in this chapter.

#### Editing a Photo in the Photoshop Workspace

*Instructions:* Start Photoshop and perform the customization steps found on pages PS 6 through PS 10. Open the Apply 1-1 Water Park file in the Chapter 01 folder from the Data Files for Students. Visit www.cengage.com/ct/studentdownload for detailed instructions or contact your instructor for information about accessing the required files.

First, you will save the photo in the PSD format, then you will crop the photo, add a white border, and save the edited photo, as shown in Figure 1–87 on the next page. Next, you will resize the photo for printing and print one copy. Finally, you will reopen your edited photo, and then you will optimize it for the Web, save it, and close it.

*Continued >*

# Textbook Walk-Through

15. Select using the Lasso Tool (PS 100)
16. Subtract from a Selection using the Magic Wand Tool (PS 102)
17. Select using the Elliptical Marquee Tool (PS 105)
18. Subtract Noncontiguous Pixels of the Same Color (PS 106)
19. Duplicate and Scale (PS 107)
20. Reselect (PS 108)

21. Fit Screen (PS 110)
22. Crop a Selection (PS 110)
23. Save a Photo in the PDF Format (PS 112)
24. Create a New Keyboard Shortcut (PS 114)
25. Test a New Keyboard Shortcut (PS 117)
26. Return to the Default Settings for Keyboard Shortcuts (PS 118)

## Apply Your Knowledge

Reinforce the skills and apply the concepts you learned in this chapter.

### Moving and Duplicating Selections

*Instructions:* Start Photoshop and perform the customization steps found on pages PS 6 through PS 10. Open the Apply 2-1 Bread file in the Chapter 02 folder from the Data Files for Students and save it, in the PSD file format, as Apply 2-1 Bread Edited. Visit www.cengage.com/ct/studentdownload for detailed instructions or contact your instructor for information about accessing the required files.

You will create a grocery advertisement featuring bakery items. First, you will select individual items from within the file, and then you will transform and move them so that the finished design looks like Figure 2–72. You will place the rest of the images from back to front.

**Figure 2–72**

---

**Apply Your Knowledge** usually requires students to open and manipulate a file from the Data Files that parallels the activities learned in the chapter.

7. To create the border:

a. If necessary, press the D key to select the default colors. Press the x key to reverse the foreground and background colors, so that white displays over black on the Tools panel.

b. Press CTRL+A to select all of the photo.

c. Use the Select menu to modify the border to 100 pixels.

d. Use the Stroke command on the Edit menu to stroke the selection with white.

e. Press CTRL+D to clear your selection when you are finished creating the border.

8. Press CTRL+S to save the Apply 1-1 Water Park Edited photo with the same file name in the same location.

9. Use the Image menu to resize the photo width to 5 inches wide to create a custom-sized photo for printing.

10. Save the resized file as Apply 1-1 Water Park for Print.

11. Print the photo and then close the file. If Photoshop displays a dialog box about saving again, click the No button.

12. Open the Apply 1-1 Water Park for Print file using the Open Recent list.

13. Save the photo for the Web, displaying it in the 4-Up tab. Select the preview that looks the best for your download speed.

14. Preview the optimized photo in your browser. Close the browser.

15. Save the optimized file with the name, Apply-1-1-Water-Park-for-Web.

16. Close the Apply 1-1 Water Park for Print file without saving it and quit Photoshop.

---

## Extend Your Knowledge

Extend the skills you learned in this chapter and experiment with new skills. You may need to use Help to complete the assignment.

### Exploring Crop Tool Options

...tomization steps found on pages PS 6 through
...n the Chapter 01 folder from the Data Files for
...nd 1-1 Arc de Triomphe Edited in the PSD file
...d
...for
...ook
...ered,

**Figure 1–88**

*Continued >*

---

**Extend Your Knowledge** *continued*

*Perform the following tasks:*

1. Use Help to read about the Crop Tool's Straighten button and the Aspect Ratio button.

2. Select the Crop Tool. On the options bar, click the Straighten button, and then drag in the photo, across a line that should be straight in the upper portion of the monument.

3. Use the 'Select a preset aspect ratio' button to choose a 5 × 7 forced ratio. Drag a corner cropping handle inward, keeping the arc within the grid. Drag the picture to center it within the cropping area.

4. Click the 'Delete cropped pixels' check box, if necessary, and then crop the photo.

5. Review Table 1–4 on page PS 38. Use the commands on the Modify submenu to set the border options of your choice. Stroke the selection with a color of your choice.

6. After viewing the resulting border, use the History panel to go back to the photo's cropped state.

7. Repeat Steps 5 and 6 several times to experiment with different border widths and colors, then apply the border that best complements the photo and save the changes to the photo.

8. Close the photo and quit Photoshop.

---

## Make It Right

Analyze a project and correct all errors and/or improve the design.

### Changing a Photo's Focus and Optimizing It for the Web

*Instructions:* Start Photoshop and perform the customization steps found on pages PS 6 through PS 10. Open the Make It Right 1-1 Young Stars file in the Chapter 01 folder from the Data Files for Students and save it on your storage device as Make It Right 1-1 Young Stars Edited in the PSD file format. Visit www.cengage.com/ct/studentdownload for detailed instructions or contact your instructor for information about accessing the required files.

Members of your Astronomy Club have selected the Young Stars photo (Figure 1–89) for the club's Web site. You are tasked with editing the photo to focus more clearly on the cluster of stars and its trailing dust blanket, and then optimizing the photo for the Web.

Source: NASA/JPL-Caltech/Harvard-Smithsonian CfA

**Figure 1–89**

View the photo in different screen modes and at different magnifications. Keeping the rule of thirds and the golden rectangle concepts in mind, crop the photo to change its focal point and resave it. Then save the photo for the Web as Make-It-Right-1-1-Young-Stars-for-Web.

---

**Extend Your Knowledge** projects at the end of each chapter allow students to extend and expand on the skills learned within the chapter. Students use critical thinking to experiment with new skills to complete each project.

**Make It Right** projects call on students to analyze a file, discover errors in it, and fix them using the skills they learned in the chapter.

# Textbook Walk-Through

6. Select a different tool so the cropping handles no longer are displayed.

7. Save the photo again with the same name.

8. Close the file and open it again using the Recent submenu.

9. Press CTRL+A to select all of the photo.

10. To create the border, do the following:

 a. On the Select menu, point to Modify, and then click Border.

 b. When the Border Selection dialog box is displayed, type 100 in the Width Box. Click the OK button.

 c. On the Select menu, open the Modify submenu, and then click Smooth.

 d. When the Smooth Selection dialog box is displayed, type 50 in the Sample Radius box to smooth the corners. Click the OK button.

 e. Press SHIFT+F5 to access the Fill command.

 f. When the Fill dialog box is displayed, click the Use box arrow and then click White in the list.

 g. Click the Mode box arrow and then click Normal in the list, if necessary.

 h. If necessary, type 100 in the Opacity box. Click the OK button.

 i. Press CTRL+D to deselect the border.

11. Save the photo again.

12. Use the Print One Copy command on the File menu to print a copy of the photo.

13. Close the document window.

14. Quit Photoshop.

15. Submit the assignment in the format specified by your instructor.

## In the Lab

**In the Lab** assignments require students to utilize the chapter concepts and techniques to solve problems on a computer.

### Lab 3: Preparing a Photo for the Web

*Problem:* As an independent consultant in Web site design, you have been hired by the Pineapple Growers Association to prepare a photo of an exotic pineapple growing in a field for use on the association's Web site. The edited photo is displayed in Figure 1–92.

*Note:* To complete this assignment, you will be required to use the Data Files for Students. Visit www.cengage.com/ct/studen___ download for detailed instructions or contact your instructor ___ information about accessing the required files.

*Instructions:* Perform the following tasks:
Start Photoshop. Perform the customization steps found on p___ PS 6 through PS 10. Open the file, Lab 1-3 Pineapple, from t___ Chapter 01 folder of the Data Files for Students. Save the file ___ the PSD format with the name Lab 1-3 Pineapple Edited. Res___ the photo to 500 pixels wide. Zoom to 50% magnification. Sea___ Photoshop Help for help related to optimization. Read about ___ optimizing for the Web. Print a copy of the help topic and the___ close the Adobe Help window.

Use the Save for Web dialog box to view the 4-Up tab. Choose the best-looking preview. Select the connection speed ___

STUDENT ASSIGNMENTS

---

**In the Lab** *continued*

your Internet connection. Save the Web version of the photo using the name, Lab-1-3-Pineapple-for-Web. For extra credit, upload the Web version to a Web server. See Appendix C for information on publishing to a Web server. See your instructor for ways to submit this assignment.

## Cases and Places

Apply your creative thinking and problem-solving skills to design and implement a solution.

*Note:* To complete these assignments, you may be required to use the Data Files for Students. Visit www.cengage.com/ct/studentdownload for detailed instructions or contact your instructor for information about accessing the required files.

### 1: Crop a Photo for a Class Directory

**Academic**
As a member of your high school reunion committee, it is your task to assemble the class photo directory. You are to edit a high school student photo and prepare it for print in the reunion directory. The photo needs to fit in a space 1.75 inches high and 1.33 inches wide. Each photo needs to have approximately .25 inches above the head. After starting Photoshop and resetting the workspace, select the photo, Case 1-1 Student, from the Chapter 01 folder of the Data Files for Students. Save the photo on your USB flash drive storage device as Case 1-1 Student Edited, using the PSD format. Resize the photo to match the requirements. Use the rulers to help you crop the photo for .25 inches above the top of the student's head. Save the photo again and print a copy for your instructor.

### 2: Create a Photo for a Social Networking Site

**Personal**
You would like to place a photo of your recent tubing adventure on your social networking page. The photo you have is of two people. You need to crop out the other person who is tubing. After starting Photoshop and resetting the workspace, select the photo, Case 1-2 Tubing, from the Chapter 01 folder of the Data Files for Students. Save the photo on your USB flash drive storage device as Case 1-2 Tubing Edited, using the PSD format. Crop the photo to remove one of the tubes, keeping in mind the rule of thirds, the golden rectangle, and the direction of the action. Save the photo for the Web and upload it to Facebook or another Web server as directed by your instructor.

### 3: Creating a Photo for a Brochure

**Professional**
You are an intern with an event planning business. The company is planning to send out a trifold brochure about local churches and chapels used for weddings. The photo named Case 1-3 Chapel is located in the Chapter 01 folder of the Data Files for Students. Save the photo on your USB flash drive storage device as Case 1-3 Chapel Edited, using the PSD format. Resize the photo to be 3.5 inches wide. Create a black border of 10 pixels. Save the file again and print a copy for your instructor.

Found within the Cases and Places exercises, the **Personal** activities call on students to create an open-ended project that relates to their personal lives.

# 1 | Editing a Photo

Adobe product screenshot(s) reprinted with permission from Adobe Systems Incorporated

## Objectives

You will have mastered the material in this chapter when you can:

- Start Photoshop and customize the Photoshop workspace

- Open a photo

- Identify parts of the Photoshop workspace

- Explain file types

- View a photo using the Zoom Tool, Navigator panel, and the Hand Tool

- Display rulers

- Crop a photo using the rule of thirds overlay

- Save a photo for both print and the Web

- Create a border

- Open a recent file

- Resize a photo

- Insert text and stroke

- Print a photo

- Access Photoshop Help

- Close a file and quit Photoshop

# 1 | Editing a Photo

## What Is Photoshop CS6?

**Photoshop CS6** is a popular image-editing software program produced by Adobe Systems Incorporated. **Image-editing software** refers to computer programs that allow you to create and modify **digital images**, or pictures in electronic form. One type of digital image is a digital **photograph**, or **photo**, which is a picture taken with a camera and stored as a digitized file. The photo then is converted into a print or a slide, or used in another file. Other types of digital images include scanned images, or electronic forms of original artwork created from scratch. Digital images are used in graphic applications, advertising, print publishing, and on the Web. Personal uses include private photos, online photo sharing, scrapbooking, blogging, and social networking, among others. Image-editing software, such as Photoshop, can be used for basic adjustments such as rotating, cropping, or resizing, as well as for more advanced manipulations, such as airbrushing, retouching, photo repair, changing the contrast of images and balancing or combining elements of different images. Because Photoshop allows you to save multilayered, composite images and then return later to extract parts of those images, it works well for repurposing a wide variety of graphic-related files.

Photoshop CS6 is part of the **Adobe Creative Suite 6** and comes packaged with most of the suite versions. It also is sold and used independently as a stand-alone application. Photoshop CS6 is available for both the PC and Macintosh computer platforms. Photoshop CS6 Extended includes all of the features of Photoshop CS6 and some new features for working with 3D imagery, motion-based content, and advanced image analysis. The chapters in this book use Photoshop CS6 on the PC platform, running the Windows 7 operating system; however, Photoshop looks very similar on the Windows and the Mac operating systems. Both versions present the same tools and similar menus. One of the main differences is in the approach to shortcut keys. Windows uses the CTRL key to access many of the shortcuts in the Adobe Creative Suite; MacOS uses the CMD key represented by the symbol ⌘ and sometimes the OPT key represented by the symbol ⌥. As system dialog boxes are presented in the chapters, the corresponding steps for Mac users are presented in Appendix G, the For Mac Users appendix.

To illustrate the features of Photoshop CS6, this book presents a series of chapters that use Photoshop to edit photos similar to those you will encounter in academic and business environments, as well as photos for personal use.

**Project Planning Guidelines**

The process of editing a photo requires careful analysis and planning. As a starting point, choose a photo that correctly expresses your desired subject or theme. Once the theme is determined, analyze the intended audience. Define a plan for editing that enhances the photo, eliminates visual clutter, improves color and contrast, and corrects defects. Always work on a duplicate of an original image. Finally, determine the file format and print style that will be most successful at delivering the message. Details of these guidelines are provided in Appendix A, Project Planning Guidelines. In addition, each chapter in this book provides practical applications of these planning considerations.

# Project — Postcard Graphic

A **postcard** is a rectangular piece of mail intended for writing and sending without an envelope. People use postcards for greetings, announcements, reminders, and business contacts. Many times, a postcard is an effective marketing tool used to generate prospective leads at a relatively low cost. One of the most popular uses for postcards involves pictures. Businesses and organizations produce a postcard with a photo or graphic on one side and a short description with room to write a brief correspondence on the other. People purchase picture postcards to mail to friends or to serve as reminders of their vacation. Sometimes a picture postcard is mailed to attract attention and direct people to Web sites or business locations. A postcard graphic must portray clearly its message or theme in an eye-catching manner, keeping in mind the relevant audience.

Most postcards are rectangular, at least 3½ inches high and 5 inches long — some are larger. A common size is 4 inches by 6 inches. A picture postcard might contain text printed over the picture or a border to add interest. A graphic designed for a postcard should be of high quality, use strong color, and deliver a message in the clearest, most attractive, and most effective way possible.

The project in this chapter uses Photoshop to enhance a photograph of an eagle and add text to create a postcard for use by a wildlife park. The original photo is displayed in Figure 1–1a. The edited photo is displayed in Figure 1–1b. The enhancements will emphasize the eagle by positioning the scene to make the layout appear more visually appealing and to crop some of the background. A gray border will frame the scene. Text will be added to identify the location. Finally, the photo will be resized to fit on a postcard and then optimized for the park's Web site.

**BTW**

**What's New in CS6?**
Photoshop CS6 has many new features, including an advanced cropping tool, Content Aware Move and Patch tools, Paragraph and Character Style panels, a new Blur gallery, as well as many others. To see more, press the F1 key and then click the What's new link.

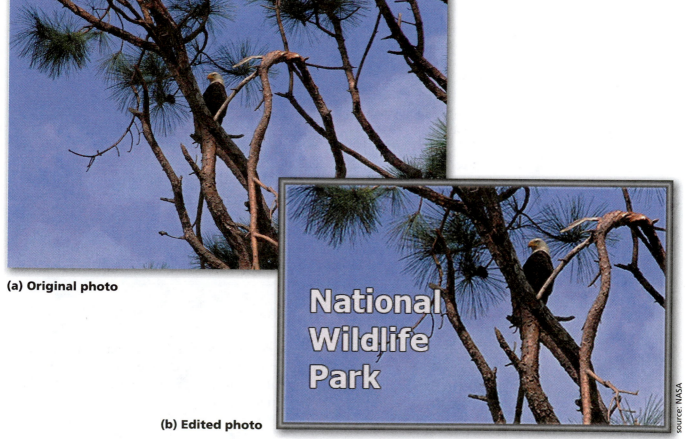

**(a) Original photo**

**(b) Edited photo**

**Figure 1–1**

**BTW**

**Screen Resolution**
If your system has a high-resolution monitor with a screen resolution of 1280 × 800 or higher, lowering that resolution to 1024 × 768 might cause some images to be distorted because of a difference in the aspect ratio. If you want to keep your high-resolution setting, be aware that the location of on-screen tools might vary slightly from the book.

# Overview

As you read this chapter, you will learn how to edit the photo shown in Figure 1–1a on the previous page by performing these general tasks:

- Customize the workspace.
- Display and navigate a photo at various magnifications.
- Crop a photo effectively.
- Create and modify a border.
- Stroke a selection.
- Resize and print a photo.
- Save, close, and then reopen a photo.
- Add stroked text to the photo.
- Save a photo for the Web.
- Use Photoshop Help.

**Plan Ahead**

**General Project Guidelines**
When editing a photo, the actions you perform and decisions you make will affect the appearance and characteristics of the finished product. As you edit a photo, such as the one shown in Figure 1–1a, you should follow these general guidelines:

1. **Find an appropriate image or photo.** Keep in mind the purpose and the graphic needs of the project when choosing an image or photo. Decide ahead of time on the file type and decide if the image will be used on the Web. An eye-catching graphic image should convey a theme that is understood universally. The photo should grab the attention of viewers and draw them into the picture, whether in print or on the Web.

2. **Determine how to edit the photo to highlight the theme.** As you edit, use standard design principles, and keep in mind your subject, your audience, the required size and shape of the graphic, color decisions, the rule of thirds, the golden rectangle, and other design principles. Decide which parts of the photo portray your message and which parts are visual clutter. Crop the photo as needed.

3. **Identify finishing touches that will further enhance the photo.** The overall appearance of a photo significantly affects its ability to communicate clearly. You might want to add text or a border.

4. **Prepare for publication.** Resize the photo as needed to fit the allotted space. Save the photo on a storage medium, such as a hard drive, USB flash drive, or CD. Print the photo or publish it to the Web.

When necessary, more specific details concerning the above guidelines are presented at appropriate points in the chapter. The chapter also will identify the actions performed and decisions made regarding these guidelines during the creation of the edited photo shown in Figure 1–1b on the previous page.

**BTW**

**By The Way Boxes**
For a complete list of the BTWs found in the margins of this book, visit the BTW chapter resource on the student companion site located at www.cengagebrain.com.

# Starting Photoshop

If you are using a computer to step through the project in this chapter, and you want your screen to match the figures in this book, you should change your screen's resolution to 1024 × 768. For information about how to change a screen's resolution, read Appendix F, the Changing Screen Resolution appendix.

## To Start Photoshop

The following steps, which assume Windows 7 is running, start Photoshop, based on a typical installation. You may need to ask your instructor how to start Photoshop for your computer.

**1**

- Click the Start button on the Windows 7 taskbar to display the Start menu.

- Type `Photoshop CS6` as the search text in the 'Search programs and files' text box, and watch the search results appear on the Start menu (Figure 1–2).

Start menu

Programs (1)

Adobe Photoshop CS6

Adobe Photoshop CS6 command

any documents containing the words, Photoshop CS6, and any files that have been opened with Photoshop CS6 may appear in your list

Windows 7 displays the results of search

**Note:** To help you locate screen elements that are referenced in the step instructions, such as buttons and commands, this book uses red boxes to point to these screen elements.

See more results

Search programs and files text box

Photoshop CS6

Shut down

Start button

Windows 7 taskbar

**Figure 1–2**

**2**

- Click Adobe Photoshop CS6 in the search results on the Start menu to start Photoshop.

- After a few moments, when the Photoshop window is displayed, if the window is not maximized, click the Maximize button next to the Close button on the Application bar to maximize the window (Figure 1–3).

Application bar

Photoshop window

with maximized window, Maximize button changes to Restore Down button

Ps  File  Edit  Image  Layer  Type  Select  Filter  3D  View  Window  Help

options bar

Feather: 0 px   Anti-alias   Style: Normal   Width:   Height:   Refine Edge...

Color  Swatches

Adjustments  Styles

Add an adjustment

Layers  Channels  Paths

workspace

Tools panel

other panels

other minimized panels

Mini Bridge  Timeline

**Figure 1–3**

**Other Ways**

1. Double-click Photoshop icon on desktop, if the icon is present

2. Click Adobe Photoshop CS6 on Start menu

**MAC** For a detailed example of this procedure using the Mac operating system, refer to the steps on page APP 76 of the For Mac Users appendix at the end of this book.

# Customizing the Photoshop Workspace

The screen in Figure 1–3 on the previous page shows how the Photoshop workspace looks the first time you start Photoshop after installation on most computers. Photoshop does not open a blank or default photo automatically; rather, the Application bar and the options bar appear across the top of the screen with a work area below the options bar. The Tools panel is displayed on the left; other panels are displayed on the right and across the bottom. The work area and panels are referred to collectively as the **workspace**.

As you work in Photoshop, the panels, the selected tool, and the options bar settings might change. Therefore, if you want your screen to match the figures in this book, you should restore the default workspace, select the default tool, and reset the options bar. In addition, users might change the default color for the workspace. For more information about how to change other advanced Photoshop settings, see the Changing Screen Resolution appendix.

Because of a default preference setting, each time you start Photoshop, the Photoshop workspace is displayed the same way it was the last time you used Photoshop. If you (or another user) move the panels while working in Photoshop, they will appear in their new locations the next time you start Photoshop. You can create and save your own workspaces, or use Photoshop's saved workspaces that show groups of panels used for certain tasks. For example, the Painting workspace displays the Brush panel, the Brush presets panel, and the Swatches panel, among others — all of which you would need when painting. You will learn more about panels later in this chapter. Similarly, if values on the options bar are changed or a different tool is selected, they will remain changed the next time you start Photoshop. If you want to return the workspace to its default settings, follow these steps each time you start Photoshop.

## To Select the Essentials Workspace

The default workspace, called Essentials, displays commonly used panels. The following steps select the Essentials workspace and reset its default values.

**1**

- Click Window on the Application bar to display the Window menu.

- Point to Workspace on the Window menu to display the Workspace submenu (Figure 1–4).

🔍 **Experiment**

- Click each of the workspaces that are displayed in the list to view the different panel configurations. Notice that Photoshop displays a check mark on the menu, next to the chosen workspace. When you are finished, click Window on the Application bar and then point to Workspace again to display the submenu.

**Figure 1–4**

**2**

• Click Essentials (Default) on the Workspace submenu to select the default workspace panels.

• Click Window on the Application bar and then point to Workspace again to display the submenu (Figure 1–5).

**Q&A**

What does the New Workspace command do?

The New Workspace command displays a dialog box where you can create a new workspace based on the currently displayed panels. You also can delete a workspace from the Workspace submenu.

Figure 1–5

**3**

• Click Reset Essentials to restore the workspace to its default settings and reposition any panels that might have been moved (Figure 1–6).

**Q&A**

My screen did not change. Did I do something wrong?

If Photoshop is a new installation on your system, you might notice few changes on your screen.

Figure 1–6

## To Select the Default Tool

The following step selects the Rectangular Marquee Tool, which is the default tool for a new installation of Photoshop. When you select a tool on the Tools panel, the options bar reflects the settings of that tool.

**1**

- If the tools on the Tools panel appear in two columns, click the double arrow at the top of the Tools panel.

- If necessary, click the second button from the top on the Tools panel to select it (Figure 1–7).

- If the button does not display a square icon, right-click the button and then click Rectangular Marquee Tool on the context menu.

**Q&A** What appears when I point to the button?

When you point to many objects in the Photoshop workspace, such as a tool or button, Photoshop displays a tool tip. A **tool tip** is a short, on-screen note associated with the object to which you are pointing, which helps you identify the object. This button's name is the Rectangular Marquee Tool.

**Figure 1–7**

| Other Ways |
| --- |
| 1. Press M |

## To Reset the Options Bar

As you work through the chapters, editing and creating images, you will find that the options bar is **context sensitive**, which means it changes as you select different tools. In addition, the options and settings are retained for the next time you use Photoshop. To match the figures in this book, you should reset the options bar, using a context menu, each time you start Photoshop. A **context menu**, or **shortcut menu**, appears when you right-click some objects in the Photoshop workspace. The menu displays commands representing the active tool, selection, or panel.

The following steps reset all tool settings in the options bar using a context menu.

**1**

- Right-click the Rectangular Marquee Tool icon on the options bar to display its context menu (Figure 1–8).

**Q&A** Why is my icon elliptical?

It is possible that a previous user has used the Elliptical Marquee Tool. Press SHIFT+M to return to the Rectangular Marquee Tool.

**Figure 1–8**

**2**

- Click Reset All Tools to display a confirmation dialog box (Figure 1–9).

**3**

- Click the OK button to restore the tools to their default settings.

**Figure 1–9**

## To Reset the Interface Color

Photoshop CS6 allows the user to choose from among four different color schemes for the interface: Black, Dark Gray, Medium Gray, and Light Gray. The color scheme you choose depends upon your personal preferences for contrast, focus, and readability.

The following steps reset the interface color to Medium Gray, which displays the work area in dark gray and the panels in medium gray.

**1**

- Click Edit on the Application bar, and then point to Preferences to display the Preferences submenu (Figure 1–10).

**Figure 1–10**

**2**

- Click Interface on the Preferences submenu to display the Preferences dialog box.

- In the Appearance area, click the third button, Medium Gray, to change the interface color (Figure 1–11).

**Q&A**

What other preferences can I change?

You can change things such as the color of certain display features, the number of states in the History panel, and the unit of measure, among others.

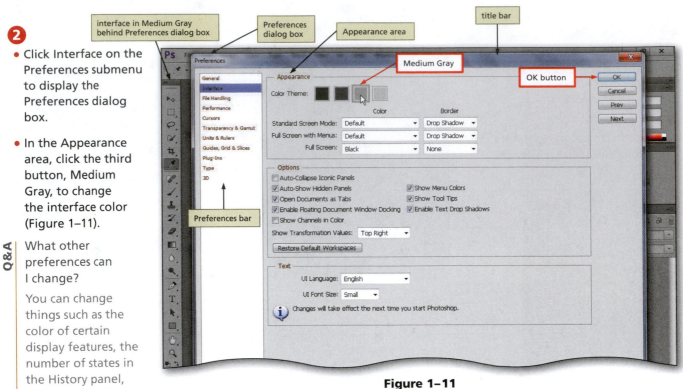

Figure 1–11

**Experiment**

- One at a time, click each of the four color schemes and notice how the interface changes. You can drag the title bar of the Preferences dialog box to move it out of the way, if necessary.

**3**

- Click the OK button in the Preferences dialog box to close the dialog box and return to the Photoshop workspace (Figure 1–12).

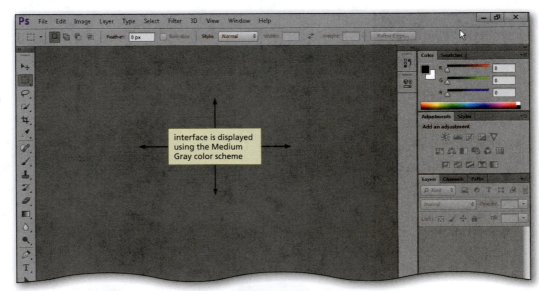

Figure 1–12

**Other Ways**

1. Press CTRL+K, click Interface on Preferences bar, click desired color scheme, click OK button

2. Right-click any button on vertical dock of panels, click Interface Options, click desired color scheme, click OK button

# Opening a Photo

To open a photo in Photoshop, it must be stored as a digital file on your computer system or on an external storage device. To **open** a photo, you bring a copy of the file from the storage location to the screen where you can **edit**, or make changes to, the photo. The changes do not become permanent, however, until you **save** or store the changed file on a storage device. The photos used in this book are included in the Data Files for Students. Visit www.cengage.com/ct/studentdownload for detailed instructions or contact your instructor for information about accessing the required files. Your instructor may designate a different location for the photos.

---

**Find an appropriate image or photo.**

Sometimes a person or business gives you a specific photo to use in a project. Other times, you are assigned a theme and asked to find or take the photo. An eye-catching graphic image should convey a visual message that is not expressed easily with words. Keep the audience in mind as you choose a photo. Photos generally fall into one of four categories:

- In advertising, a photo might show a product, service, result, model, or benefit.

- In a public service setting, a photo might represent a topic of interest, nature, signage, buildings, or a photo of historical importance.

- In industry, a photo might display a process, product, work organization, employee, facility, layout, equipment, safety, result, or culture.

- For personal or journalistic use, a photo might be a portrait, scenery, action shot, or event.

**Plan Ahead**

---

## To Open a File

The following steps open the Eagle file from the Data Files for Students. Visit www.cengage.com/ct/studentdownload for detailed instructions or contact your instructor for information about accessing the required files.

**1**

- Click File on the Application bar to display the File menu (Figure 1–13).

**Q&A** Do I need the Data Files for Students?

You will need the Data Files for Students to complete the activities and exercises in this book. See your instructor for information on how to acquire the necessary files.

**Q&A** Can I use a shortcut key to open a file?

Yes, the shortcut keys are displayed on the menu. In this textbook, the shortcut keys also are displayed at the end of each series of steps in the Other Ways box.

**Figure 1–13**

**2**

- Click Open on the File menu to display the Open dialog box.

- Click the Look in box arrow to display a list of the available storage locations on your system (Figure 1–14).

What do the other buttons in the Open dialog box do?

To the right of the Look in box arrow are buttons to help you navigate folders, create folders, and change the view. Links to common storage locations are found in the Navigation pane on the left.

**Figure 1–14**

**3**

- Click the storage location of the Data Files for Students, as specified by your instructor, to display its contents (Figure 1–15).

**Figure 1–15**

**4**

- Double-click the Photoshop folder and then double-click the Chapter 01 folder.

- Click the file, Eagle, to select the file to be opened (Figure 1–16).

**Q&A** Why is my file list different?

Your list might vary. In addition, the files in Figure 1–16 are displayed in List view. Click the View Menu button to verify your view.

**Figure 1–16**

**5**

- Click the Open button to open the selected file and display the photo in the Photoshop workspace (Figure 1–17).

**Q&A** Can I edit a printed photo?

Most of the images you will use in this book already are stored in digital format; however, when you have a print copy of a picture, rather than a digital file stored on your system, it sometimes is

**Figure 1–17**

necessary to scan the picture using a scanner. A **scanner** is a device used to convert a hard copy into a digital form for storage, retrieval, or other electronic purposes. Photoshop allows you to bring a copy from the scanner directly into the workspace.

**MAC** For a detailed example of this procedure using the Mac operating system, refer to the steps on pages APP 77 through APP 79 of the For Mac Users appendix.

**Other Ways**

1. Press CTRL+O, select file, click Open button

2. In Windows, right-click file, click Open with, click Adobe Photoshop CS6

# The Photoshop Workspace

The Photoshop workspace consists of a variety of components to make your work more efficient and to make your photo documents look more professional. The following sections discuss these components.

## The Application Bar

The Application bar appears at the top of the workspace (Figure 1–18). The Application bar contains the application button and the menu. On the far right side of the Application bar are the common window clip controls.

**Figure 1–18**

**Hidden Menu Commands**

When Photoshop first is installed, all of the menu commands within a menu appear when you click the menu name. To hide seldom-used menu commands, you can click the Menus command on the Edit menu and follow the on-screen instructions. A **hidden command** does not appear immediately on a menu.

The menu displays the Photoshop menu names. Each **menu** contains a list of commands you can use to perform tasks such as opening, saving, printing, and editing photos. To display a menu, such as the View menu, click the View menu name on the Application bar. If you point to a command on a menu that has an arrow on its right edge, a **submenu**, or secondary menu, displays another list of commands. (See Figure 1–10 on page PS 9).

## The Options Bar

The options bar (Figure 1–18) appears below the Application bar. Sometimes called the control panel, the options bar contains buttons and boxes that allow you to perform tasks more quickly than when using the Application bar and related menus. Most buttons on the options bar display words or images to help you remember their functions. When you point to a button or box on the options bar, a tool tip is displayed below the mouse pointer. The options bar changes to reflect the tool currently selected on the Tools panel. For example, a tool related to text might display a font box on the options bar, whereas a tool related to painting will display a brush button. The selected tool always appears as an icon on the left side of the options bar. As each tool is discussed, the associated options bar will be explained in more detail.

**Show All Menu Items**

If menu commands have been hidden, a Show All Menu Items command will appear at the bottom of the menu list. Click the Show All Menu Items command, or press and hold the CTRL key when you click the menu name to display all menu commands, including hidden ones.

You can **float**, or move, the options bar in the workspace by dragging the gray gripper bar on the left side of the options bar. You can **dock** or reattach the options bar below the Application bar by resetting the workspace. To hide or show the options bar, click Options on the Window menu.

## The Tools Panel

On the left side of the workspace is the Tools panel. The Tools panel is a group of **tools**, or buttons, organized into a toolbar. As with the options bar, you can float, dock, hide, or show the Tools panel. Each tool on the Tools panel displays a **tool icon**. When you point to the tool icon, a tool tip displays the name of the tool, including its shortcut key. You can expand some tools to show hidden tools beneath them. Expandable tools display a small triangle in the lower-right corner of the tool icon. Click and hold the tool button or right-click to see or select one of its hidden tools from the context menu. The default tool names and their corresponding shortcut keys are listed in Figure 1–19.

When you click a tool on the Tools panel, Photoshop selects the button and changes the options bar as necessary. When using a tool from the Tools panel, the mouse pointer changes to reflect the selected tool.

The Tools panel is organized by purpose. At the very top of the panel is a button to display the panel in two columns, followed underneath by the gripper bar. Below that, the selection tools appear, then the crop and slice tools, followed by retouching, painting, drawing and type, annotation, measuring, and navigation tools. At the bottom of the Tools panel are buttons to set colors, create a quick mask, and change screen modes.

As each tool is introduced throughout this book, its function and options bar characteristics will be explained further.

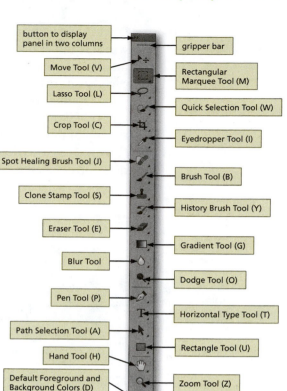

**Figure 1–19**

## The Document Window

The **document window** is the windowed area within the workspace that displays the active file or image. The document window contains the document window tab, the display area, scroll bars, and a status bar (Figure 1–20).

**Figure 1–20**

**Document Window Tab** When a file is open, Photoshop displays a **document window tab** at the top of the document window that shows the name of the file, the magnification, the color mode, and a Close button. If you have multiple files open, each has its own document window tab.

To **float** the document window in the display area, drag the document window tab. When the document window is floating, the document Window tab expands across the top of the document window and displays Minimize, Maximize, and Close buttons (Figure 1–21). To **dock** the document window again, or lock it in its previous location, drag the document window tab close to the options bar.

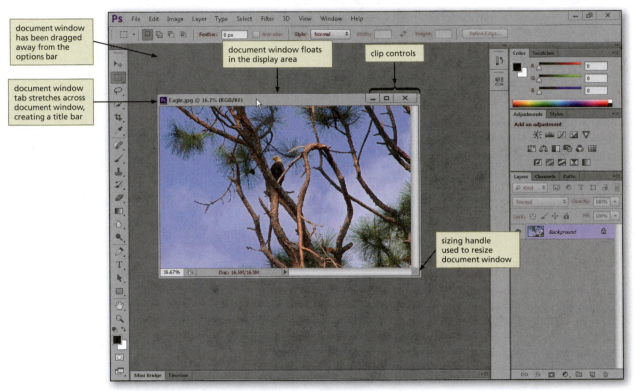

**Figure 1–21**

**BTW**

**Adobe Suite Workspaces**
The workspaces of the various applications in Adobe Creative Suite 6 share the same appearance to make it easy to move between applications. The toolbars, panels, and workspace are located in the same positions. Many shortcut keys are the same. Common menu terminology reduces the learning curve.

To **minimize** a document window, drag the document window tab away from the options bar so that the window floats, and then click the Minimize button. A minimized document window does not appear in the workspace; rather, it appears as a second Photoshop button on the Windows taskbar.

In Photoshop, a maximized document window fills the entire screen; you cannot see the menus or panels. To **maximize** a document window, drag the document window tab away from the options bar so that it floats, and then click the Maximize button. To return the document window to a floating state, click the Restore Down button on the document window title bar.

**Display Area** The **display area** is the portion of the document window that displays the photo or image. You perform most tool tasks and edit the photo in the display area.

**Scroll Bars** **Scroll bars** appear on the right and bottom of the document window. When the photo is bigger than the document window, the scroll bars become active and display scroll arrows and scroll boxes to move the image up, down, left, and right.

**Status Bar** Across the bottom of the document window, Photoshop displays the **status bar**. The status bar contains a magnification box. **Magnification** refers to the percentage of enlargement or reduction on the screen. For example, a 50% indication in the magnification box means the entire photo is displayed at 50 percent of its actual size. Changing the magnification does not change the size of the photo physically; it merely displays it on the screen at a different size. You can type a new percentage in the magnification box to display a different view of the photo.

Next to the magnification box is the **message area**. Messages can display information about the file size, the current tool, or the document dimensions. When you first start Photoshop, the message area displays information about the document size in storage.

On the right side of the status bar is the status bar menu button, which, when clicked, displays a status bar menu (Figure 1–20 on page PS 15). You use the status bar menu to change the message area or to change to other versions of the document.

Your installation of Photoshop might display rulers at the top and left of the document window. You will learn about rulers later in this chapter.

## Panels

A **panel** is a collection of graphically displayed choices and commands related to a specific tool or feature, such as those involving colors, brushes, actions, or layers (Figure 1–22). Panels help you monitor and modify your work. Each panel displays a panel tab with the name of the panel and a panel menu button. When you click the panel menu button, also called the panel menu icon, Photoshop displays a context-sensitive panel menu that allows you to make changes to the panel. Some panels have a status bar across the bottom. A panel can display buttons, boxes, sliders, scroll bars, or drop-down lists.

BTW

**Panels vs. Palettes**
In previous versions of the Adobe Creative Suite, the panels were called palettes. In all of the CS6 applications, panels can be grouped, stacked, or docked in the workspace, just as palettes were.

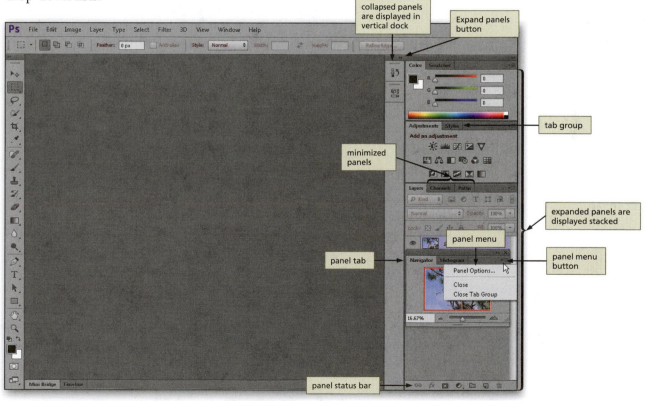

**Figure 1–22**

Several panels appear in the Essentials workspace. Some panels are expanded to display their contents, and are grouped by general purpose. A **panel group** or **tab group** displays several panels horizontally. The panel group is docked vertically on the right side of the workspace. Other open panels are displayed along the bottom or as icons or buttons in a vertical dock between the document window and the expanded panels. Panels are **collapsed** when they appear as an icon or button, or **expanded**

**BTW**

**More Panel Options**
If you want to display panels as buttons rather than as minimized or expanded pallets, right-click the panel tab, and then click Collapse to Icons on the context menu. A panel icon displays the name of the panel and its associated icon as a button.

when they display their contents. Panels are **minimized** when they display only their tab. To collapse or expand a panel group, click the double arrow at the top of the panel or double-click its tab. To close a panel, click Close on the panel menu. To redisplay the panel, click the panel name on the Window menu or use a panel shortcut key.

You can arrange and reposition panels either individually or in groups. To move them individually, drag their tabs; to move a group, drag the area to the right of the tabs. To float a panel in the workspace, drag its tab outside of the vertical dock. You can create a **stack** of floating panels by dragging a panel tab to a location below another floating panel and docking it.

Sometimes you might want to hide all the panels to display more of the document window. To hide all panels, press the TAB key. Press the TAB key again to display the panels.

Photoshop comes with 29 panels, described in Table 1–1. As each panel is introduced throughout this book, its function and characteristics will be explained further.

**BTW**

**Adobe Bridge**
When organizing your photos into folders, or if you want to rate your photos, it might be more convenient to use Adobe Bridge CS6. See Appendix E, the Using Adobe Bridge CS6 appendix, for more information.

### Table 1–1 Photoshop Panels

| Panel Name | Purpose |
|---|---|
| 3D | To show the 3D layer components, settings, and options of the associated 3D file — available in Photoshop Extended only |
| Actions | To record, play, edit, and delete individual actions |
| Adjustments | To create nondestructive adjustment layers with color and tonal adjustments |
| Brush | To select preset brushes and design custom brushes |
| Brush Presets | To create, load, save, and manage preset brush tips |
| Channels | To create and manage channels |
| Character | To provide options for formatting characters |
| Character Styles | To create, load, save, and manage character styles |
| Clone Source | To set up and manipulate sample sources for the Clone Stamp Tools or Healing Brush Tools |
| Color | To display the color values for the current foreground and background colors |
| Histogram | To view tonal and color information about an image |
| History | To jump to any recent state of the image created during the current working session |
| Info | To display color values and document status information |
| Layer Comps | To display multiple compositions of a page layout |
| Layers | To show and hide layers, create new layers, and work with groups of layers |
| Mini Bridge | To assist in navigating folders and files, and to access other modules in the suite |
| Measurement Log | To record measurement data about a measured object — available in Photoshop Extended only |
| Navigator | To change the view or magnification of the photo using a thumbnail display |
| Notes | To insert, edit, and delete notes attached to files |
| Options | To display options and settings for the currently selected tool |
| Paragraph | To change the formatting of columns and paragraphs |
| Paragraph Styles | To create, load, save, and manage paragraph styles |
| Paths | To manipulate each saved path, the current work path, and the current vector mask |
| Properties | To display characteristics about the file and to assist in creating precise, editable pixel- and vector-based masks |
| Styles | To view and select preset styles |
| Swatches | To select and store colors that you need to use often |
| Timeline | To create a sequence of images or frames, displayed as motion over time |
| Tools | To select tools |
| Tool Presets | To save and reuse tool settings |

# File Types

A **file type** refers to the internal characteristics of digital files; it designates the operational or structural characteristics of a file. Each digital file, graphic or otherwise, is stored with specific kinds of formatting related to how the file appears on the screen, how it prints, and the software it uses to do so. Computer systems use the file type to help users open the file with the appropriate software. A **file extension**, in most computer systems, is a three- or four-letter suffix after the file name that distinguishes the file type. For example, Eagle.jpg refers to a file named Eagle with the extension and file type JPG. A period separates the file name and its extension. When you are exploring files on your system, you might see the file extensions as part of the file name, or you might see a column of information about file types.

Graphic files are created and stored using many different file types and extensions. The type of file sometimes is determined by the hardware or software used to create the file. Other times, the user has a choice in applying a file type and makes the decision based on the file size, the intended purpose of the graphic file — such as whether the file is to be used on the Web — or the desired color mode.

Several common graphic file types are listed in Table 1–2.

| Table 1–2 Graphic File Types | | |
|---|---|---|
| **File Extension** | **File Type** | **Description** |
| BMP | Bitmap | BMP is a standard Windows image format used on DOS and Windows-compatible computers. BMP format supports many different color modes. |
| EPS | Encapsulated PostScript | EPS files can contain both bitmap and vector graphics. Almost all graphics, illustration, and page-layout programs support the EPS format, which can be used to transfer PostScript artwork between applications. |
| GIF | Graphics Interchange Format | GIF commonly is used to display graphics and images on Web pages. It is a compressed format designed to minimize file size and electronic transfer time. |
| JPG or JPEG | Joint Photographic Experts Group | JPG files commonly are used to display photographs on Web pages. JPG format supports many different color modes. JPG retains all color information in an RGB image, unlike GIF format. Most digital cameras produce JPG files. |
| PDF | Portable Document Format | PDF is a flexible file format based on the PostScript imaging model that is cross-platform and cross-application. PDF files accurately display and preserve fonts, page layouts, and graphics. PDF files can contain electronic document search and navigation features such as hyperlinks. |
| PSD | Photoshop Document | PSD format is the default file format in Photoshop and the only format that supports all Photoshop features. Other Adobe applications can import PSD files directly and preserve many Photoshop features because of the tight integration among Adobe products. |
| RAW | Photoshop Raw | RAW format is a flexible file format used for transferring images between applications and computer platforms. There are no pixel or file size restrictions in this format. Documents saved in the Photoshop Raw format cannot contain layers. |
| TIF or TIFF | Tagged Image File Format | TIF is a flexible bitmap image format supported by almost all paint, image-editing, and page-layout applications. This format often is used for files that are to be exchanged between applications or computer platforms. Most desktop scanners can produce TIF images. |

**BTW**

**File Extensions**
The default setting for file extensions in Photoshop is to use a lowercase three-letter extension. If you want to change the extension, do the following: Press SHIFT+CTRL+S to access the Save As dialog box. In the File name text box, type the file name, period, and new extension within quotation marks. Click the Save button.

**BTW**

**File Name Characters**
A file name can have a maximum of 260 characters, including spaces. The only invalid characters are the backslash (\), forward slash (/), colon (:), asterisk (*), question mark (?), quotation mark ("), less than symbol (<), greater than symbol (>), and vertical bar (|).

**Saving Files**
While Photoshop is saving your file, it briefly displays a Working in Background shape. In addition, your USB drive might have a light that flashes during the save process. The new file name appears on the document window tab.

# Saving a Photo

As you make changes to a file in Photoshop, the computer stores it in memory. If you turn off the computer or if you lose electrical power, the file in memory is lost. If you plan to use the photo later, you must save it on a storage device such as a USB flash drive, hard disk, or in cloud storage.

While you are editing, to preserve the most features such as layers, effects, masks, and styles, Photoshop recommends that you save photos in the **PSD format**. PSD, which stands for Photoshop Document Format, is the default file format for files created from scratch in Photoshop, and supports files up to 2 gigabytes (GB) in size. The PSD format also maximizes portability among other Adobe versions and applications.

## To Save a File in the PSD Format

The following steps save the photo on a USB flash drive using the file name, Eagle Edited. In addition to saving in the PSD format, you will save the photo with a new file name and in a new location, so that the original photo is preserved in case you need to start again. Even though you have yet to edit the photo, it is a good practice to save a copy of the file on your personal storage device early in the process. A **folder** is a specific location on a storage medium, represented visually by a file folder icon. Folders are good ways to organize files. In this book, you will create a folder for each chapter.

**1**

- With a USB flash drive connected to one of the computer's USB ports, click File on the Application bar to display the File menu (Figure 1–23).

Q&A

Do I have to save to a USB flash drive?

No. You can save to any device or folder.

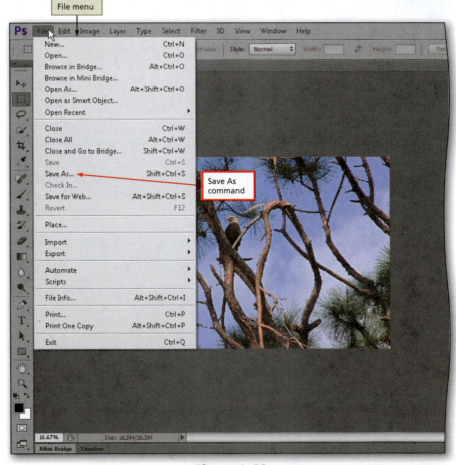

**Figure 1–23**

**2**

- Click Save As to display the Save As dialog box.

- Type `Eagle Edited` in the File name text box to change the file name. Do not press the ENTER key after typing the file name.

- Click the Save in box arrow to display the list of available drives (Figure 1–24).

What if my USB flash drive has a different name or letter?

It is very likely that your USB flash drive will have a different name and drive letter and be connected to a different port. Verify that the device in your list is correct.

**Figure 1–24**

**3**

- Click Removable Disk (F:), or the name of your USB flash drive, in the list of available storage devices to select that drive as the new save location.

- Click the Create New Folder button on the Save As dialog box toolbar to create a new folder on the selected storage device.

- When the new folder appears, type `Chapter 01` to change the name of the folder, and then press the ENTER key (Figure 1–25).

Why is my list of drives arranged and named differently?

The size of the Save As dialog box and your computer's configuration determine how the list is displayed and how the drives are named.

**Figure 1–25**

**4**

- Double-click the new folder to open it.

- Click the Format button to display the list of available file formats (Figure 1–26).

Do I have to use the same file name?

It is good practice to identify the relation-ship of this photo to the original by using at least part of the original file name with some notation about its status.

**Figure 1–26**

**5**

- Click Photoshop (*.PSD, *.PDD) to select the file type (Figure 1–27).

What is PDD?

The **PDD format** is used with images created by Photo Deluxe and other software packages. Some older digital cameras produce files with a PDD extension as well.

**Figure 1–27**

**6**

- Click the Save button to save the document on the selected drive with the new file name (Figure 1–28).

**Figure 1–28**

**Other Ways**

1. Press SHIFT+CTRL+S, choose settings, click Save button

**MAC** For a detailed example of this procedure using the Mac operating system, refer to the steps on pages APP 79 through APP 80 of the For Mac Users appendix.

# Viewing Photos

Photoshop allows you to view photos in many different ways, by adjusting the document window and by using different tools and panels. Using good navigation techniques to view images can help you edit the details of a photo or check for problems. For example, you might want to zoom in on a specific portion of the photo or move to a different location in a large photo. You might want to use a ruler to measure certain portions of the photo. Or you might want to view the image without the distraction of the panels and menu. Zooming, navigating, scrolling, and changing the screen mode are some ways to view the document window and its photo.

## Zooming

To make careful edits in a photo, you sometimes need to change the magnification, or **zoom**. Zooming allows you to focus on certain parts of the photo, such as a specific person in a crowd scene or details in a complicated picture. A magnification of 100% means the photo is displayed at its actual size. Zooming in enlarges the percentage of magnification of the photo; zooming out reduces the magnification. Note that zooming does not change the size of the photo; it merely changes the appearance of the photo in the document window.

The Zoom Tool button displays a magnifying glass icon on the Tools panel. You also can press the z key to select the Zoom Tool. Choosing one over the other is a matter of personal choice. Most people use the shortcut key. Others sometimes choose the button because of its proximity to the mouse pointer at the time.

When you use the Zoom tool, each click magnifies the image to the next preset percentage. When positioned in the photo, the Zoom Tool mouse pointer displays a magnifying glass, with either a plus sign, indicating an increase in magnification, or a minus sign, indicating a decrease in magnification. Right-clicking with the Zoom Tool in the photo displays a context menu with options to zoom in or zoom out, among others.

Figure 1–29 displays the Zoom Tool options bar, with buttons to zoom in and out. Other options include check boxes used when working with multiple photos, displaying the actual pixels, fitting the entire photo on the screen, filling the screen, and displaying the photo at its print size.

**BTW**

**Ways to Zoom**
There are many ways to zoom, including the Zoom tool, the Zoom buttons, the magnification box, and the Navigator panel. How you zoom depends on your personal preference and whether you want to change the current tool.

**BTW**

**Scrubby Zoom**
If you click the Scrubby Zoom check box, you can drag to the left in the image to zoom out, or to the right to zoom in.

**Figure 1–29**

# To Use the Zoom Tool

The following steps zoom in on the eagle for careful editing later in the chapter.

**1**

- Click the Zoom Tool button on the Tools panel to select the Zoom Tool.

- Move the mouse pointer into the document window to display the magnifying glass mouse pointer (Figure 1–30).

**Q&A**

Why does my mouse pointer display a minus sign?

Someone may have previously zoomed out and the setting has carried over. Click the Zoom In button on the options bar.

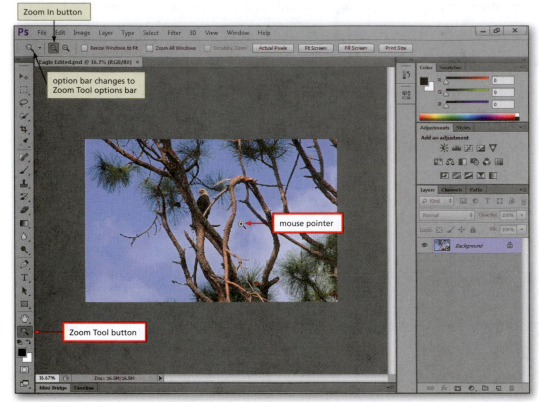

Zoom In button

option bar changes to Zoom Tool options bar

mouse pointer

Zoom Tool button

**Figure 1–30**

**2**

- Click the eagle three times to zoom in (Figure 1–31).

🔍 **Experiment**

- On the options bar, click the Zoom In button and then click the photo. Click the Zoom Out button and then click the photo. ALT+click the photo to zoom in the opposite direction from the options bar setting. Zoom to 50% magnification.

**Other Ways**

1. Press z, click document window
2. Press CTRL+PLUS SIGN (+) or CTRL+MINUS SIGN (-)
3. On View menu, click Zoom In or Zoom Out

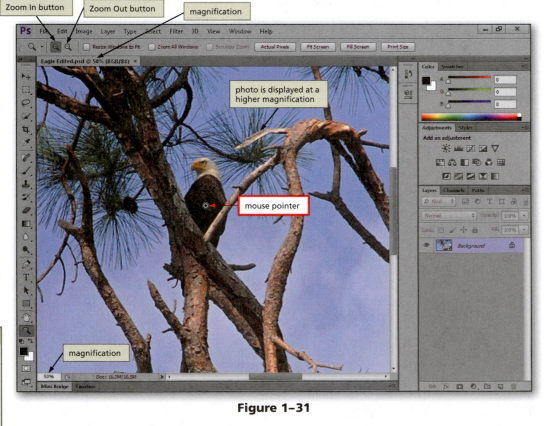

Zoom In button    Zoom Out button    magnification

photo is displayed at a higher magnification

mouse pointer

magnification

**Figure 1–31**

# The Navigator Panel

Another convenient way to zoom and move around the photo is to use the Navigator panel. The Navigator panel (Figure 1–32) is used to change the view of your document window using a thumbnail display. To display the Navigator panel, select Navigator from the Window menu.

**Figure 1–32**

The rectangle with the red border in the Navigator panel is called the **proxy view area** or **view box**, which outlines the currently viewable area in the window. Dragging the proxy view area changes the portion of the photo that is displayed in the document window. In the lower portion of the Navigator panel, you can type in the desired magnification, or you can use the slider or buttons to increase or decrease the magnification.

In Figure 1–32, the Navigator panel menu appears when you click the panel menu button. The Panel Options command displays the Panel Options dialog box.

# To Use the Navigator Panel

The following steps display and use the Navigator panel to reposition the view of the photo using the proxy view area.

**1**

- Click Window on the Application bar to display the Window menu (Figure 1–33).

**Q&A**

What two panels are already on the vertical dock of panels?

In the Essentials workspace, the History panel and Properties panel appear on the dock.

Figure 1–33

**2**

- Click Navigator on the Window menu to display the Navigator panel (Figure 1–34).

**Q&A**

Why would I choose the Navigator panel over other methods of moving around the screen?

When you are using a different tool on the Tools panel, such as a text tool or brush tool, it is easier to use the Navigator panel to zoom in or out and move around in the photo. That way, you do not have to change to the Zoom Tool, perform the zoom, and then change back to your editing tool.

Figure 1–34

**3**

- Drag the proxy view area on the Navigator Panel to display the upper-right portion of the photo (Figure 1–35).

🔎 **Experiment**

- Drag the proxy view area to display different portions of the photo. Drag the Zoom Slider and try clicking the Zoom In and Zoom Out buttons on the Navigator panel. When you are finished, return to 50% magnification, and drag the proxy view area to display the upper-right portion of the photo.

**Figure 1–35**

## To Minimize the Navigator Panel

The following step minimizes the Navigator panel so that it is displayed as a button in the vertical dock of buttons. In the right portion of the panel's title bar, the double arrow, sometimes called the Collapse to Icons button, minimizes a panel.

**1**

- Click the double arrow at the top of the Navigator panel (Figure 1–36).

**Q&A**

How would I move or close the panel?

To move the panel, drag the panel tab. To close the panel, click Close on the panel menu, or if the panel is floating, click the panel's Close button.

**Figure 1–36**

| Other Ways |
| --- |
| 1. On vertical dock, click Navigator button |

## The Hand Tool

You also can use the Hand Tool to move around in the photo if the photo has been magnified to be larger than the document window. To use the Hand Tool, click the Hand Tool button on the Tools panel, and then drag in the display area of the document window.

The Hand Tool options bar (Figure 1–37) displays boxes and buttons to assist you in scrolling and manipulating the document window.

**Figure 1–37**

## To Use the Hand Tool

The following step uses the Hand Tool to view a different part of the photo.

**1**

- Click the Hand Tool button on the Tools panel to select the Hand Tool.

- Drag in the document window to display the center portion of the photo (Figure 1–38).

**Q&A**

What is the other tool grouped with the Hand Tool?

Grouped with the Hand Tool is the Rotate View Tool. It is used to rotate the entire image, nondestructively, for fine editing.

**Figure 1–38**

| Other Ways |
| --- |
| 1. Press H, drag photo |

## To Change the Magnification

The following steps use the Magnification box on the status bar to change the magnification.

**1**
- Double-click the Magnification box on the status bar to select the current magnification (Figure 1–39).

status bar

magnification selected in Magnification box

**Figure 1–39**

**2**
- Type 20 and then press the ENTER key to change the magnification (Figure 1–40).

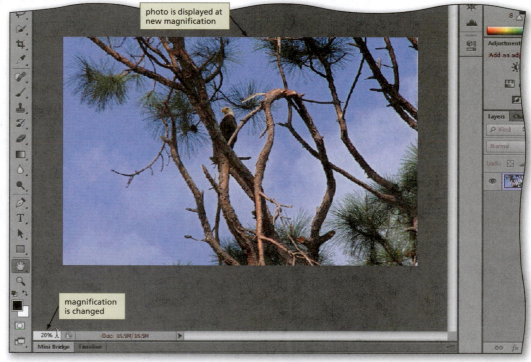

photo is displayed at new magnification

magnification is changed

20%

**Figure 1–40**

**Other Ways**

1. On Navigator panel, type percentage in Magnification box

## To Display Rulers

To make careful edits in a photo, sometimes it is necessary to use precise measurements in addition to zooming and navigating. In these cases, you should change the Photoshop document window to view the rulers. **Rulers** appear on the top and left sides of the document window. Rulers help you position images or elements precisely. As you move your mouse pointer over a photo, markers on the ruler display the mouse pointer's position.

The following steps display the rulers in the document window.

**1**

• Click View on the Application bar to display the View menu (Figure 1–41).

**Q&A**

What unit of measurement do the rulers use?

Rulers display inches by default, but you can right-click a ruler to change the increment to pixels, centimeters, or other units of measurement.

Figure 1–41

**2**

• Click Rulers to display the rulers in the document window (Figure 1–42).

**Q&A**

Is the photo really 42 × 26 inches?

The resolution from photos taken with digital cameras is measured in **megapixels** or millions of pixels. The more megapixels you have, the better the photo resolution; however, it translates to very large print sizes. You will resize the photo later in the chapter.

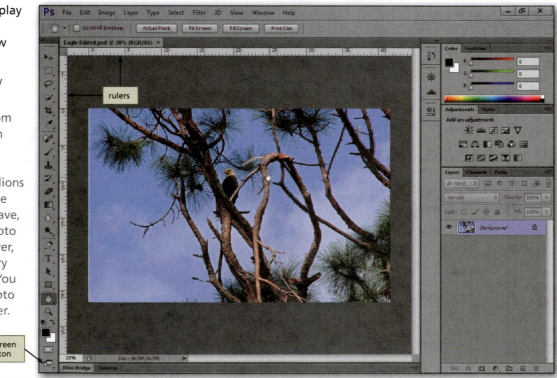

Figure 1–42

| Other Ways |
| --- |
| 1. Press CTRL+R |

## Screen Modes

To change the way the panels, bars, and document window appear, Photoshop includes three **screen modes**, or ways to view the document window. The Change Screen Mode button is located at the bottom of the Tools panel (Figure 1–42) and toggles among the screen modes. Standard screen mode displays the Application bar, document window, scroll bars, and visible panels. Full screen mode displays only the image and rulers, if they are visible, on a black background. Full screen mode with menu enlarges the document window to fill the workspace with no title bar, status bar, or scroll bars. A fourth way to view the screen is to hide the panels using the TAB key. Pressing the TAB key again redisplays the panels.

Choosing a mode depends on what you are trying to accomplish. While editing a single photo, standard screen mode may be the best, especially for beginners. If you are working on multiple files, screen space is at a premium and you might want to use one of the full screen modes.

# Editing the Photo

Editing, or making corrections and changes to a photo, involves a wide variety of tasks such as changing or emphasizing the focus of interest, recoloring portions of the photo, correcting defects, adding new artwork, or changing the file type for specific purposes. Editing also is called **post-processing**, because it includes actions you take after the picture has been processed by the camera or scanner.

Table 1–3 suggests typical categories and types of edits you might perform on photos; there are many others. These edits commonly overlap, and, when performed in combination, they can even create new editing varieties. You will learn more about edits as you work through the chapters in this book.

| Table 1–3 Photo Edits | |
|---|---|
| **Category** | **Types of Edits** |
| Transformations | Cropping, slicing, changing the aspect, rotating, leveling, mirroring, warping, skewing, distorting, flipping, and changing the perspective |
| Enhancements and Layering | Filters, layers, clones, borders, artwork, text, animation, painting, morphing, ordering, styles, masks, cutaways, selections, depth perception, anti-aliasing, moves, shapes, rasterizing |
| Color | Correction, contrast, blending, modes and systems, separations, screening, levels, ruling, trapping, matching, black and white |
| Correction | Sharpening, red-eye, tears, correcting distortion, retouching, reducing noise, blur, dodge, burn |
| File Type | Camera raw, print, Web, animated images |
| Resolution | Resampling, resizing, collinear editing, interpolation, editing pixel dimensions and document sizes |

Editing the Eagle Edited photo will involve three steps. First, you will crop the photo to remove excessive background. Next, you will add a border and stroke it with color. Finally, you will resize the photo to fit the intended use and size requirements, inserting text for the postcard.

**BTW**

**Screen Modes**
You also can use the View menu to change Screen Modes as well as pressing the F key on the keyboard.

**BTW**

**Cropping**
To evaluate an image for cropping, make a printout. Using two L shapes cut from paper, form a size and shape rectangle to isolate a portion of the image. Draw lines on the printout to use as a guide when cropping in Photoshop.

**BTW**

**When Not to Crop**
At times, cropping the photo is not desirable. For example, when you are working with older photos that convey a specific setting or location, the background might contain details that help evoke the setting, such as furniture, clothing worn by people in the background, or toys or vehicles from a particular time period. Retaining these details can help viewers recall the time and place of the original photo.

**Rotate and Crop**
You can rotate the image around the cropping area by moving the mouse pointer just outside of one of the cropping handles. When the mouse pointer changes to a curved arrow, drag to rotate. If you are using the Perspective Crop Tool, the rotation mouse pointer rotates the crop area rather than the image.

**Straighten and Crop**
If you click the Straighten button on the options bar, you can drag a line in the crop area. The image will rotate to match the angle of the line. This is useful when the image is out of alignment. You should try to drag across a natural line within the image.

**Trimming vs. Cropping**
The Trim command also crops an image by removing unwanted portions of the photo, but in a different way from the Crop Tool. The Trim command, on the Image menu, trims surrounding transparent pixels or background pixels of the color you specify.

> **Determine how to edit the photo to highlight the theme.**
> You always should perform editing with design principles in mind. Look at your photo carefully. Are there parts that detract from the central figure? Would the theme be illustrated better by only displaying a portion of the photo? If you want to emphasize a single object on a fairly solid background, you might need to crop, or trim, extraneous space around the object. Decide which parts of the photo portray your message and which parts are visual clutter.
>
> - Use the rule of thirds to position visual lines.
> - Crop the photo to remove excess background.
> - Rotate the photo if necessary.

## Cropping

The first step in editing the eagle photo is to **crop**, or cut away, some of the extra sky and branches so the photo focuses on the eagle. Photographers try to compose and capture images full-frame, which means the object of interest fills the dimensions of the photo. When that is not possible, photographers and graphic artists crop the photo either to create an illusion of full-frame, to fit unusual shapes in layouts, or to make the image more dramatic. From a design point of view, sometimes it is necessary to crop a photo to straighten an image, remove distracting elements, or simplify the subject. The goal of most cropping is to make the most important feature in the original photo stand out. Cropping sometimes is used to convert a digital photo's proportions to those typical for traditional photos.

Most photographers and graphic artists use the **rule of thirds**, also called the principle of thirds, when placing the focus of interest. Imagine that the scene is divided into thirds both vertically and horizontally. The intersections of these imaginary lines suggest four positions for placing the focus of interest. The position you select depends on the subject and its presentation in the photo. For instance, there might be a shadow, path, or visual line you wish to include. In the case of moving objects, you generally should leave space in front of them, into which they theoretically can move. When eyes are involved, it is better to leave space on the side toward which the person or animal is looking, so they do not appear to look directly out of the setting.

Because the eagle photo will be used on a postcard, the photo's orientation should be **landscape**, or horizontal. In most cases, you should try to crop to a rectangular shape with an approximate short-side to long-side ratio of 5:8. Sometimes called the **golden rectangle**, a 5:8 ratio emulates natural geometric forms such as flowers, leaves, shells, and butterflies. Most digital cameras take pictures with a similar ratio.

The Crop Tool allows you to select the portion of the photo you wish to retain. Photoshop automatically displays handles and a rule of thirds overlay for further adjustments, if necessary. Then, when you press the ENTER key, the rest of the photo is cropped, or removed. You can choose to permanently delete the cropped pixels on the options bar. The cropping handles continue to appear until you choose another tool.

The Crop Tool is grouped with the Perspective Crop Tool. In a **perspective crop**, when you drag one of the cropping handles, the other handles stay in place, which creates a distortion.

The Crop Tool options bar displays boxes and buttons to assist cropping activities (Figure 1–43). You can specify the aspect ratio, or the exact height and width of the crop. The options bar also contains buttons to rotate or straighten the photo, as well as a View button menu to change the overlay grid.

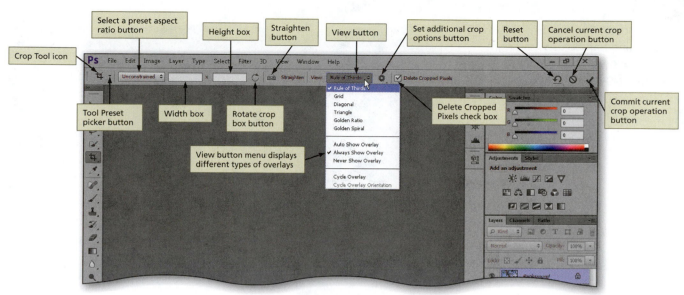

**Figure 1–43**

## To Crop a Photo

To make the eagle the focus of the photo, the extra background will be cropped to provide a line of sight to the left, keeping as much of the tree as possible. The following steps crop the photo of the eagle.

**1**

- Click the Crop Tool button on the Tools panel to select the Crop Tool.

- Click the photo to display the rule of thirds grid.

- If necessary, click the Delete Cropped Pixels check box on the options bar, so that it displays a check mark (Figure 1–44).

**Experiment**

- On the options bar, click the View button, and then, one at a time, choose different overlays. Click the photo to display the overlay each time. When you are finished, click the View button again and then click Rule of Thirds.

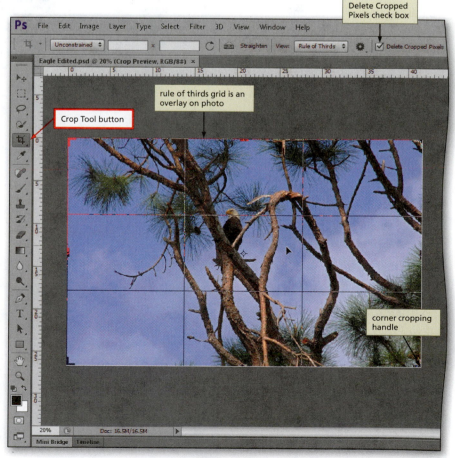

**Figure 1–44**

**2**

- SHIFT+CTRL+drag the lower-right cropping handle until the right vertical gridline aligns with the eagle (Figure 1–45).

**Q&A**

Why should I hold down the SHIFT and CTRL keys while dragging?

SHIFT+CTRL+dragging maintains the aspect ratio of both the grid overlay and the image.

**Figure 1–45**

**3**

- Within the cropping area, drag the photo straight up, until the upper-right intersection of the grid is centered over the eagle (Figure 1–46).

**Q&A**

What if I change my mind or make a mistake when cropping?

If you make a mistake while dragging the cropping area and want to start over, you can click the Cancel current crop operation button or press the ESC key, which cancels the selection. If you already have performed the crop and then change your mind, you have several choices. You can click the Undo command on the Edit menu, or you can press CTRL+Z to undo the last edit.

**Figure 1–46**

**4**

- Press the ENTER key to complete the crop (Figure 1–47).

🔍 **Experiment**

- If you want to practice cropping, drag a cropping handle again. After each crop, press CTRL+Z to undo the crop.

**Other Ways**

1. Press C, drag in photo, on options bar click 'Commit current crop operation' button
2. Select portion of image, on Image menu click Crop, press ENTER key

**Figure 1–47**

## To Select the Default Tool Again

If you do not want to use the Crop Tool any longer, or you do not want to see the cropping handles, select any other tool on the Tools panel. The following step selects the default tool again, as you did at the beginning of the chapter.

**1** On the Tools panel, click the Rectangular Marquee Tool button to select the tool.

# Creating a Border

A **border** is a decorative edge on a photo or a portion of a photo. Photoshop provides many ways to create a border, ranging from simple color transformations around the edge of the photo to predefined decorated layers to stylized photo frames.

A border helps define the edge of the photo, especially when the photo might be set on colored paper or on a Web page with a background texture. A border visually separates the photo from the rest of the page, while focusing the viewer's attention. Rounded borders soften the images in a photo. Square borders are more formal. Decorative borders on a static photo can add interest and amusement but easily can detract from the focus on a busier photo. **Blended borders** are not a solid fill; rather, they blend a fill color from the outer edge toward the middle, sometimes providing a three-dimensional effect. A border that complements the photo in style, color, and juxtaposition is best. In the eagle photo, you will create a border using selections of 75 black pixels with 25 pixels of overlapping white. A **pixel** is an individual dot of light that is the basic unit used to create digital images.

**BTW**

**Selections**
When you select all, Photoshop displays the photo with a marquee around all four edges. The selection tools on the Tools panel also can help you make selections in the photo. The Rectangular Marquee, Lasso, Quick Selection, and Magic Wand tools will be discussed in Chapter 2.

> **Identify finishing touches that will further enhance the photo.**
> Adding a border or decorative frame around a photo sometimes can be an effective way to highlight or make the photo stand out on the page. A border should frame the subject, rather than become the subject. If a border is required by the customer or needed for layout placement, choose a color and width that neither overwhelms nor overlaps any detail in the photo. Using a border color that complements one of the colors already in the photo creates a strong, visually connected image. For more information about graphic design concepts, read Appendix B, Graphic Design Overview.

**Plan Ahead**

## To Create a Selection

Specifying or isolating an area of your photo for editing is called making a **selection**. Selecting specific areas allows you to edit and apply special effects to portions of your image, while leaving the unselected areas untouched.

Selections can be simple shapes such as rectangles or ovals, or unusually shaped areas of a photo, outlining specific objects. Selections can be the entire photo or as small a portion as one pixel. A selection displays a marquee in Photoshop. A **marquee** is a flashing or pulsating border, sometimes called marching ants.

In the case of the Eagle Edited photo, you will make a selection around the edge of the photo to create a border. The steps on the next page select the photo.

**1**

● On the Application bar, click Select to display the Select menu (Figure 1–48).

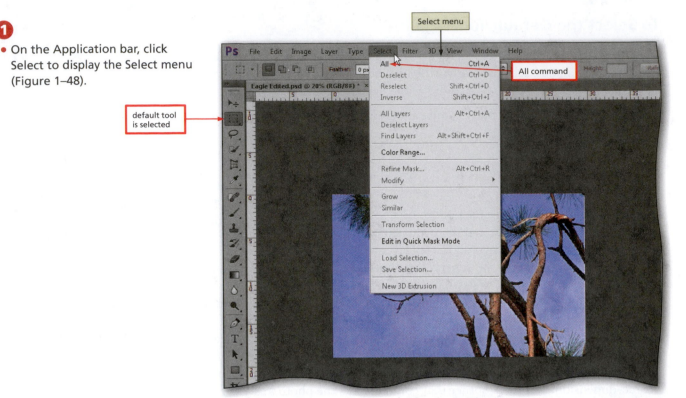

**Figure 1–48**

**2**

● On the Select menu, click the All command to display the selection marquee around the entire photo (Figure 1–49).

**Q&A**

Am I selecting all of the photo?

You are identifying the pixels along the edge of the image. Some commands apply to all of the pixels within the selection border, such as copying, deleting, or filling; other commands, such as stroking, apply only to the pixels along the edge of the selection.

**Figure 1–49**

| Other Ways |
| --- |
| 1. To select all, press CTRL+A |

## To Stroke a Selection

A **stroke** is a colored outline or edge. When stroking a selection, you must specify the number of pixels to include in the stroke and the desired color. You also must decide whether to apply the stroke outside the selection border, inside the selection border, or centered on the selection border. Other stroke settings include blending modes and opacity, which you will learn about in a later chapter. The following steps stroke a selection.

**1**

• With the photograph still selected, click Edit on the Application bar to display the Edit menu (Figure 1–50).

Edit menu

Stroke command

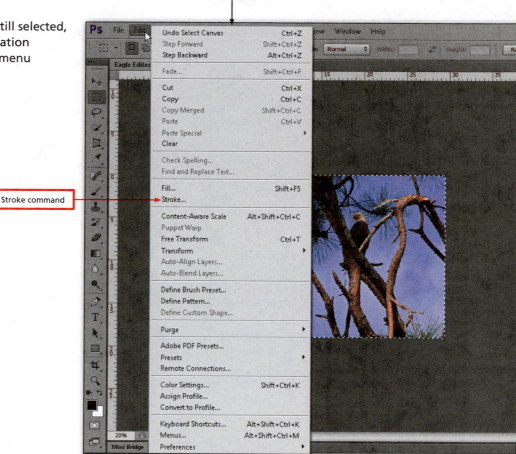

**Figure 1–50**

**2**

• Click Stroke to display the Stroke dialog box.

• Type 75 in the Width box (Figure 1–51).

**Q&A**

Do I need to select a color?

No, the default value is the foreground color, black. If your foreground color is not black, click the Cancel button, press the D key to choose the default colors and start again with Step 1.

**Figure 1–51**

**3**

- Click the OK button in the Stroke dialog box to apply the stroke (Figure 1–52).

**Q&A**

What does the asterisk mean in the document window tab?

The asterisk means you have made changes to the photo since your last save. Once you save the file, the asterisk no longer is displayed.

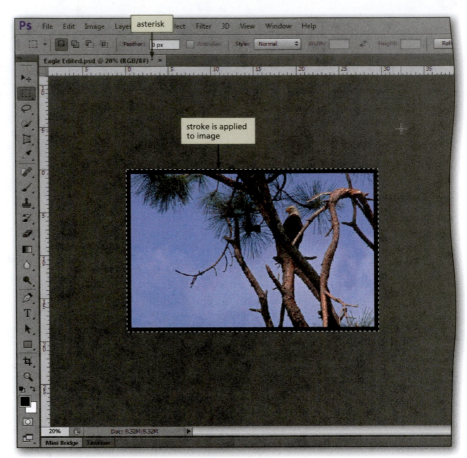

**Figure 1–52**

**Reviewing Your Edits**
Each edit or state of the photo is recorded sequentially in the History panel. If you want to step back through the edits or go back to a particular state, such as the previous crop, click the state in the History panel. You will learn more about the History panel in a future chapter.

# Modifying Selections

You can modify the selection in several different ways. In the eagle photo, you will modify the selection border by increasing the number of pixels along the border so you can add a second color at that location. Table 1–4 displays the Modify commands on the Select menu.

| Table 1–4 Modify Commands | |
|---|---|
| **Type of Modification** | **Result** |
| Border | This command allows you to select a width of pixels, from 1 to 200, to be split evenly on either side of the existing selection marquee. |
| Smooth | This command allows you to select a number of pixels in a radius around the selection. Photoshop adds or removes pixels in that radius to smooth sharp corners and jagged lines, reducing patchiness. |
| Expand | The border is increased by a number of pixels from 1 to 100. |
| Contract | The border is decreased by a number of pixels from 1 to 100. |
| Feather | This command creates a feather edge with a width from 0 to 250 pixels. |

## To Modify a Selection

The following steps modify the selection by changing the border selection area.

**1**

• On the Application bar, click Select, and then point to Modify to display the Modify submenu (Figure 1–53).

**Figure 1–53**

**2**

• Click Border on the Modify submenu to display the Border Selection dialog box.

**Q&A**

Could I use the Contract command to contract the selection?

No, you must specify the border first. The Contract command is **grayed out**, or **unavailable**, so you cannot select it, before choosing the Border command.

• Type 50 in the Width box to create a border selection on each side of the marquee (Figure 1–54).

**Figure 1–54**

**3**

● Click the OK button in the Border Selection dialog box to define the selection (Figure 1–55).

**Q&A**

My display shows two marquees around the photo. Did I do something wrong?

No. Your version of Photoshop might be using a different screen mode or resolution.

**Experiment**

● To practice smoothing the border, click the Select menu, point to Modify, and then click Smooth. Enter a value in the Sample Radius box and then click the OK button. Notice the change in the marquee. Press CTRL+Z to undo the Smooth command.

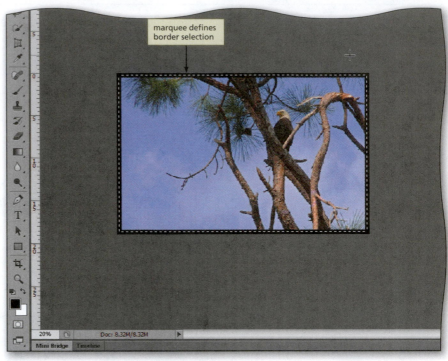

marquee defines border selection

**Figure 1–55**

## To Switch Foreground and Background Colors

On the Tools panel, the default foreground color is black and the default background color is white. Photoshop uses the default foreground color in strokes, fills, and brushes — in the previous steps when you stroked, the pixels became black. To create a rounded gray border, you will use a white, overlapping stroke. The following step switches the foreground and background colors so white is over black.

**1**

● Click the Switch Foreground and Background Colors button to reverse the colors (Figure 1–56).

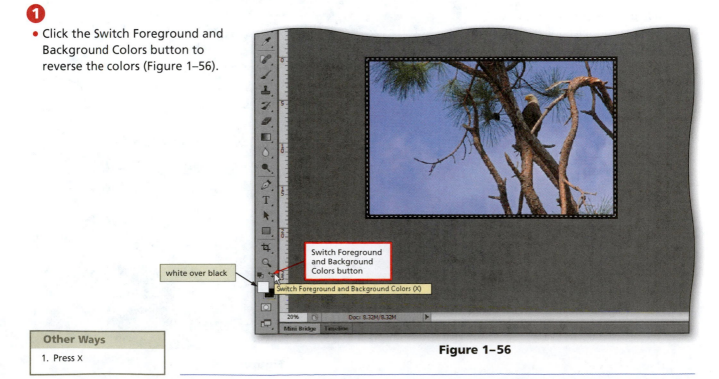

Switch Foreground and Background Colors button

white over black

Switch Foreground and Background Colors (X)

**Other Ways**

1. Press X

**Figure 1–56**

## To Stroke Again

To create the gray border, you will stroke the selection again, this time with white, and using a narrower width.

**1** Click Edit on the Application bar to display the Edit menu.

**2** Click Stroke to display the Stroke dialog box.

**3** Type 25 in the Width box to set the width of the stroke.

**4** Click the OK button to apply the stroke (Figure 1–57).

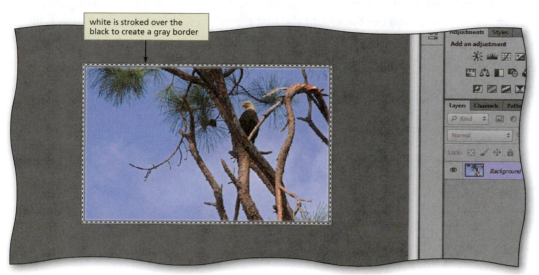

white is stroked over the black to create a gray border

**Figure 1–57**

## To Deselect

Because the border is complete, you should remove the selection indicator, or **deselect** it, so the marquee no longer appears. The following step removes the selection.

**1**

• Click Select on the Application bar, and then click Deselect to remove the selection (Figure 1–58).

selection no longer is displayed

**Figure 1–58**

**Other Ways**

1. Press CTRL+D

### To Switch Foreground and Background Colors Again

The following step switches the foreground and background colors back to black over white.

**1** On the Tools panel, click the Switch Foreground and Background Colors button again to reverse the colors.

**Saving Photos**
When you save a photo on a storage device, it also remains in main memory and is displayed on the screen.

# Saving a Photo with the Same File Name

Because you have made many edits to the photo, it is a good idea to save the photo again. When you saved the document the first time, you assigned the file name, Eagle Edited. When you use the following procedure, Photoshop automatically assigns the same file name to the photo, and it is stored in the same location.

## To Save a File with the Same File Name

The following step saves the Eagle Edited file with the changes you made.

**1**
- On the Application bar, click File to display the File menu, and then click Save to save the photo with the same file name.

| Other Ways |
| --- |
| 1. Press CTRL+S |

## To Close a File

The following step closes the Eagle Edited document window without quitting Photoshop.

**1**
- Click the Close button on the document window tab (Figure 1–59) to close the document window and the image file.

- If Photoshop displays a dialog box asking you to save again, click the No button.

Close button

**Figure 1–59**

**MAC** For a detailed example of this procedure using the Mac operating system, refer to the steps on page APP 81 of the For Mac Users appendix.

| Other Ways | |
| --- | --- |
| 1. Press CTRL+W | 2. On File menu, click Close |

**Break Point:** If you wish to take a break, this is a good place to do so. You can quit Photoshop now. To resume at a later time, start Photoshop, and continue following the steps from this location forward.

# Opening a Recent File in Photoshop

Once you have created and saved a document, you may need to retrieve it from your storage medium. For example, you might want to edit the photo further or print it. Photoshop maintains a list of recently used files to give you quick access to them for further editing. The list is maintained from session to session.

## To Open a Recent File

Earlier in this chapter, you saved your edited photo on a USB flash drive, using the file name, Eagle Edited. The following steps open the Eagle Edited file using the Open Recent list.

**1**

• Click File on the Application bar and then point to Open Recent to display the Open Recent submenu (Figure 1–60).

**Q&A** What does the Clear Recent File List command do?

If you click the Clear Recent File List command, your Recent list will be emptied. To open a file, you then would have to click Open on the File menu and navigate to the location of the file.

**Figure 1–60**

**2**

- Click the Eagle Edited file to open it.

- If necessary, change the magnification to 25% (Figure 1–61).

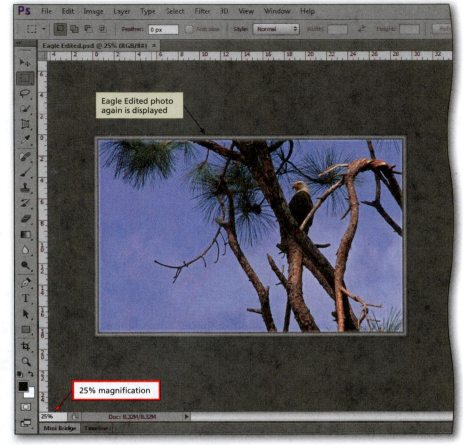

**Figure 1–61**

**Other Ways**

1. Click Open on file menu, navigate to file, click Open button

2. Press CTRL+O, navigate to file, click Open button

3. Press CTRL+O, navigate to file, double-click file

**Document Size**

Cropping reduces the storage size of the document, which is the size of the saved, flattened file in Adobe Photoshop format. The document window status bar displays the new document size after cropping.

# Changing Image Sizes

Sometimes it is necessary to resize an image to fit within certain space limitations. **Resize** means to scale or change the dimensions of the photo. Zooming in or dragging a corner of the document window to change the size is not the same as actually changing the dimensions of the photo. Resizing in a page layout program, such as Publisher, QuarkXPress, or InDesign, merely stretches the pixels. In Photoshop, resizing means adding to or subtracting from the number of pixels.

Photoshop uses a mathematical process called **interpolation**, or **resampling**, when it changes the number of pixels. The program interpolates or calculates how to add new pixels to the photo to match those already there. Photoshop samples the pixels and reproduces them to determine where and how to enlarge or reduce the photo.

When you resize a photo, you must consider many things, such as the type of file, the width, the height, and the resolution. **Resolution** refers to the number of pixels per inch, printed on a page or displayed on a monitor. Not all photos lend themselves to resizing. Some file types lose quality and sharpness when resized. Fine details cannot be interpolated from low-resolution photos. Resizing works best for small changes where exact dimensions are critical. If possible, it usually is better to take a photo at the highest feasible resolution or rescan the image at a higher resolution rather than resize it later.

In those cases where it is impossible to create the photo at the proper size, Photoshop helps you resize or **scale** your photos for print or online media.

**Prepare for publication.**
**Plan**
**Ahead**

Keep in mind the golden rectangle of well-designed photos and the limitations of your space. Resize the photo. Print a copy and evaluate its visual appeal. If you are going to publish the photo to the Web, determine the following:

- Typical download speed of your audience

- Browser considerations

- Number of colors

- File type

Finally, save the photo with a descriptive name indicating its completion.

## To Resize the Image

Because the eagle photo will be printed on a postcard at a specific size, you will change the height to 4 inches. The following steps resize the image to create a custom-sized photo for printing.

**1**

- Click Image on the Application bar to display the Image menu (Figure 1–62).

**Q&A** What is the difference between Image Size and Canvas size?

Increasing the canvas size adds space around an existing image. Decreasing the canvas size is the same as cropping.

**Figure 1–62**

**2**

- Click Image Size to display the Image Size dialog box.

- In the Document Size area, double-click the value in the Height box and then type 4 to replace the previous value (Figure 1–63).

**Q&A** Why did the width change?

When you change the width or height, Photoshop automatically adjusts the other dimension to maintain the proportions of the photo. Your exact width might differ slightly depending on how closely you cropped the original photo.

**Figure 1–63**

**3**

- Click the OK button to finish resizing the image.

- Change the magnification to 100% (Figure 1–64).

🔍 **Experiment**

- Click the status bar menu button and then click Document Dimensions to verify that the image size has been changed. Then, click the status bar menu button again and then click Document Sizes to redisplay the document size.

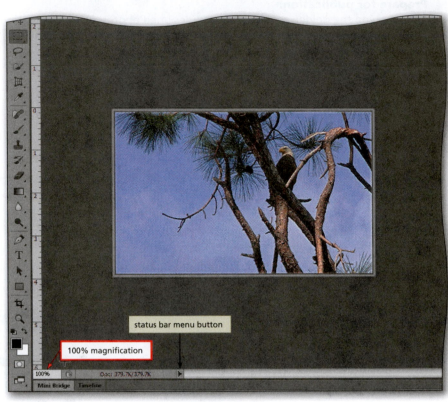

**Figure 1–64**

**Other Ways**

1. Press ALT+CTRL+I, change settings, click OK button

# Inserting Text

The next steps use a type tool to create text for the postcard. On the Tools panel, the default type tool is the Horizontal Type Tool. The options bar for the Horizontal Type Tool (Figure 1–65) includes boxes and buttons typical of those found in a word processing toolbar, including font family, font style, font size, and justification. A Create warped text button allows you to create text in specialized formations, similar to the WordArt tool in Microsoft Word. On the right side of the options bar are buttons to cancel and commit editing changes. In a future chapter, you will learn about the Character and Paragraph panels that provide additional tools for manipulating text.

**Figure 1–65**

## To Select the Horizontal Type Tool

The following step selects the Horizontal Type Tool on the Tools panel.

**1**

- Click the Horizontal Type Tool on the Tools panel to select it (Figure 1–66).

- If the solid T icon does not appear on the button, right-click the button to display its context menu, then click Horizontal Type Tool in the list.

Horizontal Type Tool button

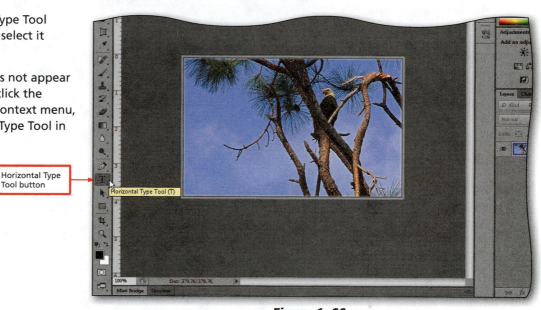

**Figure 1–66**

| Other Ways |
|---|
| 1. Press T |

## To Set Font Options

The following steps select font settings on the options bar. In addition to the font and alignment options, when you click the 'Set the text color' box, Photoshop uses color picker tools, such as a color field and color model boxes, to help you select the text color.

**1**

- On the options bar, click the 'Set the font family' box arrow to display the list of font families.

- Scroll in the list to display the Tahoma font family (Figure 1–67).

Set the font family box arrow

list of available fonts

Tahoma font family

scroll box

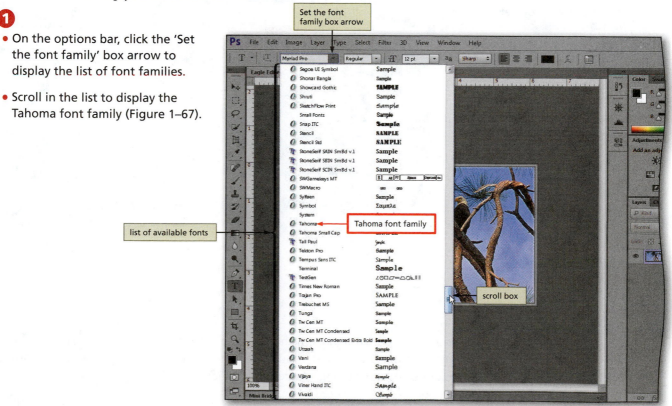

**Figure 1–67**

**2**
- Click Tahoma or a similar font in the list.

- Click the 'Set the font style' box arrow to display the list of font styles (Figure 1–68).

**Q&A**
Why does the list not include other styles, such as italics?

Available font styles depend on the chosen font and the capability of the printer to reproduce that font. This font has only regular and bold styles.

**Figure 1–68**

**3**
- Click Bold to choose a bold font style.

- Select the value in the 'Set the font size' box, and then type 36 to replace the size (Figure 1–69).

**Figure 1–69**

**4**
- Click the 'Set the text color' box to open the Color Picker (Text Color) dialog box.

- Click a white color in the upper-left corner of the color field (Figure 1–70).

**Q&A**
What do the numerical boxes indicate?

Each color mode uses a numerical method called a color model, or color space, to describe the color. Some companies use specific numbers to create exact colors for branding purposes.

**Figure 1–70**

**5**
- Click the OK button in the Color Picker (Text Color) dialog box to apply white as the text color on the options bar.

## To Insert Text

With the type tool selected, you drag a bounding box in the document window to insert text. A **bounding box** is similar to a text box in other applications, with a dotted outline and sizing handles. As you drag, the mouse pointer changes to a small, open book outline. After typing the text in the bounding box, you use the 'Commit any current edits' button to complete the entry. Then, if the size of the bounding box needs to be adjusted, you can drag the sizing handles. The mouse pointer becomes an insertion point when positioned over the text. You will learn about other type tools and features in a later chapter.

The following steps enter text on the postcard.

**1**

- With the Horizontal Type Tool still selected, drag a bounding box in the lower-right portion of the photo, approximately 2.5 inches wide and 2 inches tall, as shown in Figure 1–71.

**Q&A** What is the new notation on the Layers panel?

When you create a bounding box, Photoshop separates the text from the rest of the picture in its own layer. You will learn more about layers in a future chapter.

**Figure 1–71**

**2**

- Type National and then press the ENTER key.

- Type Wildlife and then press the ENTER key.

- Type Park to complete the text (Figure 1–72).

**Q&A** Can I make changes and corrections to the text?

Yes, you can click anywhere in the text box, use the ARROW keys, the BACKSPACE key, and the DELETE key just as you do in word processing. If your bounding box is too small, you can drag the sizing handles.

**Figure 1–72**

**3**

- On the options bar, click the 'Commit any current edits' button to finish the new layer.

## To Stroke Text

Earlier in this chapter, you added a stroke of color to a selection as you created a border for the postcard. The following steps stroke the text with black to make the letters stand out. You will use the Layer Style dialog box to create the stroke.

**1**

- With the new layer still selected on the Layer's panel, click the 'Add a layer style' button on the Layers panel status bar (Figure 1–73).

**Q&A**

Could I use the Stroke command on the Edit menu to stroke text?

No. The Stroke command on the Edit menu is for selections only. Because this is an entire layer, you need to use a layer style.

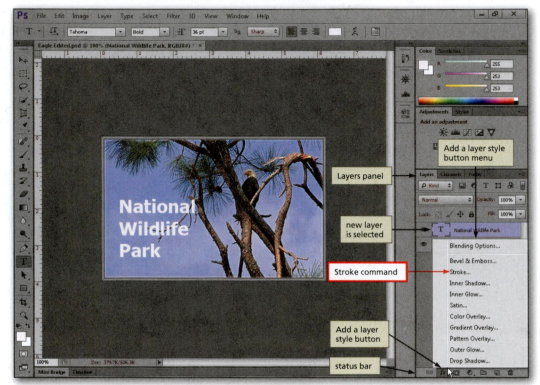

**Figure 1–73**

**2**

- Click Stroke in the list of layer styles to display the Layer Style dialog box.

- Type 1 in the Size box to create 1 pixel of black stroke (Figure 1–74).

**Q&A**

What should I do if my color does not appear as black?

Black is the default color; however, a previous user on your computer may have changed the color. Click the Color box to display a Color Picker dialog box. Click black and then click the OK button.

**Figure 1–74**

**3**

- Click the OK button in the Layer Style dialog box to accept the settings and add the stroke (Figure 1–75).

- Press the D key to reset the default colors on the Tools panel.

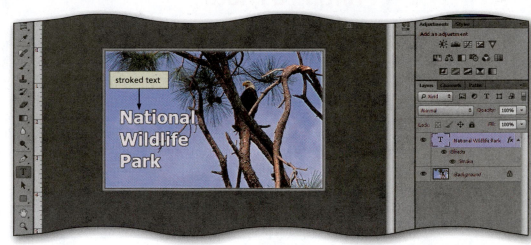

**Figure 1–75**

## To Save a File with a Different Name

Many graphic designers will save multiple copies of the same photo with various edits. Because this photo has been resized to print properly, you need to save it with a different name, as performed in the following step.

**1**

- Click File on the Application bar and then click Save As to display the Save As dialog box.

- In the Save As dialog box, type Eagle Resized with Text in the File name text box.

- If necessary, click the Save in box arrow and then click Removable Disk (F:), or the location of your USB flash drive and appropriate folder in the list.

- If necessary, click the Format button and then click Photoshop (*.PSD, *.PDD) to select the format type (Figure 1–76).

**Figure 1–76**

- Click the Save button to save the image with the new name.

- If Photoshop displays a Photoshop Format Options dialog box, click the OK button to accept the settings and close the dialog box.

# Printing a Photo

The photo now can be printed, saved, taken to a professional print shop, or sent online to a printing service. A printed version of the photo is called a **hard copy** or **printout**. You can print one copy using the Print One Copy command on the File menu, or to display the Print dialog box, you can click Print on the File menu, which offers you more printing options.

The Print One Copy command sends the printout to the default printer. If you are not sure which printer is your default printer, choose the Print command. In the Print dialog box, click the Printer box arrow and choose your current printer. You will learn more about the Print dialog box in Chapter 2.

## To Print a Photo

The following steps print the photo created in this chapter.

**1**

- Ready the printer according to the printer instructions.

- Click File on the Application bar, and then click Print to display the Print dialog box.

- If necessary, click the Printer box arrow and then select your printer from the list. Do not change any other settings (Figure 1–77).

**Q&A**

Does Photoshop have a Print button?

No. Photoshop's Print commands are available on the File menu or by using shortcut keys.

**Figure 1–77**

**2**

- In the Print dialog box, click the Print button to start the printing process. If your system displays a second Print dialog box or a Print Settings dialog box, unique to your printer, click its Print button.

- When the printer stops, retrieve the hard copy of the photo.

| **Other Ways** | |
|---|---|
| 1. To print one copy, press ALT+SHIFT+CTRL+P | 2. To display Print dialog box, press CTRL+P |

# Saving a Photo for Use on the Web

When preparing photos for the Web, you often need to compromise between the quality of the display and the file size. Web users do not want to wait while large photos load from Web servers to their individual computer systems. To solve this problem, Photoshop provides several commands to compress the file size of an image while optimizing its online display quality. Additionally, Photoshop allows you to save the photo in a variety of formats such as **GIF**, which is a compressed graphic format designed to minimize file size and electronic transfer time, or as an **HTML** (Hypertext Markup Language) file, which contains all the necessary information to display your photo in a Web browser.

Therefore, you have two choices in Photoshop for creating Web images: the Zoomify command and the Save for Web command. When you **zoomify**, you create a high-resolution image for the Web, complete with a background and tools for navigation, panning, and zooming. To zoomify, click Export on the File menu and then click Zoomify. In the Zoomify Export dialog box, you set various Web and export options. Photoshop creates the HTML code and accompanying files for you to upload to a Web server.

If you do not want the extra HTML files for the background, navigation, and zooming, you can create a single graphic file by using the Save for Web command. The resulting graphic can be used on the Web or on a variety of mobile devices.

**Optimization** is the process of changing the photo to make it most effective for its purpose. The Save for Web command allows you to preview optimized images in different file formats, and with different file attributes, for precise optimization. You can view multiple versions of a photo simultaneously and modify settings as you preview the image.

BTW

**Reviewing the HTML Code**
If you want to review the HTML code later, you can either open the file in Photoshop, access the Save for Web dialog box, and then click the Preview button; or, you can double-click the HTML file to open it in a browser, click View on the Browser's menu bar, and then click Source.

## To Preview using the Save for Web Dialog Box

To optimize the eagle photo for use on the Web, you need to make decisions about the file size, and how long it might take to load on a Web page, as you preview the image. These kinds of decisions must take into consideration the audience and the nature of the Web page. For example, Web pages geared for college campuses probably could assume a faster download time than those that target a wide range of home users. An e-commerce site that needs high-quality photography to sell its product will make certain choices in color and resolution.

The hardware and software of Web users also is taken into consideration. For instance, if a Web photo contains more colors than the user's monitor can display, a browser might **dither**, or approximate, the colors that it cannot display, by blending colors that it can. Dithering might not be appropriate for some Web pages, because it increases the file size and, therefore, causes the page to load more slowly.

Many other appearance settings play a role in the quality of Web graphics, some of which are subjective in nature. As you become more experienced in Photoshop, you will learn how to make choices about dithering, colors, texture, image size, and other settings.

The step on the next page uses the Save for Web command to display previews for four possible Web formats.

**1**

- With the Eagle Resized with Text photo open, click File on the Application bar to display the File menu and then click Save for Web to display the Save for Web dialog box.

- Click the 4-Up tab to display four versions of the photo (Figure 1–78).

**Q&A**

Why are there four frames?

Photoshop displays four previews — the original photo and three others that are converted to different resolutions to optimize download times.

Figure 1–78

## To Choose a Download Speed

For faster downloads when the photo is displayed as a Web graphic, you can choose a download speed that will be similar to that of your target audience. The **annotation area** below each preview in the Save for Web dialog box provides optimization information such as the size of the optimized file and the estimated download time using the selected modem speed. You will learn more about other settings in the Save for Web dialog box in a later chapter.

The following steps change the download speed to 512 kilobytes per second (Kbps).

**1**

- Click the upper-right preview, if necessary, to choose a high quality version of the photo.

- In the annotation area below the upper-right preview, click the 'Select download speed' button to display the list of connection speeds (Figure 1–79).

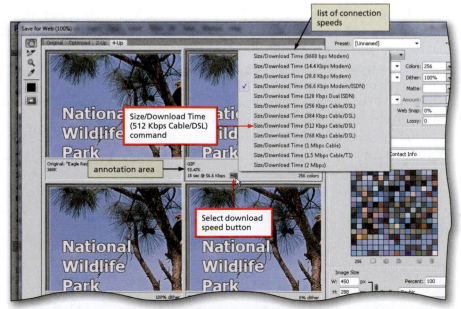

Figure 1–79

**2**

- In the list, click Size/Download Time (512 Kbps Cable/DSL) or another appropriate speed (Figure 1–80).

**Q&A**

How fast will the picture download?

In Figure 1–78, the speed was 18 seconds at 56.6 Kbps. At 512 Kbps, the photo will download in 3 seconds, as shown in Figure 1–80. Your download times might differ slightly.

🔍 **Experiment**

- Click the Select download speed button to display the list of connection speeds and then click various connection speeds to see how the download times are affected. When finished, click Size/Download Time (512 Kbps Cable/DSL) in the list.

Figure 1–80

**Other Ways**

1. Right-click annotation area, select download speed

**BTW**

**Save for Web Preview**
If you want the entire photo to display in the Save for Web dialog box, click the Zoom Level box arrow and then click Fit in View.

## To Preview the Photo on the Web

Before uploading a photo to the Web, it is always a good idea to preview it to check for errors. When Photoshop displays a Web preview of any photo, it also displays the characteristics of the file and the HTML code used to create the preview. The steps on the next page preview the image in a browser.

**1**
- Click the Preview button (shown in Figure 1–80 on the previous page) to display the photo in a Web browser.

- If necessary, double-click the browser's application bar to maximize the browser window (Figure 1–81).

**Q&A**
When I clicked the Preview button, the HTML code displayed in Notepad. Should it open in a browser?

If Photoshop cannot detect a default browser on your system, you may have to click the box arrow next to the Preview button (Figure 1–80), and then click Edit List to add your browser.

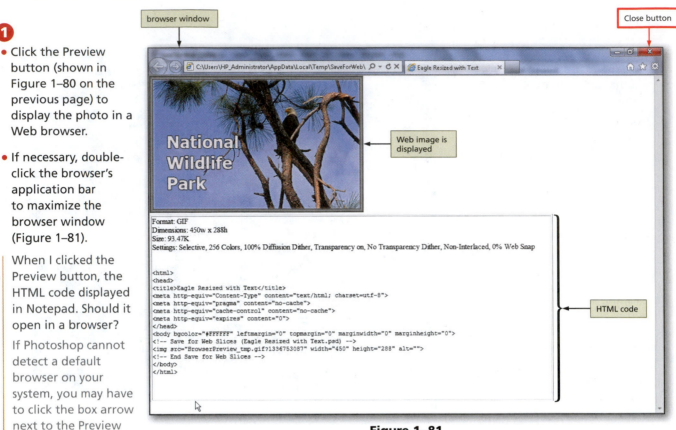

Figure 1–81

**Q&A**
How would I use the HTML code?

As a Web designer, you might copy and paste the code into a text editor or Web creation software, replacing BrowserPreview with the name of the file. After saving, the code, the HTML file, and the photo would need to be uploaded to a server.

**2**
- Click the Close button on the browser's application bar to close the browser window. If necessary, click the Adobe Photoshop CS6 button on the Windows taskbar to return to the Save for Web dialog box.

---

**BTW**

**Saving for Web**
In the Save Optimized As dialog box, you can click the Format button to choose one of three ways to save for the Web. The Images only option saves the photo itself in a Web-friendly format as a GIF file. The HTML only option saves the coding that creates the Web page, but not the photo. The HTML and Images option saves the Web page and creates an accompanying folder named Images to go with the Web page file. Inside the Images folder is a GIF version of the photo.

**BTW**

**CS6 Device Central**
Device Central, available in Photoshop CS6, the extended version, enables you to preview how Photoshop files will look on a variety of mobile devices. An emulator or mock-up displays the device and preview. Photoshop supports most cell phone displays, portable electronic devices, and MP3 players with video. In the Device Central window, you can adjust settings for lighting, scaling, and alignment.

## To Save the Photo for the Web

When you click the Save button in the Save for Web dialog box, Photoshop displays the Save Optimized As dialog box, where you will name the Web file. The following steps save the Photo for the Web.

**1**

- In the Save for Web dialog box (Figure 1–80 on page PS 55), click the Save button to display the Save Optimized As dialog box.

- Type Eagle-for-Web in the File name text box.

- If necessary, click the Save in box arrow and then click Removable Disk (F:), or the location of your USB flash drive. Double-click the appropriate folder in the list (Figure 1–82).

**Q&A** Why are the words in the file name hyphenated?

For ease of use, it is standard for Web graphics to have no spaces in their file names.

**Figure 1–82**

**2**

- Click the Save button in the Save Optimized As dialog box to save the file.

# Photoshop Help

At anytime while you are using Photoshop, you can get answers to questions by using **Photoshop Help**. You activate Photoshop Help either by clicking Help on the Application bar or by pressing the F1 key. The Help menu includes commands to display more information about your copy of Photoshop, as well as a list of how-to guides for common tasks. The Photoshop Online Help command connects you, through the Adobe Photoshop Support Center on the Web, to a wealth of assistance, including tutorials with detailed instructions accompanied by illustrations and videos. Used properly, this form of online assistance can increase your productivity and reduce your frustration by minimizing the time you spend learning how to use Photoshop. Additional information about using Photoshop Help is available in Appendix D, the Using Photoshop Help appendix.

**BTW**

**Community Help**
Community Help is an integrated Web environment that includes Photoshop Help and gives you access to community-generated content moderated by Adobe and industry experts. Comments from users help guide you to an answer.

## To Access Photoshop Help

The next step displays Photoshop Help online. You must be connected to the Web if you plan to perform these steps on a computer.

**1**

- With Photoshop open on your system, press the F1 key to access the Photoshop Help / Help and tutorials page.

- If necessary, double-click the application bar to maximize the window (Figure 1–83).

**Q&A**

My page looks different. Did I do something wrong?

No. Adobe updates the Help pages frequently. Your page will differ.

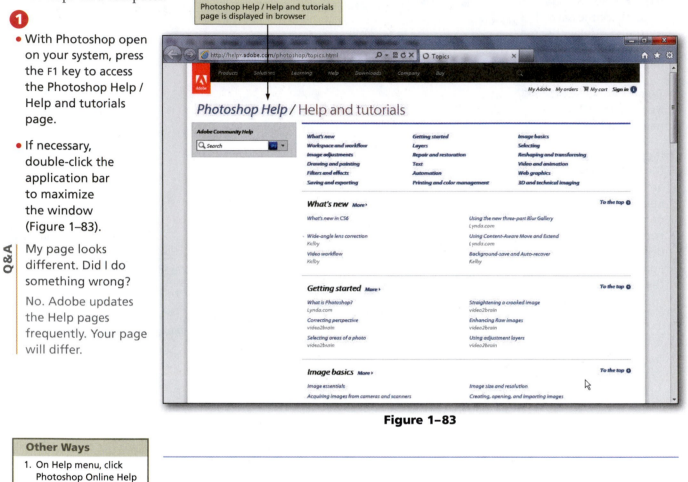

Photoshop Help / Help and tutorials page is displayed in browser

**Figure 1–83**

**Other Ways**

1. On Help menu, click Photoshop Online Help

## To Use the Help Search Box

The Search box allows you to type words or phrases about which you want additional information and help, such as cropping or printing images. When you press the ENTER key, Photoshop Help responds by displaying a list of topics related to the word or phrase you typed.

The following steps use the Search box to obtain information about the Tools panel.

**1**
• Click the Search
box and then type
`Tools panel` to
enter the search topic
(Figure 1–84).

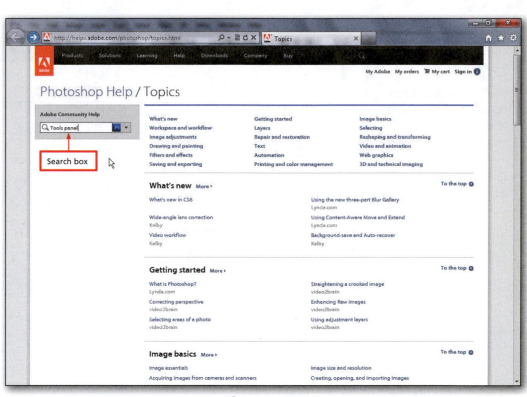

**Figure 1–84**

**2**
• Press the ENTER key to
display the relevant
links (Figure 1–85).

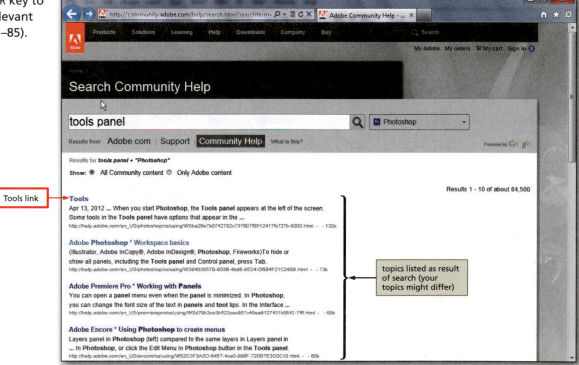

**Figure 1–85**

**3**

- Click the link, Tools, to display the contents (Figure 1–86).

- Scroll as necessary to read the information about tools.

🔍 **Experiment**

- Click other links to view more information, or search for other topics using the Search box.

**4**

- In the browser application bar, click the Close button to close the window, and then, if necessary, click the Adobe Photoshop CS6 button on the taskbar to return to Photoshop.

Close button

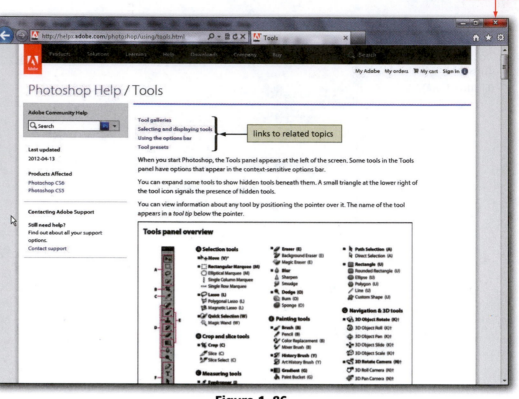

**Figure 1–86**

**Other Ways**

1. On Help menu, click Photoshop Online Help, enter search topic

## To Quit Photoshop

The following step quits Photoshop and returns control to Windows.

**1**

- Click the Close button on the right side of the Application bar to close the window.

- If Photoshop displays a dialog box asking you to save changes, click the No button.

**MAC** For a detailed example of this procedure using the Mac operating system, refer to the steps on page APP 82 of the For Mac Users appendix.

**Other Ways**

1. On File menu, click Exit
2. Press CTRL+Q

# Chapter Summary

In this chapter, you gained a broad knowledge of Photoshop. First, you learned how to start Photoshop. You were introduced to the Photoshop workspace. You learned how to open a photo, change the magnification, zoom, and display rulers. You learned about design issues related to the placement of visual points of interest. You then learned how to crop a photo to eliminate extraneous background. After you added a blended border, you resized the image and added text. Once you saved the photo, you learned how to print it. You used the Save for Web command to optimize and save a Web version. You learned how to use Adobe Help to research specific help topics. Finally, you learned how to quit Photoshop.

The items listed below include all the new Photoshop skills you have learned in this chapter:

1. Start Photoshop (PS 4)
2. Select the Essentials Workspace (PS 6)
3. Select the Default Tool (PS 8)
4. Reset the Options Bar (PS 8)
5. Reset the Interface Color (PS 9)
6. Open a File (PS 11)
7. Save a File in the PSD Format (PS 20)
8. Use the Zoom Tool (PS 24)
9. Use the Navigator Panel (PS 26)
10. Minimize the Navigator Panel (PS 27)
11. Use the Hand Tool (PS 28)
12. Change the Magnification (PS 29)
13. Display Rulers (PS 30)
14. Crop a Photo (PS 33)
15. Create a Selection (PS 35)
16. Stroke a Selection (PS 36)
17. Modify a Selection (PS 39)
18. Switch Foreground and Background Colors (PS 40)
19. Deselect (PS 41)
20. Save a File with the Same File Name (PS 42)
21. Close a File (PS 42)
22. Open a Recent File (PS 43)
23. Resize the Image (PS 45)
24. Select the Horizontal Type Tool (PS 47)
25. Set Font Options (PS 47)
26. Insert Text (PS 48)
27. Stroke Text (PS 50)
28. Save a File with a Different Name (PS 51)
29. Print a Photo (PS 52)
30. Preview using the Save for Web Dialog Box (PS 53)
31. Choose a Download Speed (PS 54)
32. Preview the Photo on the Web (PS 55)
33. Save the Photo for the Web (PS 56)
34. Access Photoshop Help (PS 58)
35. Use the Help Search Box (PS 58)
36. Quit Photoshop (PS 60)

## Apply Your Knowledge

Reinforce the skills and apply the concepts you learned in this chapter.

### Editing a Photo in the Photoshop Workspace

*Instructions:*   Start Photoshop and perform the customization steps found on pages PS 6 through PS 10. Open the Apply 1-1 Water Park file in the Chapter 01 folder from the Data Files for Students. Visit www.cengage.com/ct/studentdownload for detailed instructions or contact your instructor for information about accessing the required files.

First, you will save the photo in the PSD format, then you will crop the photo, add a white border, and save the edited photo, as shown in Figure 1–87 on the next page. Next, you will resize the photo for printing and print one copy. Finally, you will reopen your edited photo, and then you will optimize it for the Web, save it, and close it.

*Continued >*

Source: Mali Jones

**Figure 1–87**

*Perform the following tasks:*

1. On the File menu, click Save As. When Photoshop displays the Save As dialog box, navigate to your storage device and then double-click the appropriate folder, if necessary. In the File name box, type `Apply 1-1 Water Park Edited`. Click the Format button and choose the PSD file format. Click the Save button to save the file.

2. Use the Zoom Tool to zoom the photo to 50% magnification, if necessary.

3. Use the Hand Tool to reposition the photo in the workspace to view different areas of the zoomed photo.

4. Use the Navigator panel to zoom out to 16.67%.

5. Use the Crop Tool to crop the photo, retaining the top patio of the water slide and the child on the right slide as shown in Figure 1–87. When using the Crop Tool, you might want to use the 'Rotate the crop box between portrait and landscape orientation' button. Include more water than sky. Use the rule of thirds guide to position the child in the lower-right intersection. (*Hint:* If your cropping selection does not look correct, you can press the ESC key to clear the selection before you press the ENTER key. Immediately after cropping the photo, you can click Undo on the Edit menu to undo the crop action.)

6. Select a different tool so the cropping handles no longer are displayed.

7. To create the border:

   a. If necessary, press the D key to select the default colors. Press the x key to reverse the foreground and background colors, so that white displays over black on the Tools panel.

   b. Press CTRL+A to select all of the photo.

   c. Use the Select menu to modify the border to 100 pixels.

   d. Use the Stroke command on the Edit menu to stroke the selection with white.

   e. Press CTRL+D to clear your selection when you are finished creating the border.

8. Press CTRL+S to save the Apply 1-1 Water Park Edited photo with the same file name in the same location.

9. Use the Image menu to resize the photo width to 5 inches wide to create a custom-sized photo for printing.

10. Save the resized file as Apply 1-1 Water Park for Print.

11. Print the photo and then close the file. If Photoshop displays a dialog box about saving again, click the No button.

12. Open the Apply 1-1 Water Park for Print file using the Open Recent list.

13. Save the photo for the Web, displaying it in the 4-Up tab. Select the preview that looks the best for your download speed.

14. Preview the optimized photo in your browser. Close the browser.

15. Save the optimized file with the name, Apply-1-1-Water-Park-for-Web.

16. Close the Apply 1-1 Water Park for Print file without saving it and quit Photoshop.

## Extend Your Knowledge

Extend the skills you learned in this chapter and experiment with new skills. You may need to use Help to complete the assignment.

### Exploring Crop Tool Options

*Instructions:*  Start Photoshop and perform the customization steps found on pages PS 6 through PS 10. Open the Extend 1-1 Arc de Triomphe file in the Chapter 01 folder from the Data Files for Students and save it on your storage device as Extend 1-1 Arc de Triomphe Edited in the PSD file format. Visit www.cengage.com/ct/studentdownload for detailed instructions or contact your instructor for information about accessing the required files.

The photo (Figure 1–88) is to be added to a book about Paris; therefore, the structure should be centered, straightened, and display in a 5 × 7 format.

**Figure 1–88**

*Continued >*

**Extend Your Knowledge** *continued*

*Perform the following tasks:*

1. Use Help to read about the Crop Tool's Straighten button and the Aspect Ratio button.

2. Select the Crop Tool. On the options bar, click the Straighten button, and then drag in the photo, across a line that should be straight in the upper portion of the monument.

3. Use the 'Select a preset aspect ratio' button to choose a 5 × 7 forced ratio. Drag a corner cropping handle inward, keeping the arc within the grid. Drag the picture to center it within the cropping area.

4. Click the 'Delete cropped pixels' check box, if necessary, and then crop the photo.

5. Review Table 1–4 on page PS 38. Use the commands on the Modify submenu to set the border options of your choice. Stroke the selection with a color of your choice.

6. After viewing the resulting border, use the History panel to go back to the photo's cropped state.

7. Repeat Steps 5 and 6 several times to experiment with different border widths and colors, then apply the border that best complements the photo and save the changes to the photo.

8. Close the photo and quit Photoshop.

## Make It Right

Analyze a project and correct all errors and/or improve the design.

### Changing a Photo's Focus and Optimizing It for the Web

*Instructions:* Start Photoshop and perform the customization steps found on pages PS 6 through PS 10. Open the Make It Right 1-1 Young Stars file in the Chapter 01 folder from the Data Files for Students and save it on your storage device as Make It Right 1-1 Young Stars Edited in the PSD file format. Visit www.cengage.com/ct/studentdownload for detailed instructions or contact your instructor for information about accessing the required files.

Members of your Astronomy Club have selected the Young Stars photo (Figure 1–89) for the club's Web site. You are tasked with editing the photo to focus more clearly on the cluster of stars and its trailing dust blanket, and then optimizing the photo for the Web.

Source: NASA/JPL–Caltech/Harvard-Smithsonian CFA

**Figure 1–89**

View the photo in different screen modes and at different magnifications. Keeping the rule of thirds and the golden rectangle concepts in mind, crop the photo to change its focal point and resave it. Then save the photo for the Web as Make-It-Right-1-1-Young-Stars-for-Web.

## In the Lab

Design and/or create a project using the guidelines, concepts, and skills presented in this chapter. Labs are listed in order of increasing difficulty.

### Lab 1: Cropping a Photo and Adding a Smooth Border

*Problem:*   An extreme sports magazine has accepted the submission of your parasailing photo, but they would like you to crop the photo more, add a smooth border, and resize it. The edited photo is displayed in Figure 1–90.

*Note:*   To complete this assignment, you will be required to use the Data Files for Students. Visit www.cengage.com/ct/studentdownload for detailed instructions or contact your instructor for information about accessing the required files.

**Figure 1–90**

*Instructions:*   Perform the following tasks:

1. Start Photoshop.

2. Click Window on the application bar, point to Workspace, and then click Essentials (Default). Repeat the process and click Reset Essentials to reset the Essentials workspace.

3. Select the second button on the Tools panel to reset the Tools panel.

4. Right-click the Rectangular Marquee Tool icon on the options bar, and then click Reset all Tools to reset the options bar.

5. Press the D key to select the default colors. If black is not over white at the bottom of the Tools panel, click the Switch foreground and background colors button.

6. Open the file, Lab 1-1 Parasailing, from the Chapter 01 folder of the Data Files for Students or from a location specified by your instructor.

7. Click Save As on the File menu, and then type the new file name, Lab 1-1 Parasailing Edited. Navigate to your storage location, if necessary. Click the Format button and choose the PSD format. Click the Save button.

8. Use the Magnification box to zoom the photo to 25% magnification, if necessary.

9. If the rulers do not appear, press CTRL+R to view the rulers.

10. Select the Crop Tool. Click the photo to display the rule of thirds grid. SHIFT+drag the lower-right cropping handle until the sail is positioned at the upper-right intersection of the rule of thirds grid.

11. Press the ENTER key. If your crop does not seem correct, click the Undo command on the Edit menu and repeat Step 10.

12. Select another tool so the cropping handles no longer are displayed.

13. Save the photo again.

14. Press CTRL+A to select all of the photo. Click Select on the Application bar, point to Modify to display the Modify submenu, and then click Border to display the Border Selection dialog box. Type 100 in the Width box, and then click the OK button.

*Continued >*

*In the Lab continued*

15. Display the Modify submenu again, and click Smooth. Type 5 0 in the Smooth Radius box, and then click the OK button to create a second marquee with smoothed corners.

16. If white is not the foreground color, press the x key to switch the foreground and background colors. Click Edit on the Application bar and then click Stroke. Type 5 0 in the Width box. Click the Inside option button in the Location area. Click the OK button to stroke the selection. Press CTRL+D to deselect.

17. Click the Image Size command on the Image menu. When the Image Size dialog box is displayed, in the Document Size area, type 4 in the Width box. Click the OK button.

18. Press CTRL+S to save the file again.

19. Use the Print One Copy command on the File menu to print a copy of the photo.

20. Close your file and quit Photoshop.

21. Send the photo as an e-mail attachment to your instructor, or submit it in the format specified by your instructor.

## In the Lab

### Lab 2: Creating a Smoothed Border

*Problem:* The local hockey team is preparing a flyer to advertise its next game. The marketing department would like you to take one of the pictures from the last game and crop it to show just the face-off players and the official. Because the flyer will be printed on white paper, you should create a white border, so the photo blends into the background and adds to the ice rink effect. The edited photo is displayed in Figure 1–91.

**Figure 1–91**

*Note:* To complete this assignment, you will be required to use the Data Files for Students. Visit www.cengage.com/ct/studentdownload for detailed instructions or contact your instructor for information about accessing the required files.

*Instructions:* Perform the following tasks:

1. Start Photoshop. Perform the customization steps found on pages PS 6 through PS 10.

2. Open the file, Lab 1-2 Hockey, from the Chapter 01 folder of the Data Files for Students or from a location specified by your instructor.

3. Use the Save As command on the File menu to save the file on your storage device with the name, Lab 1-2 Hockey Edited, in the PSD format.

4. Click the Zoom Tool button on the Tools panel. Click the official in the photo to center the photo in the display. Zoom as necessary so you can make precise edits.

5. Crop the picture to display only the official and the two hockey players ready for the face-off. The vertical line of the hockey stick and the visual line of the official should be positioned using the rule of thirds.

6. Select a different tool so the cropping handles no longer are displayed.

7. Save the photo again with the same name.

8. Close the file and open it again using the Recent submenu.

9. Press CTRL+A to select all of the photo.

10. To create the border, do the following:

    a. On the Select menu, point to Modify, and then click Border.

    b. When the Border Selection dialog box is displayed, type 100 in the Width Box. Click the OK button.

    c. On the Select menu, open the Modify submenu, and then click Smooth.

    d. When the Smooth Selection dialog box is displayed, type 50 in the Sample Radius box to smooth the corners. Click the OK button.

    e. Press SHIFT+F5 to access the Fill command.

    f. When the Fill dialog box is displayed, click the Use box arrow and then click White in the list.

    g. Click the Mode box arrow and then click Normal in the list, if necessary.

    h. If necessary, type 100 in the Opacity box. Click the OK button.

    i. Press CTRL+D to deselect the border.

11. Save the photo again.

12. Use the Print One Copy command on the File menu to print a copy of the photo.

13. Close the document window.

14. Quit Photoshop.

15. Submit the assignment in the format specified by your instructor.

## In the Lab

### Lab 3: Preparing a Photo for the Web

*Problem:* As an independent consultant in Web site design, you have been hired by the Pineapple Growers Association to prepare a photo of an exotic pineapple growing in a field for use on the association's Web site. The edited photo is displayed in Figure 1–92.

*Note:* To complete this assignment, you will be required to use the Data Files for Students. Visit www.cengage.com/ct/student-download for detailed instructions or contact your instructor for information about accessing the required files.

*Instructions:* Perform the following tasks:
Start Photoshop. Perform the customization steps found on pages PS 6 through PS 10. Open the file, Lab 1-3 Pineapple, from the Chapter 01 folder of the Data Files for Students. Save the file in the PSD format with the name Lab 1-3 Pineapple Edited. Resize the photo to 500 pixels wide. Zoom to 50% magnification. Search Photoshop Help for help related to optimization. Read about optimizing for the Web. Print a copy of the help topic and then close the Adobe Help window.

Use the Save for Web dialog box to view the 4-Up tab. Choose the best-looking preview. Select the connection speed of

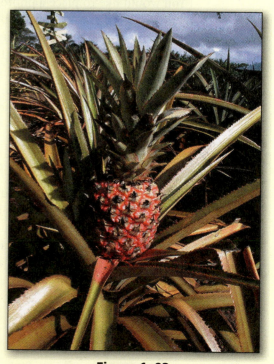

**Figure 1–92**

*Continued >*

**In the Lab** *continued*

your Internet connection. Save the Web version of the photo using the name, Lab-1-3-Pineapple-for-Web. For extra credit, upload the Web version to a Web server. See Appendix C for information on publishing to a Web server. See your instructor for ways to submit this assignment.

## Cases and Places

Apply your creative thinking and problem-solving skills to design and implement a solution.

*Note:* To complete these assignments, you may be required to use the Data Files for Students. Visit www.cengage.com/ct/studentdownload for detailed instructions or contact your instructor for information about accessing the required files.

### 1: Crop a Photo for a Class Directory

**Academic**

As a member of your high school reunion committee, it is your task to assemble the class photo directory. You are to edit a high school student photo and prepare it for print in the reunion directory. The photo needs to fit in a space 1.75 inches high and 1.33 inches wide. Each photo needs to have approximately .25 inches above the head. After starting Photoshop and resetting the workspace, select the photo, Case 1-1 Student, from the Chapter 01 folder of the Data Files for Students. Save the photo on your USB flash drive storage device as Case 1-1 Student Edited, using the PSD format. Resize the photo to match the requirements. Use the rulers to help you crop the photo for .25 inches above the top of the student's head. Save the photo again and print a copy for your instructor.

### 2: Create a Photo for a Social Networking Site

**Personal**

You would like to place a photo of your recent tubing adventure on your social networking page. The photo you have is of two people. You need to crop out the other person who is tubing. After starting Photoshop and resetting the workspace, select the photo, Case 1-2 Tubing, from the Chapter 01 folder of the Data Files for Students. Save the photo on your USB flash drive storage device as Case 1-2 Tubing Edited, using the PSD format. Crop the photo to remove one of the tubes, keeping in mind the rule of thirds, the golden rectangle, and the direction of the action. Save the photo for the Web and upload it to Facebook or another Web server as directed by your instructor.

### 3: Creating a Photo for a Brochure

**Professional**

You are an intern with an event planning business. The company is planning to send out a trifold brochure about local churches and chapels used for weddings. The photo named Case 1-3 Chapel is located in the Chapter 01 folder of the Data Files for Students. Save the photo on your USB flash drive storage device as Case 1-3 Chapel Edited, using the PSD format. Resize the photo to be 3.5 inches wide. Create a black border of 10 pixels. Save the file again and print a copy for your instructor.

# 2 | Using Selection Tools and Shortcut Keys

Adobe product screenshot(s) reprinted with permission from Adobe Systems Incorporated

## Objectives

You will have mastered the material in this chapter when you can:

- Explain the terms layout, perspective, and storyboard

- Describe selection tools

- Select objects using the marquee tools

- Move and duplicate selections

- Use the History panel

- Use the Grow command and Refine Edges to adjust selections

- Employ the lasso tools

- Subtract areas from selections

- Use grids, guides, and snapping

- Select objects using the Quick Selection and Magic Wand Tools

- Print to a PDF file

- Use, create, and test new keyboard shortcuts

# 2 | Using Selection Tools and Shortcut Keys

## Introduction

In Chapter 1, you learned about the Photoshop interface, as well as navigation and zooming techniques. You cropped and resized a photo, added a border and text, and saved the photo for both Web and print media. You learned about Online Help, along with opening, saving, and printing photos. This chapter continues to emphasize those topics and presents some new ones.

Recall that when you make a selection, you are specifying or isolating an area of your photo for editing. By selecting specific areas, you can edit and apply special effects to portions of your image, while leaving the unselected areas untouched. The new topics covered in this chapter include the marquee tools used to select rectangular or elliptical areas, the lasso tools used to select free-form segments or shapes, and the Quick Selection and Magic Wand Tools used to select consistently colored areas. You will learn how to use the Move Tool to duplicate and scale. Finally, you will print to a PDF file and create a new keyboard shortcut.

## Project — Advertisement Graphic

An advertisement, or ad, is a form of communication that promotes a product or service to a potential customer. An advertisement tries to persuade consumers to purchase a product or service. An advertisement typically has a single message directed toward a target audience.

A graphic designed for advertising, sometimes called an **advertising piece**, needs to catch the customer's eye and entice him or her to purchase the product. A clear graphic with strong contrast, item repetition, and visual lines tells the story and enhances text that might be added later. Chapter 2 illustrates the creation of a retail store advertising piece. You will begin with the image in Figure 2–1a that shows individual wicker baskets. You then will manipulate the image by selecting, editing, and moving the objects to produce a more attractive layout, creating Figure 2–1b for use in the advertisement.

### Overview

As you read this chapter, you will learn how to create the advertisement graphic shown in Figure 2–1b by performing these general tasks:

- Select portions of the photo.
- Copy, move, and scale selections.
- Eliminate white space in and among objects in selected areas.
- Retrace editing steps using the History panel.
- Refine edges of selections.
- Print to a PDF file.
- Create a new shortcut key.

**(a) Original image**

**(b) Edited image**

**Figure 2–1**

**Plan
Ahead**

**General Project Guidelines**

When editing a photo, the actions you perform and decisions you make will affect the appearance and characteristics of the finished product. As you edit a photo, such as the one shown in Figure 2–1a, you should follow these general guidelines:

1. **Choose the correct tool.** When you need to copy and paste portions of your photo, consider carefully which Photoshop selection tool to use. You want the procedure to be efficient and produce a clear image. Keep in mind the shape and background of the photo you want to copy, as well as your expertise with various tools.

2. **Plan your duplications.** Use a storyboard or make a list of the items you plan to duplicate, and then decide whether it will be an exact duplication or a manipulated one, called a **transformed copy**. The decision depends on the visual effect you want to achieve and the customer requirements.

3. **Use grids and guides.** When you are working with exact measurements, close cropping and moving, or just want to align things easily, use grids and guides to display nonprinting lines across the document window. Use the Photoshop snapping function to align selections. Visual estimations of size and location are easier to perceive when using these guides.

4. **Create files in portable formats.** You might have to distribute your artwork in a variety of formats, depending on its use. Portability is an important consideration. It usually is safe to begin work in the Photoshop PSD format and then use the Save as command or Print command to convert your work to the PDF format. PDF files are platform and software independent.

When necessary, more specific details concerning the above guidelines are presented at appropriate points in the chapter. The chapter also will identify the actions performed and decisions made regarding these guidelines during the creation of the edited photo shown in Figure 2–1b.

# Creating an Advertising Piece

Figure 2–2 illustrates the design decisions made to create the advertising piece. Using an attractive layout containing multiple objects is a good marketing strategy; such a piece visually and subconsciously can encourage the viewer to purchase more than one item. **Layout** refers to placing visual elements into a pleasing and understandable arrangement; in the basket advertisement, the layout is suggestive of how the product or products might look in a buyer's home. Advertising artists and product designers try to determine how the target consumer will use the product and group objects accordingly in the layout.

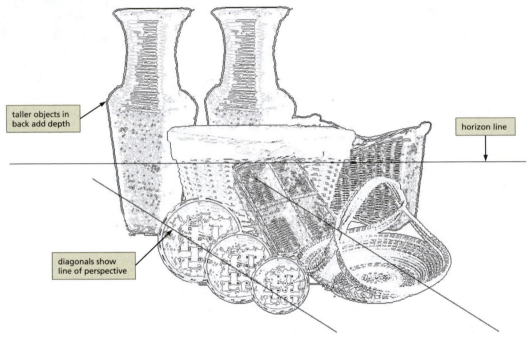

Figure 2–2

From a design point of view, creating visual diagonal lines creates perspective. **Perspective** is the technique photographers, designers, and artists use to create the illusion of three dimensions on a flat or two-dimensional surface. Perspective is a means of fooling the eye by making it appear as if there is depth or receding space in an image. Adjusting the sizes and juxtaposing the objects creates asymmetrical balance and visual tension between the featured products. For example, in Figure 2–2, the height of the tall baskets leads the viewer's eye to the background, as does the diagonal alignment of smaller pieces in front of the larger ones.

The **horizon line** in perspective drawing is a virtual horizontal line across the picture. The placement of the horizon line determines from where the viewer seems to be looking, such as down from a high place or up from close to the ground. In the basket advertisement, the horizon line runs across the middle of the drawing.

Using white space, or nonimage area, is effective in directing the viewer to notice what is important. The products grouped this way are, in a sense, framed by the white space.

This product layout also helps other members of the design team when it is time to make decisions about type placement. The group of products can be shifted up or down, as one image, to accommodate the layout and text, including the font sizes, placement, title, description, and price information. Recall that the rule of thirds offers a useful means to make effective layouts for images and text.

Designing a preliminary layout sketch, similar to Figure 2–2, to help you make choices about placement, size, perspective, and spacing, is referred to as creating a **storyboard** or **rough**.

## To Start Photoshop

If you are stepping through this project on a computer and you want your screen to match the figures in this book, then you should change your computer's resolution to 1024 × 768 and reset the panels, tools, and colors. For more information about how to change the resolution on your computer and other advanced Photoshop settings, read Appendix F, the Changing Screen Resolution appendix.

The following steps, which assume Windows 7 is running, start Photoshop based on a typical installation. You may need to ask your instructor how to start Photoshop for your system.

**1** Click the Start button on the Windows 7 taskbar to display the Start menu and then type `Photoshop CS6` in the 'Search programs and files' box.

**2** Click Adobe Photoshop CS6 in the list to start Photoshop.

**3** If the Photoshop window is not maximized, click the Maximize button next to the Close button on the Application bar to maximize the window.

## To Reset the Workspace

As discussed in Chapter 1, it is helpful to reset the workspace so that the tools and panels appear in their default positions. The following steps select the Essentials workspace.

**1** Click Window on the Application bar to display the Window menu, and then point to Workspace to display the Workspace submenu.

**2** Click Essentials (Default) on the Workspace submenu to select the default workspace panels.

**3** Click Window on the Application bar, and then point to Workspace again to display the list.

**4** Click Reset Essentials to restore the workspace to its default settings and reposition any panels that may have been moved.

## To Reset the Tools and the Options Bar

Recall that the Tools panel and the options bar retain their settings from previous Photoshop sessions. The following steps select the Rectangular Marquee Tool and reset all tool settings in the options bar.

**1** If the tools in the Tools panel appear in two columns, click the double arrow at the top of the Tools panel.

**2** If necessary, click the Rectangular Marquee Tool button on the Tools panel to select it.

**3** Right-click the Rectangular Marquee Tool icon on the options bar to display the context menu, and then click Reset All Tools. When Photoshop displays a confirmation dialog box, click the OK button to restore the tools to their default settings.

## To Set the Interface and Default Colors

Recall that Photoshop retains the interface color scheme, as well as the foreground and background colors, from session to session. The following steps set the interface to Medium Gray and the foreground and background colors to black over white.

 Click Edit on the Application bar to display the Edit menu. Point to Preferences and then click Interface on the Preferences submenu to display the Preferences dialog box.

**2** If necessary, click the third button, Medium Gray, to change the interface color scheme.

**3** Click the OK button to close the Preferences dialog box.

**4** Press the D key to reset the default foreground and background colors. If black is not over white on the Tools panel, press the X key.

## To Open a File

To open a file in Photoshop, it must be stored as a digital file on your computer system or on an external storage device. To complete this assignment, you will be required to use the Data Files for Students. Visit www.cengage.com/ct/studentdownload for detailed instructions or contact your instructor for information about accessing the required files. The following steps open the Baskets file from the Data Files for Students.

**1** With the Photoshop window open, click File on the Application bar, and then click Open to display the Open dialog box.

**2** In the Open dialog box, click the Look in box arrow to display the list of available locations, and then click the location of the Photoshop Data Files for Students.

**3** Double-click the Chapter 02 folder to display its contents. Double-click the file, Baskets, to open it.

**4** When Photoshop displays the image in the document window, if the magnification shown on the status bar is not 60%, double-click the magnification box on the document window status bar, type 60, and then press the ENTER key to change the magnification (Figure 2–3).

**BTW**

**Document Window Status Bar**
The status bar of the document window in Figure 2–3 shows the current document size. To display the document dimensions, click the status bar menu button, and then click Document Dimensions.

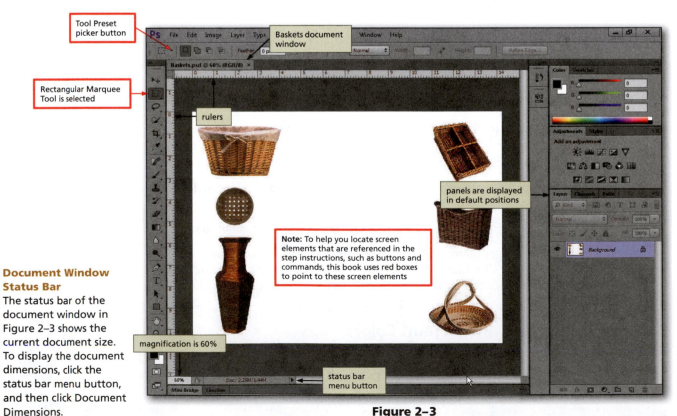

**Figure 2–3**

## To View Rulers

The following steps display the rulers in the document window to facilitate making precise measurements.

**1** If the rulers are not shown on the top and left sides of the document window, press CTRL+R to display the rulers in the workspace.

**2** If necessary, right-click the horizontal ruler and then click Inches on the context menu to display the rulers in inches.

## To Save a Photo

Even though you have yet to edit the photo, it is a good practice to save the file on your personal storage device early in the process. The following steps save the photo with the name Baskets Edited in a new folder named Chapter 02.

**1** With your USB flash drive connected to one of the computer's USB ports, click File on the Application bar to display the File menu and then click Save As to display the Save As dialog box.

**2** In the File name text box, type `Baskets Edited` to rename the file. Do not press the ENTER key after typing the file name.

**3** Click the Save in box arrow, and then click Removable Disk (F:), or the location associated with your USB flash drive, in the list, if necessary.

**4** On the Save As dialog box toolbar, click the Create New Folder button to create a new folder on the selected storage device.

**5** When the new folder appears, type `Chapter 02` to change the name of the folder, and then press the ENTER key. Double-click the new folder to open it.

**6** Click the Save button in the Save As dialog box to save the file in the new folder.

# The Marquee Tools

The **marquee tools** allow you to draw a marquee that selects a portion of the document window. Marquee tools are useful when the part of an image or photo that you wish to select fits into a rectangular or an elliptical shape. Photoshop has four marquee tools that appear in a context menu when you click the tool and hold down the mouse button, or when you right-click the tool. You can select any of the marquee tools from this context menu. Recall that Photoshop offers the added flexibility of selecting a tool with a single letter shortcut key. Pressing the M key activates the current marquee tool.

The Rectangular Marquee Tool is the default marquee tool that selects a rectangular or square portion of the image or photo. The Elliptical Marquee Tool allows you to select an ellipsis, oval, or circular area.

Dragging with the Rectangular or Elliptical Marquee Tools creates a marquee drawn from a corner. If you press the SHIFT key while dragging a marquee, Photoshop constrains the proportions of the shape, creating a perfect square or circle. If you press the ALT key while drawing a selection, Photoshop creates the marquee from the center. Pressing SHIFT+ALT starts from the center and constrains the proportions.

**BTW**

**Marquee Tool Selection**
If you are using a different tool and want to activate the marquee tools, you can click the Rectangular Marquee Tool button on the Tools panel or press the M key on the keyboard to select the tool. Once the tool is selected, pressing SHIFT+M toggles between the Rectangular and Elliptical Marquee tools. You must choose the Single Row and Single Column Marquee tools from the context menu – there are no keyboard shortcuts.

The Single Row Marquee Tool allows you to select a single row of pixels. The Single Column Marquee Tool allows you to select a single column of pixels. A single click in the document window then creates the selection. Because a single row or column of pixels is so small, it is easier to use these two marquee tools at higher magnifications.

**Plan Ahead**

**Choose the correct tool.**

When you need to copy, paste, and move portions of your photo, consider carefully which selection tool to use. You want the procedure to be efficient and produce a clear image. Keep in mind the following as you choose a selection tool:

- The shape of the selection
- The background around the selection
- The contrast between the selection and its surroundings
- The proximity of the selection to other objects
- Your expertise in using the tool
- The availability of other pointing devices, such as a graphics tablet
- The destination of the paste

Table 2–1 describes the four marquee tools.

**BTW**

**Single Row and Single Column Marquee Tools**
To create interesting backgrounds, wallpapers, and color ribbons using the Single Row or Single Column Marquee tools, choose a colorful photo and create a single row or single column marquee. Press CTRL+T to display the bounding box. Then drag the sizing handles until the selection fills the document window.

### Table 2–1 The Marquee Tools

| Tool | Purpose | Shortcut | Button |
|------|---------|----------|--------|
| Rectangular Marquee | Selects a rectangular or square portion of the document window | M SHIFT+M toggles to Elliptical Marquee | |
| Elliptical Marquee | Selects an elliptical, oval, or circular portion of the document window | M SHIFT+M toggles to Rectangular Marquee | |
| Single Row Marquee | Selects a single row of pixels in the document window | (none) | |
| Single Column Marquee | Selects a single column of pixels in the document window | (none) | |

The options bar associated with each of the marquee tools contains many buttons and settings to draw effective marquees (Figure 2–4). The options bar displays an icon for the chosen marquee on the left, followed by the Tool Preset picker. The Tool Preset picker allows you to save and reuse toolbar settings.

**Figure 2–4**

The next four buttons to the right adjust the selection. When selected, the New selection button allows you to start a new marquee.

The 'Add to selection' button draws a rectangle or ellipsis and adds it to any current selection. The 'Add to selection' button is useful for selecting the extra corners of an L-shaped object or for shapes that do not fit within a single rectangle or ellipsis. To activate the 'Add to selection' button, you can click it on the options bar, or press and hold the SHIFT key while dragging a second selection. When adding to a selection, the mouse pointer changes to a crosshair with a plus sign.

The 'Subtract from selection' button allows you to deselect or remove a portion of an existing selection. The new rectangle or ellipsis is removed from the original selection. It is useful for removing block portions of the background around oddly shaped images, or for deselecting ornamentation in an object. To activate the 'Subtract from selection' button, you can click it on the options bar, or press and hold the ALT key while dragging. When subtracting from a selection, the mouse pointer changes to a crosshair with a minus sign.

The 'Intersect with selection' button allows you to draw a second rectangle or ellipsis across a portion of the previously selected area, resulting in a selection border only around the area in which the two selections overlap. To activate the 'Intersect with selection' button, you click it on the options bar, or hold down the SHIFT and ALT keys while dragging. When creating an intersection, the mouse pointer changes to a crosshair with an X.

To the right of the selection buttons, the options bar displays a Feather box. **Feathering** softens the edges of the selection. In traditional photography, feathering is called **vignetting,** which creates a soft-edged border around an image that blends into the background. Feathering sometimes is used in wedding photos or when a haloed effect is desired. The width of the feather is measured in pixels. When using the Elliptical Marquee Tool, you can further specify blending by selecting the Anti-alias check box. **Anti-aliasing** softens the block-like, staircase look of rounded corners. Figure 2–5 shows a rectangle with no feathering, one with 10 pixels of feathering, an ellipsis with no anti-aliasing, and one created with a check mark in the Anti-alias check box.

BTW

**The Tool Preset Picker**
Most tools display a Tool Preset picker on the options bar. When you click the button, Photoshop displays a list of settings used during the current Photoshop session or previously saved options bar settings. The list makes it easier to save and reuse tool settings. You can load, edit, and create libraries of tool presets in conjunction with the Tool Presets panel. To choose a tool preset, click the Tool Preset picker in the options bar, and then select a preset from the list.

Rectangle with no feathering

Rectangle with 10 pixels of feathering

ellipsis with no anti-aliasing

ellipsis with anti-aliasing

**Figure 2–5**

BTW

**Anti-Aliasing**
Anti-aliasing is available for the Elliptical Marquee Tool, the Lasso Tool, the Polygonal Lasso Tool, the Magnetic Lasso Tool, and the Magic Wand Tool. You must specify this option before applying these tools. Once a selection is created, you cannot add anti-aliasing.

**Scrubby Sliders**
You can drag some options bar labels in Photoshop. When you point to the label, a **scrubby slider** that looks like a pointing finger appears. Dragging the scrubby slider changes the value in the accompanying text box on the options bar. For example, the Feather box label on the Rectangular Marquee Tool options bar is a scrubby slider.

**Layers**
A layer is a portion of the image superimposed, or separated, from other parts of the document. Think of layers as sheets of clear film stacked one on top of the other. In Chapter 3, you will learn how to change the composition of an image by changing the order and attributes of layers.

**Deleting Selections**
You can delete a selection by pressing the DELETE key on the keyboard. Photoshop will display a Fill dialog box. Click the OK button. If you delete by accident, press CTRL+Z to bring the selection back.

When using the Rectangular Marquee Tool or the Elliptical Marquee Tool, you can click the Style button (Figure 2–4 on page PS 76) to choose how the size of the marquee selection is determined. A Normal style sets the selection marquee proportions by dragging. A Fixed Ratio style sets a height-to-width ratio using decimal values. For example, to draw a marquee twice as wide as it is high, enter 2 for the width and 1 for the height, and then drag in the photo. A Fixed Size style allows you to specify exact pixel values for the marquee's height and width. Photoshop enables the Width box and Height box when you choose a style other than Normal. A button between the two boxes swaps the values, if desired.

Sometimes you need to make subtle changes to a selection marquee. For example, if the border or edge of a selection seems to be jagged or hazy, or if the colors at the edge of a selection bleed slightly across the marquee, you can use the Refine Edge button. When clicked, it opens a dialog box in which you can increase or decrease the radius of the marquee, change the contrast, and smooth the selection border.

Once you have drawn a marquee, you can choose from other options for further manipulation of the selected area. Right-clicking a selection displays a context menu that provides access to many other useful commands such as deselecting, reselecting, or selecting the **inverse**, which means selecting everything in the image outside of the current selection. The context menu also enables you to create layers, apply color fills and strokes, and make other changes that you will learn about in future chapters.

If you make a mistake or change your mind when drawing a marquee, you can do one of three things:

1. If you want to start over, and the New selection button is selected on the options bar, you can click somewhere else in the document window to deselect the marquee; then simply draw a new marquee. Deselecting also is available as a command on the Select menu and on the context menu. The shortcut for deselecting is CTRL+D.

2. If you have already drawn the marquee but want to move or reposition it, and the New selection button is selected on the options bar, you can drag the selection to the new location.

3. If you want to reposition while you are creating the marquee, do not release the mouse button. Press and hold the SPACEBAR key, drag the marquee to the new location, and then release the SPACEBAR key. At that point, you can continue dragging to finish drawing the marquee. Repositioning in this manner can be done while using any of the four selection adjustment buttons on the options bar.

## To Use the Rectangular Marquee Tool

The following step selects the tall basket in the lower-left corner of the Baskets Edited image using the Rectangular Marquee Tool. You will use the Elliptical Marquee Tool later in this chapter.

**1**

- With the Rectangular Marquee Tool selected on the Tools panel, drag to draw a rectangle around the tall basket in the lower-left corner to create a marquee selection. Drag close to the basket itself, as shown in Figure 2–6.

🔍 **Experiment**

- Practice drawing rectangular and elliptical marquees. Press SHIFT+M to switch between the two. SHIFT+DRAG to look at the effects. Press and hold the SPACEBAR key while you drag to reposition the current marquee. When you are finished, redraw a rectangle around the basket.

**Q&A**

What was the black box that appeared as I created the marquee?

That was the Transformation Values indicator to help show you exactly where you are in the image.

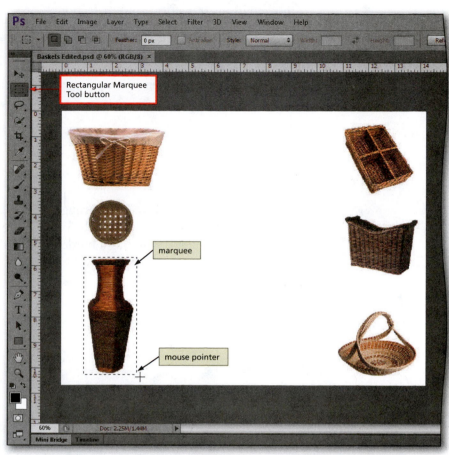

**Figure 2–6**

**Other Ways**

1. Press M key or SHIFT+M until Rectangular Marquee Tool is active, drag selection

# The Move Tool

The Move Tool on the Photoshop Tools panel is used to move or make other changes to selections. Activating the Move Tool by clicking the Move Tool button, or by pressing the v key on the keyboard, enables you to move the selection border and its contents by dragging in the document window. When you first use the Move Tool, the mouse pointer displays a black arrowhead with scissors. To move the selection in a straight line, press and hold the SHIFT key while dragging. If you press and hold the ALT key while dragging, you duplicate or move only a copy of the selected area, effectively copying and pasting the selection. While duplicating, the mouse pointer changes to a black arrowhead with a white arrowhead behind it.

When you move selections, you need to be careful about overlapping images. As you will learn in Chapter 3, Photoshop might layer or overlap portions of images when you move them. While that sometimes is preferred when creating collages or composite images, it is undesirable if an important object is obscured. Close tracing while creating selections and careful placement of moved selections will prevent unwanted layering.

The Move Tool options bar displays tools to help define the scope of the move (Figure 2–7). Later, as you learn about layers, you will use the Auto-Select check box to select layer groupings or single layers. The Show Transform Controls check box causes Photoshop to display transformation controls on the selection. The align and distribute buttons and the Auto-Align Layers button also are used with layers. The 3D mode buttons transform a 3-D selection.

**Figure 2–7**

As you use the Move Tool throughout this chapter, be careful to position your mouse pointer inside the selection before moving. Do not try to move a selection by dragging its border. If you drag a border by mistake, press the ESC key.

## To Use the Move Tool

The following steps use the Move Tool to move the basket up and to the right.

**1**
- With the basket still selected, click the Move Tool button on the Tools panel to activate the Move Tool.

- If necessary, on the options bar, click the Auto-Select check box so it does not display a check mark. If necessary, click the Show Transform Controls check box so it does not display a check mark (Figure 2–8).

**Q&A**

Are there any other tools nested with the Move Tool?

No, the Move Tool does not have a context menu. Tools with a context menu display a small black rectangle in the lower-right corner.

**Figure 2–8**

**2**
● Position your mouse pointer over
the basket, within the marquee.
Drag the selection to a position in
the upper-center portion of the
photo (Figure 2–9). Do not press
any other keys.

**Q&A**

My document window shows
a black square. What did I do
wrong?

It is possible that the default colors
on your system were changed
by another user. Press CTRL+Z to
undo the move. Press the D key to
select the default foreground and
background colors. If black is not
on top at the bottom of the Tools
panel, press the X key to exchange
the black and white colors.

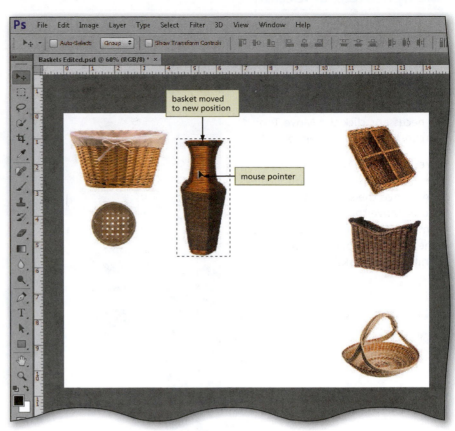

**Figure 2–9**

**Other Ways**

1. Press V, drag selection

### Plan your duplications.

Creating a storyboard, either by hand or by using software, allows you to plan your
image and make decisions about copies and placement. Some graphic artists annotate
each copy in the storyboard with information about size, shape, location, and the tool
they plan to use (Figure 2–2 on page PS 72). For example, when you paste or drag a new
copy of an image into a photo, you have two choices. You can keep the copy as an exact
duplicate, or you can transform the copy. The choice depends on the visual effect you
want to achieve and the customer requirements. Notating those requirements on your
storyboard ahead of time will facilitate creating your image.

Use an exact copy of a logo or border to create a tiled background. Commercial
applications may create duplications to represent growth; or several duplications beside
each other can emphasize a brand. Sometimes artists will duplicate an item several times
when creating a quick sketch or a rough draft. Across photos, exact duplicates maintain
consistency and product identification.

Transforming a copy or section provides additional flexibility and diversity. You
might want to create the illusion of multiple, different items to promote sales. Scaling,
skewing, warping, and distorting provide interest and differentiation, and sometimes
can correct lens errors. Flipping, rotating, or changing the perspective of the copy adds
visual excitement to reproductions and creates the illusion of three dimensions.

**Plan
Ahead**

## To Duplicate a Selection

Recall that pressing and holding the ALT key while dragging with the Move Tool creates a copy, or duplicates, the selection. SHIFT+dragging moves the selection in a straight line. Using both the SHIFT and ALT keys while dragging duplicates and moves the copy in a straight line. The following step accesses the Move Tool and creates a copy of the selected basket.

**1**

- If necessary, click the Move Tool button to select the Move Tool.

- Press and hold the SHIFT and ALT keys while dragging to duplicate and move the selection to the right. Move the selection just far enough that the white portion of the selection does not overlap the original tall basket (Figure 2–10).

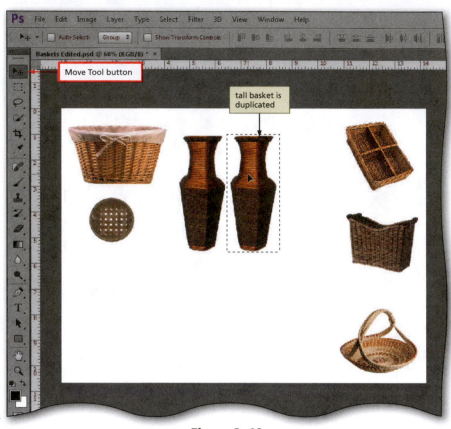

Figure 2–10

**Other Ways**

1. Press CTRL+C, press CTRL+V, press V, drag selection
2. Press V, ALT+drag selection

## To Deselect

The following step deselects the baskets.

**1** On the Select menu, click Deselect.

# The Quick Selection Tool

The Quick Selection Tool draws a selection quickly using the mouse. As you drag, Photoshop creates a selection automatically, expanding outward to find and follow the defined edges in the image. The Quick Selection Tool is nested with the Magic Wand Tool on the Tools panel. You can access either tool from the context menu or by pressing the W key; if the Magic Wand Tool has been used previously, press SHIFT+W to access the Quick Selection Tool.

Dragging a quick selection is almost like painting a stroke with a brush. The Quick Selection Tool does not create a rectangular or oval selection; rather, it looks for a contrast in color and aligns the selection border to that contrast. It is most useful for isolated objects or parts of an image that contain a contrasting background. When using the Quick Selection Tool, the mouse pointer changes to a brush tip that displays a circle with a centered cross inside. You can decrease or increase the size of the brush tip by using the LEFT BRACKET ([) or RIGHT BRACKET (]) keys respectively, or by using the options bar.

The Quick Selection Tool options bar (Figure 2–11) displays the size of the brush and contains some of the same buttons as other selection tools. It also contains an Auto-Enhance check box that reduces roughness in the selection boundary when the box is checked.

**Figure 2–11**

## To Use the Quick Selection Tool

The following steps use the Quick Selection Tool to select the basket in the middle on the right.

**1**

• Click the Quick Selection Tool button on the Tools panel to select it. If the tool icon does not display a brush, right-click the button and then click Quick Selection Tool on the context menu.

• On the options bar, click the New selection button, if necessary.

• Click the Auto-Enhance check box so it displays a check mark (Figure 2–12).

**Q&A**  What does the Auto-Enhance feature do?

Auto-Enhance reduces the block-like edges in the selection border and adjusts the selection further toward the edges of the image.

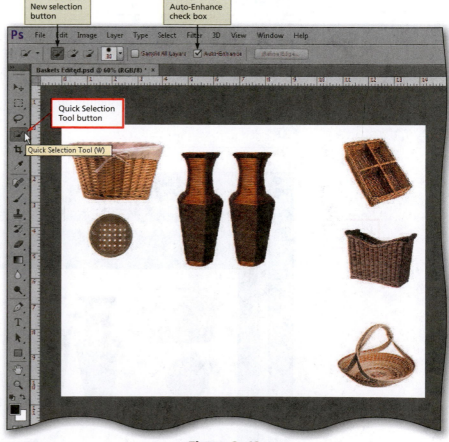

**Figure 2–12**

**2**

• Move the mouse pointer to the lower-right corner of the middle basket on the right, and then slowly drag up and left to select only the basket (Figure 2–13).

**Q&A**

What should I do if I make a mistake with the Quick Selection Tool?

If you make a mistake and want to start over, you can deselect by pressing CTRL+D, and then begin again.

### Experiment

• Practice resizing the mouse pointer by using the LEFT BRACKET ([) key to decrease the size or the RIGHT BRACKET (]) key to increase the size.

**Figure 2–13**

**Other Ways**

1. Press W or SHIFT+W until Quick Selection Tool is active, drag selection

## To Move a Selection

The following steps move the basket using the Move Tool. If you make a mistake while moving, press CTRL+Z and then move the basket again.

**1** On the Tools panel, click the Move Tool button to select the tool.

**2** Drag the selection left and slightly up, as shown in Figure 2–14. Do not press any other keys.

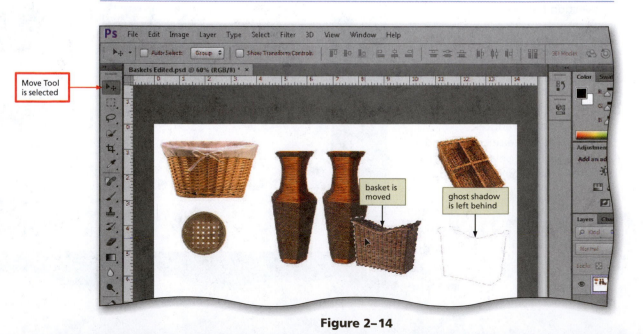

**Figure 2–14**

# The History Panel

The History panel appears when you click the History button on the vertical dock of minimized panels. The History panel records each step, called a **state**, as you edit a photo (Figure 2–15). Photoshop displays the initial state of the document at the top of the panel. Each time you apply a change to an image, the new state of that image is added to the bottom of the panel. Each state lists the name of the tool or command used to change the image.

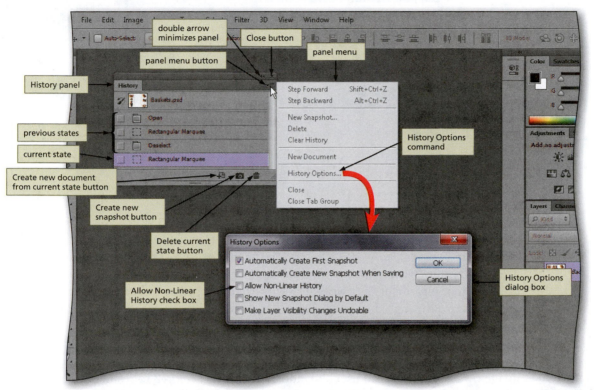

**Figure 2–15**

Like the Navigator panel that you learned about in Chapter 1, the History panel also has a panel menu where you can clear all states, change the history settings, or dock the panel. Buttons on the History panel status bar allow you to create a new document from a state, save the selected state, or delete it. The panel can be minimized by clicking the History button on the vertical dock or by clicking the double arrow at the top of the panel. To redisplay a minimized History panel, click the History button on the vertical dock, or choose it from the Window menu.

BTW

**Using the History Panel Menu**
The History panel menu has commands you can use to step forward and step backward through the listed states on the History panel.

## To Display the History Panel

The following step displays the History panel.

**1**

• Click the History button on the vertical dock of minimized panels (Figure 2–16).

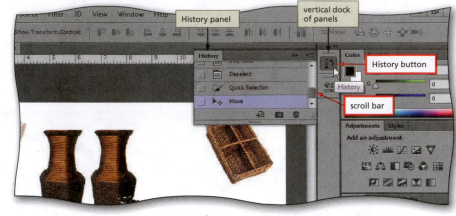

**Figure 2–16**

**Other Ways**

1. On Window menu, click History

## Using the History Panel

You can use the History panel in several different ways. When you select one of the states, Photoshop displays the image the way it looked at that point, when that change first was applied. Some users access the History panel to undo mistakes. Others use it to try out or experiment with different edits. By clicking a state, you can view the state temporarily or start working again from that point. You can step forward and backward through the states in the History panel by clicking them, or by pressing CTRL+SHIFT+Z or CTRL+ALT+Z, respectively.

Selecting a state and then changing the image in any way eliminates all the states in the History panel that came after it; however, if you select a state and change the image by accident, you can use the Undo command or CTRL+Z to restore the eliminated states. If you select the Allow Non-Linear History check box in the History Options dialog box (Figure 2–15 on the previous page) deleting a state deletes only that state.

You can use the History panel to jump to any recent state of the image created during the current working session by clicking the state. Alternatively, you also can give a state a new name, called a **snapshot**. Naming a snapshot identifies a state and distinguishes it from other states. Snapshots are stored at the top of the History panel and make it easy to compare effects. For example, you can take a snapshot before and after a series of transformations. Then, by clicking between the two snapshots in the History panel, you can see the total effect, or choose the before snapshot and start over. To create a snapshot, right-click the state and then click New Snapshot on the context menu, or click the Create new snapshot button on the History panel status bar. Snapshots do not save with the image; closing an image deletes its snapshots.

Not all steps appear in the History panel. For instance, changes to panels, color settings, actions, and preferences are not displayed in the History panel, because they are not changes to a particular image.

By default, the History panel lists the previous 20 states. You can change the number of remembered states by changing a preference setting (see the Changing Screen Resolution appendix). Photoshop deletes older states automatically to free more memory. Once you close and reopen the document, all states and snapshots from the last working session are cleared from the panel.

## To Undo Changes Using the History Panel

Notice in Figure 2–14 on page PS 84 that a shadow appears in the previous location of the basket. This shadow, called a ghost shadow, sometimes occurs when using any of the selection tools, especially when fringe pixels are faded — they were not included in the selection marquee. Therefore, you need to return to the previous state and try again. The following step uses the History Panel to undo the Move command.

**1**

• If necessary, scroll down in the History panel to display the last few states.

• Click the Quick Selection state in the History panel to go back one step and undo the move (Figure 2–17). Do not press any other keys.

**Q&A** Could I have pressed CTRL+Z to undo the move?

Yes, if you only need to undo one step, pressing CTRL+Z will work. If you need to go back more than one step, you can press CTRL+ALT+Z or use the History panel.

**Q&A** What is the box to the left of each state?

When selected, that box sets the source for painting a clone-like image using the Art History Brush Tool.

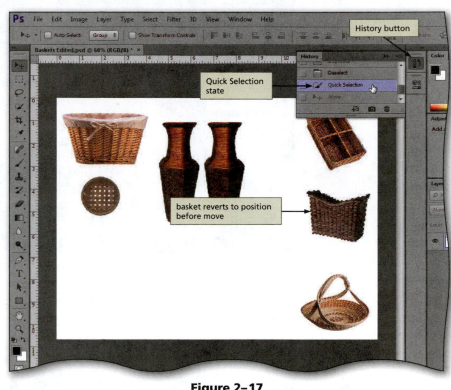

Figure 2–17

## To Minimize the History Panel

Recall in Chapter 1 that you minimized the Navigator panel by clicking the double arrow at the top of the panel. You also can minimize a panel by clicking the panel button on the vertical dock, as demonstrated in the following step.

**1** Click the History button to minimize the panel.

# Refining Edges

Each of the selection tools has a Refine Edge button located on its options bar, as shown in Figure 2–11 on page PS 83. Clicking the Refine Edge button displays a dialog box where you can make choices about improving selections with jagged edges, soft transitions, hazy borders, or fine details, and improve the quality of a selection's edges. Additionally, it allows you to view the selection on different backgrounds to facilitate editing (Figure 2–18 on the next page).

**BTW**

**Moving Among History Panel States**
Photoshop uses many function keys to move easily among the states in the History panel. To step forward, press SHIFT+CTRL+Z. To step backward, press CTRL+ALT+Z. You also can use the History panel menu to step forward and backward.

**Figure 2–18**

**BTW**

**Flipping Selections**
When you flip a selection, Photoshop creates a mirror image with a horizontal flip, or an upside-down version of the selection with a vertical flip. Flipping is available on the Edit menu and its Transform submenu or on the context menu when you right-click a selection. Flip transformations do not have to be committed.

Table 2–2 displays some of the controls in the Refine Edge dialog box and their functions.

| Table 2–2 Controls and Buttons in the Refine Edge Dialog Box | |
|---|---|
| **Control or Button** | **Function** |
| View Mode | Allows you to choose the background of the selection and show the radius, original, or both views |
| Smart Radius check box | Adjusts the radius edges automatically |
| Radius slider | Adjusts the size of the selection boundary by pixels |
| Smooth slider | Reduces irregular areas in the selection boundary to create a smoother outline with values from 0 to 100 pixels |
| Feather slider | Softens the edges of the selection for blending into backgrounds using values from 0 to 250 pixels |
| Contrast slider | Sharpens the selection edges to remove any hazy or extraneous pixels, sometimes called fuzzy artifacts or noise; increasing the contrast percentage can remove excessive noise near selection edges caused by a high radius setting |
| Shift Edge | Moves soft-edged borders helping remove or include background colors from selection edges |
| Decontaminate Colors check box | Replaces fringe color |
| Output To | Sets the output to a mask, layer, or new document |
| Remember Settings check box | Saves all settings in the dialog box for use on another selection |
| Zoom Tool button | Zooms selection in or out |
| Hand Tool button | Moves portion of the document window that is displayed |
| Refine Radius Tool button | Precisely adjusts the border area in which edge refinement occurs; pressing SHIFT+E toggles to the Erase Refinements Tool button |
| Erase Refinements Tool button | Precisely adjusts the border area in which edge refinement occurs; pressing SHIFT+E toggles to the Refine Radius Tool button |

The various settings in the Refine Edge dialog box take practice to use intuitively. The more experience you have adjusting the settings, the more comfortable you will feel with the controls. To improve selections for images on a contrasting background, you should first increase the radius and then increase the contrast to sharpen the edges. For grayscale images or selections where the colors of the object and the background are similar, try smoothing first, then feathering. For all selections, you might need to adjust the Contract/Expand slider.

## To Refine Edges

The following steps refine the edge of the selection.

**1**

- On the Tools panel, click the Quick Selection Tool button to select it (Figure 2–19).

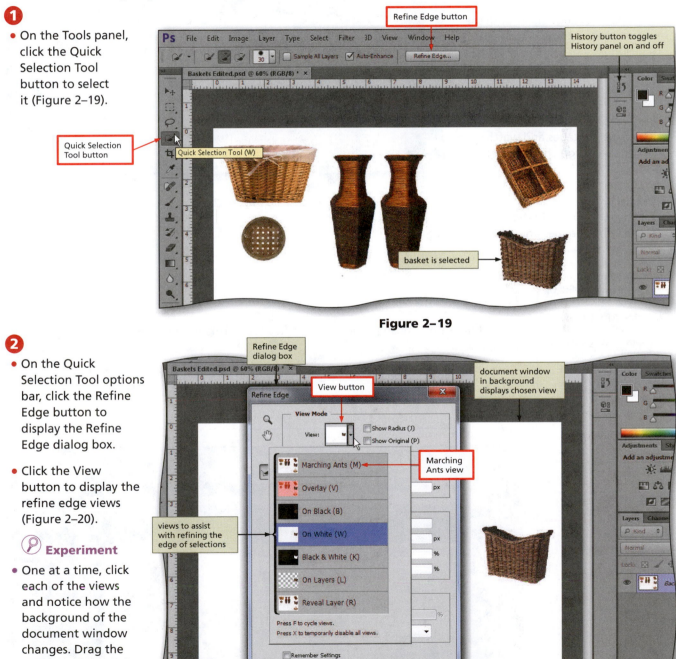

**Figure 2–19**

**2**

- On the Quick Selection Tool options bar, click the Refine Edge button to display the Refine Edge dialog box.

- Click the View button to display the refine edge views (Figure 2–20).

🔎 **Experiment**

- One at a time, click each of the views and notice how the background of the document window changes. Drag the title bar of the dialog box, if necessary to move the dialog box out of the way.

**Figure 2–20**

**3**

- Double-click Marching Ants to view the selection as a marquee.

- Drag the Radius slider until the Radius box displays approximately 20 pixels to increase the radius of the selection.

- Drag the Contrast slider until the Contrast box displays 40% to increase the contrast between the selection and its surrounding.

- Drag the Shift Edge slider until the percentage is approximately 75% to include a wider range of border colors (Figure 2–21).

### Experiment

- Drag the Shift Edge slider to various percentages and watch how the selection changes. Return the slider to 75%.

**Figure 2–21**

**4**

- Click the OK button in the Refine Edge dialog box to apply the changes and close the dialog box.

**Other Ways**

1. Press ALT+CTRL+R, choose settings, click OK button
2. Right-click selection, click Refine Edge, choose settings, click OK button
3. On Select menu, click Refine Edge, choose settings, click OK button

## To Move Again

The following steps move the basket again, this time without leaving behind a shadow.

**1** On the Tools panel, click the Move Tool button to activate the Move Tool.

**2** Drag the selection left and slightly up, as shown in Figure 2–22.

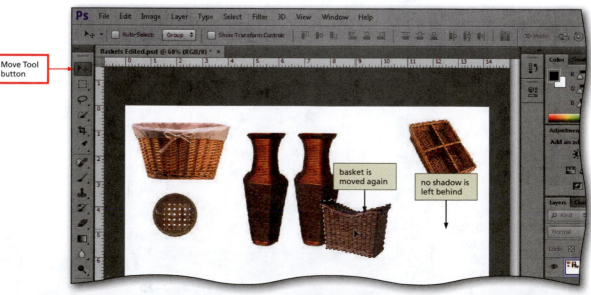

**Figure 2–22**

## To Deselect Using a Shortcut Key

The following step deselects the selection using a shortcut key.

**1** Press CTRL+D to deselect.

## To Zoom

To facilitate selecting other baskets, the following steps zoom to the upper-left portion of the document window.

**1** On the Tools panel, click the Zoom Tool button to select the tool.

**2** Click the upper-left corner of the document window twice to zoom that portion of the window to 100% (Figure 2–23).

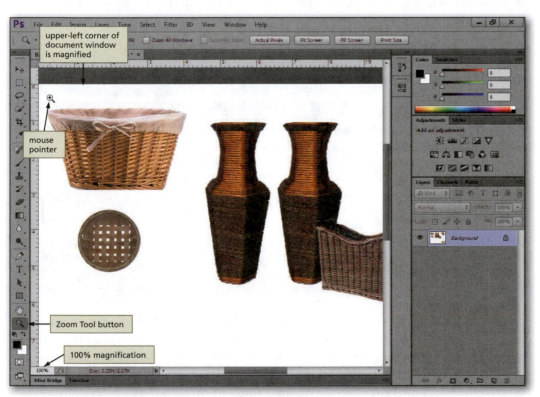

**Figure 2–23**

# The Lasso Tools

The **lasso tools** draw freehand selection borders around objects. The lasso tools provide more flexibility than the marquee tools with their standardized shapes, and might be more suitable than the Quick Selection Tool when the object has a noncontrasting background. Photoshop provides three kinds of lasso tools. The first is the default Lasso Tool, which allows you to create a selection by using the mouse to drag around any object in the document window. You select the Lasso Tool button on the Tools panel. You then begin to drag around the desired area. When you release the mouse, Photoshop connects the selection border to the point where you began dragging, finishing the loop. The Lasso Tool is useful for a quick, rough selection.

**BTW**

**Lasso Tool Selection**
If you are using a different tool, and want to activate a lasso tool, you can click the Lasso Tool button on the Tools panel or press the L key on the keyboard to select the Lasso Tool. After selecting the Lasso Tool, pressing SHIFT+L cycles through the three lasso tools.

**BTW**

**Completing Lassos**
To complete a selection using the Lasso tool, simply release the mouse button. To complete a selection using the Polygonal Lasso or Magnetic Lasso, double-click. Alternatively, you can move the mouse pointer close to the starting point. When a small circle appears on the edge of the mouse pointer, single-click to complete the lasso.

The Polygonal Lasso Tool is similar to the Lasso Tool in that it draws irregular shapes in the image; however, the Polygonal Lasso Tool uses straight line segments. To use the Polygonal Lasso Tool, choose the tool, click in the document window, release the mouse button, and then move the mouse in straight lines, clicking each time you turn a corner. When you get back to the beginning of the polygon, double-click to complete the selection.

The Magnetic Lasso Tool allows you to click close to the edge of the object you want to select. The Magnetic Lasso Tool tries to find the edge of the object by looking for the nearest color change. It then attaches the marquee to the pixel on the edge of the color change. As you move the mouse, the Magnetic Lasso Tool follows that color change with a magnetic attraction. The Magnetic Lasso Tool's marquee displays fastening points on the edge of the object. You can create more fastening points by clicking as you move the mouse, to force a change in direction or to adjust the magnetic attraction. When you get all the way around the object, you click at the connection point to complete the loop, or double-click to have Photoshop connect the loop for you. Because the Magnetic Lasso Tool looks for changes in color to define the edges of an object, it might not be as effective to create selections in images with a busy background or images with low contrast. Each of the lasso tools displays its icon as the mouse pointer.

Table 2–3 describes the three lasso tools.

#### Table 2–3 The Lasso Tools

| Tool | Purpose | Shortcut | Button |
|------|---------|----------|--------|
| Lasso | Used to draw freeform loops, creating a selection border | L<br>SHIFT+L toggles through all three lasso tools | |
| Polygonal Lasso | Used to draw straight lines, creating segments of a selection border | L<br>SHIFT+L toggles through all three lasso tools | |
| Magnetic Lasso | Used to draw a selection border that snaps to the edge of contrasting color areas in the image | L<br>SHIFT+L toggles through all three lasso tools | |

Each of the lasso tools displays an options bar similar to the marquee options bar, with buttons to add to, subtract from, and intersect with the selection; the ability to feather the border; and, an Anti-alias check box to smooth the borders of a selection (Figure 2–24). Unique to the Magnetic Lasso Tool options bar, however, is a Contrast box to enter the **contrast**, or sensitivity of color that Photoshop evaluates in making the path selection. A higher value detects only edges that contrast sharply with their surroundings; a lower value detects lower-contrast edges. The Width box causes the Magnetic Lasso Tool to detect edges only within the specified distance from the mouse pointer. A Frequency box allows you to specify the rate at which the lasso sets fastening points. A higher value anchors the selection border in place more quickly. A tablet pressure button on the right changes the pen width when using a graphic drawing tablet instead of a mouse.

**Figure 2–24**

## To Select using the Polygonal Lasso Tool

The following steps select the upper-left, lined basket by drawing lines around it with the Polygonal Lasso Tool. You will use the other lasso tools later in the chapter.

**1**
- In the document window, scroll as necessary to display the lined basket in the upper-left corner.
- Right-click the Lasso Tool button on the Tools panel to display the context menu (Figure 2–25).

**Figure 2–25**

**2**
- Click Polygonal Lasso Tool to activate the lasso.
- If necessary, on the options bar, click the New selection button (Figure 2–26).

**Experiment**
- Practice using the Polygonal Lasso Tool to draw a triangle by doing the following: in a blank area of the photo, click to begin; move the mouse pointer to the right; and then click to create one side. Move the mouse pointer up, and then click to create a second side. Move the mouse pointer to the beginning point, and then click to complete the lasso. When you are finished experimenting, press CTRL+D to deselect.

**Figure 2–26**

**3**
- Using the tip of the black arrow on the mouse pointer, click the top of the lined basket near the left side.
- Move the mouse pointer to the right to create the first line.
- Click the upper-right corner of the basket at a location before the basket's edge begins to curve downward (Figure 2–27).

**Q&A**
Can I reposition the starting point if I make a mistake?

Yes. Press the ESC key and then start again.

**Figure 2–27**

**4**

- Continue creating line segments by moving the mouse pointer and clicking each time you need to change direction.

- When you complete the lines all the way around the basket, move the mouse pointer until a small circle is visible, and then click to complete the selection (Figure 2–28).

**Q&A**

What was the small circle that appeared when I moved close to the beginning of the polygonal lasso?

When the mouse pointer moves close to where you started the polygonal lasso, Photoshop displays a small circle, which means you can single-click to complete the lasso. Otherwise, you have to double-click to complete the lasso.

**Figure 2–28**

**Other Ways**

1. Press L or SHIFT+L until Polygonal Lasso Tool is active, click photo, move mouse

**BTW**

**The Similar Command**
The Similar command increases the selection to include pixels throughout the selection, not just adjacent ones, which fall within the specified tolerance range. Choosing the Similar command more than once will increase the selection in increments.

## To Grow the Selection

A quick way to increase the size of a selection without using the Refine Edge dialog box is to use the Grow command on the Select menu. The Grow command will increase, or grow, the selection border to include all adjacent pixels falling within the tolerance range as specified on the options bar of most selection tools. Choosing the Grow command more than once will increase the selection on increments. Similar to refining the edge, the Grow command helps to avoid leaving behind a shadow when you move the selection.

The following steps grow the selection around the basket, to prevent a shadow when moving.

**1**

- Click Select on the Application bar to display the Select menu (Figure 2–29).

**Q&A**

Will I notice a big difference after I use the Grow command?

You might not see the subtle change in the selection marquee; however, growing the border helps ensure that you will not leave behind a shadow when you move the selection.

**2**

- Click Grow to increase the selection border.

**Figure 2–29**

## To Save using a Shortcut Key

The following step saves the image again, with the same file name, using a shortcut key.

**1** Press CTRL+S to save the Baskets Edited file with the same name.

**Break Point:** If you wish to take a break, this is a good place to do so. To resume at a later time, start Photoshop, open the file called Baskets Edited, select the upper-left basket, and continue following the steps from this location forward.

# Grids, Guides, and Snapping

Photoshop can show a **grid** of lines that appears as an overlay on the image. The grid is useful for laying out elements symmetrically or positioning them precisely. The grid can appear as nonprinting lines or dots. To display the grid, click Show on the View menu and then click Grid.

**BTW**

**Guides and Grids**
You can change the color or style of guides and grids. On the Edit menu, point to Preferences, and then click Guides, Grid, & Slices.

> **Use grids and guides.**
> Showing grids in your document window gives you multiple horizontal and vertical lines with which you can align selections, copies, and new images. Grids also can help you match and adjust sizes and perspective.
>
> Create guides when you have an exact margin, location, or size in mind. Because selections will snap to guides, you easily can create an upper-left corner to use as a boundary when you move and copy. Grids and guides do not print and are turned on and off without difficulty.

**Plan Ahead**

A **guide** is a nonprinting ruler line or dashed line that graphic designers use to align objects or mark key measurements. To create a guide, you turn on the ruler display and then drag from the horizontal ruler at the top of the document window or from the vertical ruler at the left side of the document window. When you release the mouse, a light, blue-green line appears across the image.

Table 2–4 displays various ways to manipulate guides.

**Table 2–4 Manipulating Guides**

| Action | Steps |
|---|---|
| Change color and style | Double-click guide. |
| Clear all guides | On the View menu, click Clear Guides. |
| Convert between horizontal and vertical guide | Select the Move Tool, ALT+click guide. |
| Create | Drag from ruler into document window, or, on the View menu, click New Guide, and then enter the orientation and position. |
| Lock in place | On the View menu, click Lock Guides. |
| Move | Select the Move Tool, and then drag the guide to a new location. |
| Remove | Select the Move Tool, and then drag the guide to the ruler. |
| Snap guide to ruler tick | SHIFT+drag the ruler. |
| Turn on/off display | On the Application bar, click View Extras, and then click Show Guides, or, on the View menu, point to Show, and then click Guides; or press CTRL+SEMICOLON (;). |

**Displaying Extras**
On the View menu is an Extras command with which you can show or hide selection edges, guides, target paths, slices, annotations, layer borders, and smart guides. You also can use CTRL+H to show or hide those items.

The term **snapping** refers to the ability of objects to attach to, or automatically align with, a grid or guide. For example, if you select an object in your image and begin to move it, as you get close to a guide, the object's selection border will attach itself to the guide. It is not a permanent attachment. If you do not want to leave the object there, simply keep dragging. To turn on or off snapping, click Snap on the View menu.

In a later chapter, you will learn about smart guides that automatically appear when you draw a shape or move a layer. Smart guides further help align shapes, slices, selections, and layers. The Changing Screen Resolution appendix describes how to set guide and grid preferences using the Edit menu.

## To Display a Grid

The following steps display the grid.

**1**

• On the Application bar, click View to display the View menu, and then point to Show to display the Show submenu (Figure 2–30).

**Q&A**

What does the Show Extras Options command do?

That command displays a dialog box where you can choose to display many different options such as grids, guides, layer edges, brush previews, and others. The choices you make then directly affect the Extras command on the View menu.

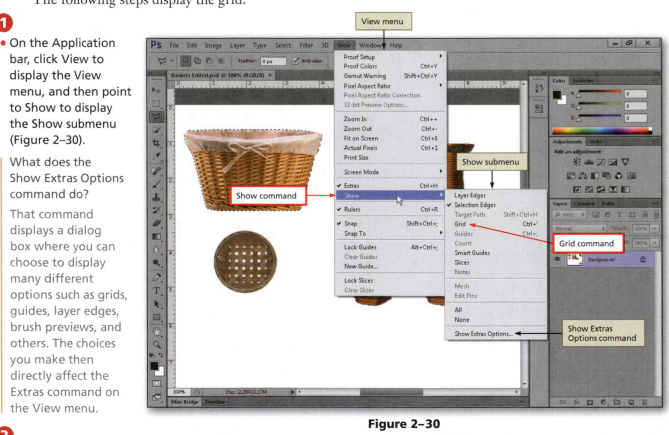

**Figure 2–30**

**2**

• Click the Grid command to display the grid (Figure 2–31).

**Figure 2–31**

**Other Ways**

1. Press CTRL+APOSTROPHE (')

## To Turn Off the Grid Display

The display of a grid is a **toggle**, which means that you turn it off in the same manner that you turned it on; in this case, with the same command.

 On the Application bar, click View to display the View menu, and then point to Show to display the Show submenu.

❷ Click Grid to remove the check mark and remove the grid from the display.

## To Create a Guide

The following steps will create a guide to help you position the lined basket on the same horizontal plane as the previous basket.

**❶**

- Position the mouse pointer in the horizontal ruler at the top of the document window.

- Drag down to create a guide, and stop at 6 inches as measured on the vertical ruler (Figure 2–32).

**Q&A** What is the black box that appears as I drag?

It is a mouse pointer tool tip that shows the location as you drag.

**❷**

- Release the mouse button.

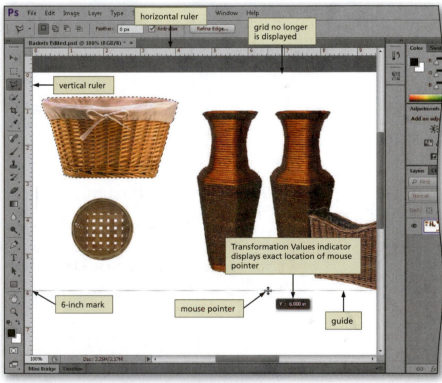

**Figure 2–32**

**BTW**

**Transformation Values Indicator**
You can change the display of the Transformation Values indicator, or turn it off completely, by clicking Edit on the Application bar, pointing to Preferences, and then clicking Interface. In the Preferences dialog box, click the Show Transformation Values box arrow and then click the desired location of the indicator or click Never in the list.

**Other Ways**

1. To show or hide guides, press CTRL+SEMICOLON (;)

2. To show or hide guides, point to Show on View menu, click Guides

3. To create guide, on View menu click New Guide, enter value, click OK button

## To Snap a Selection to the Guide

The following steps move the selection, snapping it to the guide.

**1**

- Press the V key to activate the Move Tool.

- Slowly drag the selection to a location in front of the tall baskets until the bottom of the selection snaps to the guide (Figure 2–33).

**2**

- Press CTRL+D to deselect.

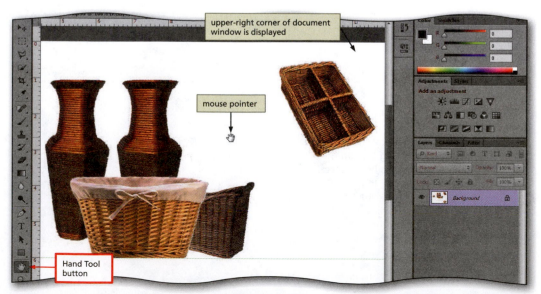

**Other Ways**

1. To turn on or off snapping, press SHIFT+CTRL+SEMICOLON (;)

**Figure 2–33**

## To Reposition the Document Window

The following steps reposition the document window so that you can select the basket in the upper-right corner.

**1** On the Tools panel, click the Hand Tool button.

**2** Drag in the document window down and left until the basket in the upper-right corner is displayed, as shown in Figure 2–34.

**Figure 2–34**

## To Select using the Magnetic Lasso Tool

The following steps use the Magnetic Lasso Tool to select the divided basket in the upper-right corner of the document window. Recall that the Magnetic Lasso Tool selects by finding the edge of a contrasting color and creating fastening points.

**1**

- Right-click the current lasso tool button, and then click Magnetic Lasso Tool to select it from the context menu.

- If necessary, on the options bar, click the New selection button to select the tool.

- Click the lower-left corner of the basket to start the selection (Figure 2–35).

**Figure 2–35**

**2**

- Move, rather than drag, the mouse pointer slowly along the bottom edge of the basket to create a selection marquee (Figure 2–36).

**Q&A** How do I correct a mistake?

As you use the Magnetic Lasso Tool, if you make a mistake, press the ESC key and begin again.

**Figure 2–36**

**3**

- Continue moving the mouse pointer around the edge of the basket. Click the mouse when turning a corner to create an extra fastening point.

- When you get to the lower-left corner again, double-click to finish the lasso (Figure 2–37).

**Q&A** When I double-clicked, the selection disappeared. What did I do wrong?

If your mouse pointer is exactly on the fastening point, a small circle indicates you are back at the beginning. In that case, a single-click finishes the lasso. If your selection disappears, press CTRL+Z to undo the double-click; the selection then should appear as shown in Figure 2–37.

**Figure 2–37**

**Other Ways**

1. Press L or SHIFT+L until Magnetic Lasso Tool is active, click photo, move mouse

## To Move a Selection using a Shortcut Key

The following steps move the selection.

**1**

- Press the V key to activate the Move Tool.

- Slowly drag the selection to a location in front of the other baskets as shown in Figure 2–38.

**Q&A**

Should I redo the move if a shadow is left behind?

You can press CTRL+Z to undo the move and then use the Grow command on the Select menu; however, later in the chapter you will crop the photo, which will remove any shadows that are left behind.

**2**

- Press CTRL+D to deselect.

**Figure 2–38**

## To Navigate using a Shortcut Key

The following steps reposition the document window so that you can select the basket in the lower-right corner.

**1** Press the H key to activate the Hand Tool.

**2** Drag in the document window until the handled basket in the lower-right corner is displayed.

## To Select using the Lasso Tool

The following steps use the Lasso Tool to create a selection by dragging around the object. As you will notice, the Lasso Tool leaves white space around the basket and inside the handle.

**1**

- Right-click the current lasso tool button on the Tools panel to display the context menu and then click Lasso Tool to select it.

- If necessary, on the options bar, click the New selection button to select the tool.

- Drag partway around the handled basket to start the lasso. Do not release the mouse button (Figure 2–39).

Figure 2–39

**2**

- Continue dragging around the basket to create a completed lasso, and then release the mouse button to finish the loop (Figure 2–40).

**Q&A**

How will I know if the lasso is complete?

When you release the mouse button, Photoshop completes the Lasso Tool selection, no matter where you are in the image.

Figure 2–40

**Other Ways**

1. Press L or SHIFT+L until Lasso Tool is active, drag selection

**Anti-Aliasing**
The Anti-alias check box smooths the jagged edges of a selection by softening the color transition between edge pixels and background pixels. While anti-aliasing is useful when cutting, copying, and pasting selections to create composite images, it might leave behind a shadow after cutting or moving a selection.

# The Magic Wand Tool

The Magic Wand Tool lets you select a consistently colored area with a single click. For example, if you wanted to select the blue sky in an image, clicking with the Magic Wand Tool would select it automatically, no matter what the shape of the blue area. When you use the Magic Wand Tool and click in the image or within a selection, Photoshop selects every pixel that contains the same or similar colors as the location you clicked. The Magic Wand Tool mouse pointer appears as a small line with a starburst on the end, similar to a magic wand.

The Magic Wand Tool options bar (Figure 2–41) contains the same selection adjustment buttons as the marquee tools, including the ability to create a new selection, add to or subtract from a selection, and intersect selections. The Magic Wand Tool options bar also has a Tolerance box that allows you to enter a value that determines the similarity or difference in the color of the selected pixels. A low value selects the few colors that are very similar to the pixel you click. A higher value selects a broader range of colors.

**Figure 2–41**

**Cutting and Pasting**
Just as you do in other applications, you can use the Cut, Copy, and Paste commands from the Edit menu or shortcut keys to make changes to selections. Unless you predefine a selection area by dragging a marquee, the Paste command pastes to the center of the document window. Both the commands and the shortcut keys create a new layer when they copy or paste.

When checked, the Contiguous check box selects only adjacent areas with the same color. Otherwise, Photoshop selects all pixels in the entire image that use the same color. Finally, the Sample All Layers check box selects colors using data from all visible layers. Otherwise, the Magic Wand Tool selects colors from the active layer only. You will learn about layers in a future chapter.

Besides using the options bar, the Magic Wand Tool can be used with many shortcut keys. Holding the SHIFT key while clicking adds to a Magic Wand Tool selection. Holding the ALT key while clicking subtracts from the selection. Holding the CTRL key while dragging with the Magic Wand Tool moves the selection.

## To Subtract from a Selection using the Magic Wand Tool

The following steps use the Magic Wand Tool to eliminate the white background in the selection, leaving only the basket inside the marquee.

**1**

- With the basket still selected, right-click the Quick Selection Tool button on the Tools panel to display the context menu (Figure 2–42).

**Figure 2–42**

**2**

- Click Magic Wand Tool to activate it.

- On the options bar, click the 'Subtract from selection' button. Click the Anti-alias check box so it does not display a check mark.

- If necessary, type 3 2 in the Tolerance box, and, if necessary, click to display a check mark in the Contiguous check box (Figure 2–43).

**Q&A** Could I press the w key to choose the Magic Wand Tool?

Yes, if the Magic Wand Tool appears on the Tools panel, you can press the w key to activate it; however, if the Quick Selection Tool appears on the Tools panel, you have to press SHIFT+W.

**Figure 2–43**

**3**

- Using the tip of the Magic Wand Tool mouse pointer, click the white space outside the basket, but inside the selection marquee, to remove the white color from the selection (Figure 2–44).

**Q&A** What is the minus sign next to the mouse pointer?

The minus sign appears whenever you choose to subtract from a selection. A plus sign would indicate an addition to the selection, and an X indicates an intersection. Photoshop displays these signs so you do not have to glance up at the options bar to see which button you are using while you drag the selection.

**Figure 2–44**

**4**

- Click the white spaces inside the basket's handle to remove them from the selection (Figure 2–45).

**Q&A**

Could I have removed the Contiguous check mark and just clicked the white area to remove all white areas?

Yes, but doing so would remove pixels because there is some white on the basket itself. It was better to remove the contiguous white spaces around the basket and within the handles.

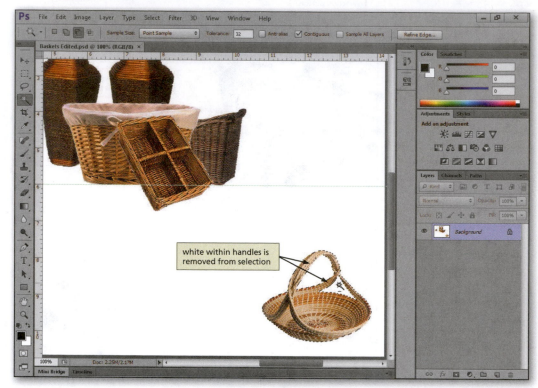

white within handles is removed from selection

**Figure 2–45**

| Other Ways |
|---|
| 1. Press W or SHIFT+W until Magic Wand Tool is active, click 'Subtract from selection' button, click selection     2. Select Magic Wand Tool, ALT+CLICK selection     3. Select Magic Wand Tool, right-click photo, click Subtract From Selection |

## To Move the Basket

The following steps move the basket.

**1** Press the V key to activate the Move Tool.

**2** Drag the basket to a location to the right of the previous selection, as shown in Figure 2–46.

**3** Press CTRL+D to deselect.

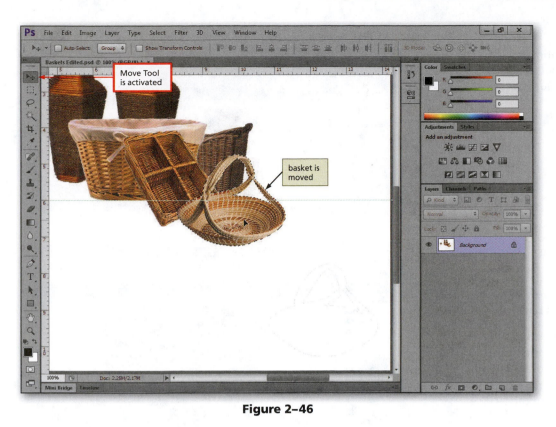

**Figure 2–46**

## To Select using the Elliptical Marquee Tool

The following steps use the Elliptical Marquee Tool to draw a circle around the final basket to select it. Recall that SHIFT+dragging with a marquee tool maintains proportions, in this case creating a circle rather than an oval. In addition, you can press and hold the SPACEBAR key to move a selection while you create it.

**1**

• Scroll to the left until the entire round basket is displayed (Figure 2–47).

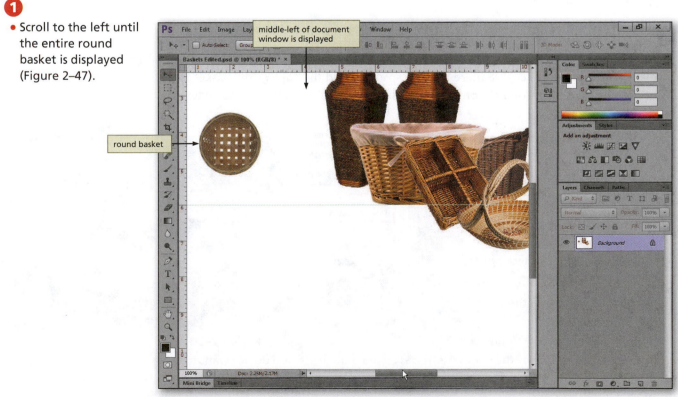

**Figure 2–47**

**2**

- Right-click the current marquee tool on the Tools panel to display the context menu (Figure 2–48).

**Figure 2–48**

**3**

- Click Elliptical Marquee Tool to activate the tool.

- If necessary, click the New selection button on the options bar.

- Position the mouse pointer at the upper-left edge of the round basket and then SHIFT+drag down and to the right to create a circle selection. Do not release the SHIFT key or mouse button.

- If necessary, press and hold the SPACEBAR key and then drag the selection into position.

- Release the mouse button before releasing the SHIFT and SPACEBAR keys (Figure 2–49).

**Figure 2–49**

## To Subtract Noncontiguous Pixels of the Same Color

The following step uses the Magic Wand Tool and the 'Subtract from selection' button to remove white pixels in the selection. Because there is white space around the edge of the basket and within the basket, you will subtract from the selection noncontiguously. You also will change the tolerance level.

**1**

- On the Tools panel, click the Magic Wand Tool button to select it.

- On the options bar, click the 'Subtract from selection' button if necessary. Double-click the Tolerance box and then type 10 to replace the current setting. Click the Contiguous check box to remove its check mark.

- Click the white area in the selection (Figure 2–50).

**Figure 2–50**

**Q&A**

How does the tolerance setting work?

In this selection, some of the edges of the basket are quite light. You do not want to leave them behind as a shadow when you move the basket; therefore, you are subtracting a more narrow range of color — the pixels that are closest in color to the strong white background.

## To Move the Round Basket

The following steps move the round basket.

**1** Press the V key to activate the Move Tool.

**2** Drag the selection to a location in front of the lined basket as shown in Figure 2–51. Do not deselect.

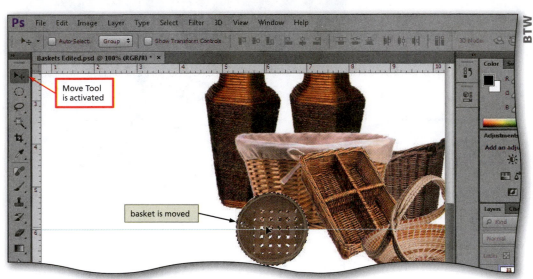

**Figure 2–51**

## To Duplicate and Scale

The following steps create a smaller copy of the selected basket. When you click the Show Transform Controls check box on the Move Tool options bar, Photoshop displays a bounding box with sizing handles. To resize, drag one of the sizing handles. To resize proportionally, SHIFT+drag one of the sizing handles. When you change the size of a selection, it is called **scaling**.

**1**
- With the Move Tool still selected, ALT+drag the selection to a location slightly down and to the right of the original selection. The copy will overlap the original round basket slightly.

- On the options bar, click the Show Transform Controls check box to display a check mark (Figure 2–52).

**Q&A** Could I just use the Copy and Paste commands?

Yes, however those commands create a new layer in the photo and increase the file size.

**Figure 2–52**

**2**

• SHIFT+drag a corner sizing handle toward the center of the basket to scale it down approximately 10 percent smaller (Figure 2–53).

**Q&A**

Why did the options bar change?

The options bar changed to the Transform options bar — an options bar not associated with any one specific tool. You will learn more about the Transform options bar in a future chapter.

**Figure 2–53**

**Q&A**

How do I know what 10 percent smaller is?

You can drag until the option bars display approximately 90% in the W and H boxes.

**3**

• On the options bar click the 'Commit transform (Enter)' button to accept the transformation.

• Press CTRL+D to deselect.

## To Reselect

When you deselect on purpose or by accident, you can return to the previous selection by using the **Reselect** command. The following steps reselect the copy of the round basket.

**1**

• Click Select on the Application bar to display the Select menu (Figure 2–54).

**Figure 2–54**

**2**
- Click Reselect to display the previous selection (Figure 2–55).

Figure 2–55

**Other Ways**

1. Press SHIFT+CTRL+D

## To Create and Scale Another Copy

The following steps create another copy of the basket.

**1** Select the Move Tool if necessary. ALT+drag the selection to a location slightly down and right of the previous selection. The copy will overlap slightly.

**2** SHIFT+drag a corner sizing handle to scale the selection down by approximately 10 percent (Figure 2–56).

**3** On the options bar, click the 'Commit transform (Enter)' button to accept the transformation, and then deselect.

Figure 2–56

## To Fit Screen

In moving around the screen in this project, you have zoomed, scrolled and used the Hand Tool. The following step uses the Fit Screen button on the Zoom Tool options bar to display the entire document window.

- Select the Zoom Tool.

- Click the Fit Screen button on the Zoom Tool options bar (Figure 2–57).

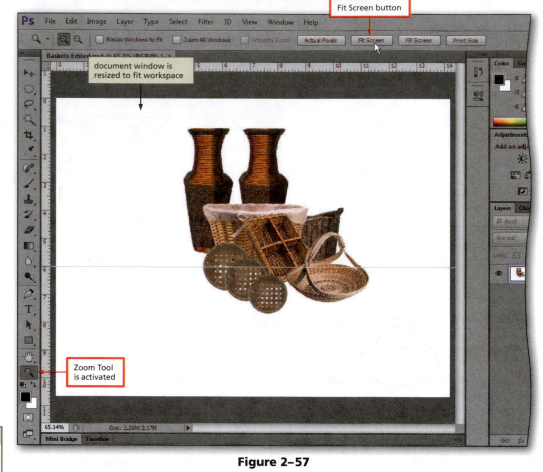

**Figure 2–57**

### Other Ways

1. Press CTRL+0 (zero)
2. On View menu, click Fit on Screen

## To Turn Off Guides using a Shortcut Key

The following step turns off the display of the green ruler guide.

**1** Press CTRL+SEMICOLON (;) to turn off the display of guides.

## To Crop a Selection

Finally, you will crop the advertisement to center the baskets, including a minimal amount of border space. In Chapter 1, you activated the Crop Tool and then adjusted the size of the selection. In the following steps, you will select first, and then crop.

**1**

- Press SHIFT+M to select the Rectangular Marquee Tool.

- Drag a rectangular marquee that leaves an even amount of white space on all four sides of the baskets.

- Press the C key to activate the Crop Tool (Figure 2–58).

**Q&A**

Why did I have to use SHIFT+M to activate the Rectangular Marquee Tool?

Previously, the Elliptical Marquee Tool had been selected. Pressing the M key would have activated it. Pressing SHIFT+M toggles through all of the marquee tools.

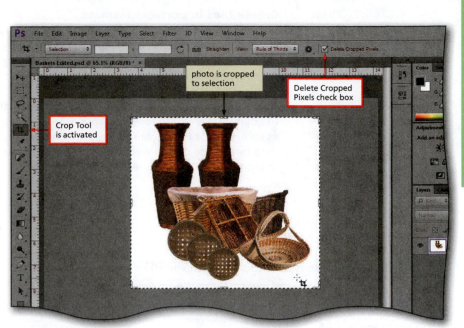

**Figure 2–58**

**2**

- On the options bar, click the Delete Cropped Pixels check box so it displays a check mark, if necessary.

- Press the ENTER key twice to accept the cropping selection and to complete the crop.

- Press the M key to return to the Rectangular Marquee Tool.

## To Save Again

The following step saves the image again, with the same file name, using a shortcut key.

**1**  Press CTRL+S to save the Baskets Edited file with the same name.

**Break Point:** If you wish to take a break, this is a good place to do so. To resume at a later time, start Photoshop, open the file named Baskets Edited, and continue following the steps from this location forward.

# Creating PDF Files

The final step is to create a PDF file of the advertising image for document exchange. **PDF** stands for **Portable Document Format**, a flexible file format based on the PostScript imaging model that is compatible across platforms and applications. PDF files accurately display and preserve fonts, page layouts, and graphics. There are two ways to create a PDF file in Photoshop. First, you can save the file in the PDF format. Alternatively, you can use the Print command to create the PDF format, allowing you to make some changes to the settings before saving.

**Plan Ahead**

**Create files in portable formats.**
You might need to distribute your artwork in a variety of formats for customers, print shops, Webmasters, and e-mail attachments. The format you choose depends on how the file will be used, but portability is always a consideration. The document might need to be used with various operating systems, monitor resolutions, computing environments, and servers.

It is a good idea to discuss with your customer the types of formats he or she might need. It usually is safe to begin work in the Photoshop PSD format and then use the Save as command or Print command to convert the files. PDF is a portable format that can be read by anyone on the Web with a free reader. The PDF format is platform and software independent. Commonly, PDF files are virus free and safe as e-mail attachments.

## To Save a Photo in the PDF Format

The following steps save the photo in the PDF format for ease of distribution.

**1**
- Click File on the Application bar, and then click Save As to display the Save As dialog box.

- Click the Format button to display the various formats you can use to save Photoshop files (Figure 2–59).

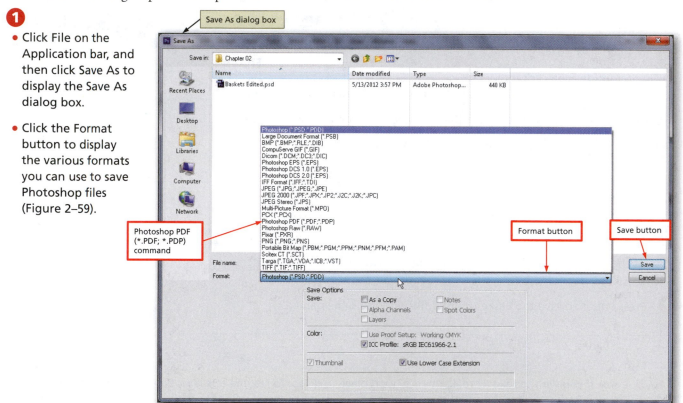

**Figure 2–59**

**2**
- Click Photoshop PDF (*.PDF;*.PDP) in the list to select the PDF format, and then click the Save button to continue the saving process (Figure 2–60).

**Figure 2–60**

**3**

- Click the OK button to display the Save Adobe PDF dialog box (Figure 2–61).

**Q&A** The Save Adobe PDF dialog box did not appear. What happened?

If you have multiple windows open on your system, the dialog box might be behind some of the other windows. In that case, minimize the other windows until the dialog box appears.

**Figure 2–61**

**4**

- Click the Save PDF button to continue the saving process and display a second Save Adobe PDF dialog box (Figure 2–62).

**Q&A** Will the PDF version have the same name?

Yes. After you save the file, you will see the name Baskets Edited.pdf on the document window tab because Photoshop can edit PDF files directly. The file also can be viewed with Adobe Acrobat or any PDF reader.

**Figure 2–62**

**5**

- Click the Yes button to finish saving.

**Other Ways**

1. Press CTRL+P, click Document box arrow, click Adobe PDF, click Print

### To Close a Photo without Closing Photoshop

Recall that when you are finished editing a photo or file, you should close it to help save system resources. You can close a photo after you have saved it and continue working in Photoshop. The following steps close the Baskets Edited.pdf file without quitting Photoshop.

**1** Click the Close button on the document window tab to close the Baskets Edited.pdf file.

**2** If Photoshop displays a dialog box, click the No button to ignore the changes since the last time you saved the photo.

# Keyboard Shortcuts

Recall that a **keyboard shortcut**, or **shortcut key**, is a way to activate menu or tool commands using the keyboard rather than the mouse. For example, pressing the L key on the keyboard immediately selects the current lasso tool without having to move your mouse away from working in the image. Shortcuts that combine two keystrokes are common as well, such as the use of CTRL+A to select an entire image. Shortcuts are useful when you do not want to take the time to traverse the menu system or when you are making precise edits and selections with the mouse and do not want to go back to any of the panels to change tools or settings. A Quick Reference summary describing Photoshop's keyboard shortcuts is included in the back of the book.

While many keyboard shortcuts already exist in Photoshop, there might be times when additional shortcuts would be useful. For instance, the Single Row and Single Column Marquee Tools have no shortcut key. If you frequently use those tools, adding the Single Row and Single Column Marquee Tools to the M keyboard shortcut might be helpful. Photoshop allows users to create, customize, and save keyboard shortcuts in one of three areas: menus, panels, and tools. When you create keyboard shortcuts, you can add them to Photoshop's default settings, save them in a personalized set for retrieval in future editing sessions, or delete them from your system.

## Creating a Keyboard Shortcut

**BTW**

**Photoshop Help**
The best way to become familiar with Photoshop Help is to use it. Appendix D includes detailed information about Photoshop Help and exercises that will help you gain confidence in using it.

To create a new keyboard shortcut, Photoshop provides a dialog box interface, which is accessible from the Edit menu. Using that dialog box, you can select one of the three shortcut areas. Then you can assign a shortcut key or combination of keys. For menu commands, your shortcut keystrokes must include a combination of the CTRL key or a function key followed by a single keyboard character. When creating shortcuts for tools, you must use a single alphabetic character. To avoid conflicting duplications, Photoshop immediately warns you if you have chosen a keyboard shortcut used somewhere else in the program.

### To Create a New Keyboard Shortcut

In the following steps, you will create a shortcut to display the Essentials workspace. While that command is accessible on the Window menu, a shortcut would save time when you need to choose the workspace.

**1**

- Click Edit on the Application bar to display the Edit menu, and then click Keyboard Shortcuts to display the Keyboard Shortcuts and Menus dialog box.

- Click the Shortcuts For box arrow, and then click Application Menus in the list, if necessary.

- In the Application Menu Command list, scroll down, and then click the triangle to the left of the Window command to display the list of Window menu commands (Figure 2–63).

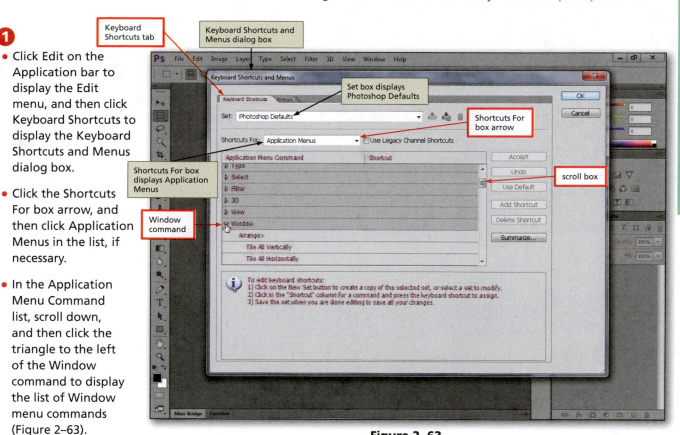

Figure 2–63

**2**

- Scroll down to display Workspace under the Window menu commands, and then click Essentials (Default) to display a shortcut key box (Figure 2–64).

**Q&A**

How are the buttons at the top of the dialog box used?

The 'Save all changes to the current set of shortcuts' button allows you to name the set for future retrieval. The 'Create a new set based on the current set of shortcuts' button creates a copy of the current keyboard shortcut settings. The 'Delete the current set of shortcuts' button deletes the set.

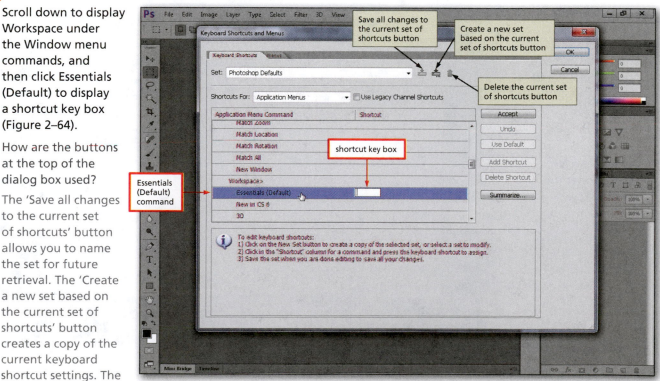

Figure 2–64

**3**

• Press the F12 key to enter a new shortcut keystroke for the Essentials (Default) command (Figure 2–65).

**Q&A**

How can I find out which shortcuts keys still are available?

When you click the Summarize button, Photoshop creates a Web page with all of the keyboard shortcuts in the set. You can save that file on your system or print it.

function key F12 is entered

warning message

Summarize button

F12 is already in use and will be removed from File > Revert if accepted.

**Figure 2–65**

**4**

• Because Photoshop warns you that the F12 key already is being used as a shortcut for a different command, press CTRL+SLASH (/) to enter a new shortcut (Figure 2–66).

**5**

• Click the Accept button to set the shortcut key.

• Click the OK button to close the dialog box.

OK button

Accept button

combination keys CTRL+/ are entered

no warning message

**Figure 2–66**

**Other Ways**

1. Press ALT+SHIFT+CTRL+K, edit settings, click OK button

## To Test a New Keyboard Shortcut

The next steps test the new keyboard shortcut.

**1**

• Click Window on the Application bar and point to Workspace to verify the shortcut key assignment (Figure 2–67).

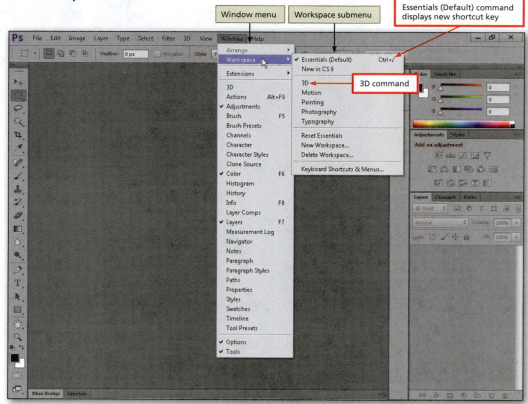

**Figure 2–67**

**2**

• Click the 3D command to change to the 3D workspace (Figure 2–68).

**Q&A**

Will the new shortcut become permanent?

The new shortcut will be saved on your system in the Photoshop Defaults (modified) set. That set will be in effect the next time you start Photoshop. If you want to remove it, you can edit that specific shortcut, or delete the set by clicking the 'Delete the current set of shortcuts' button.

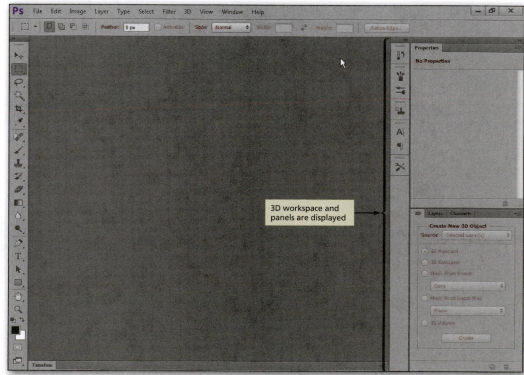

**Figure 2–68**

**3**

- Press CTRL+SLASH (/) to test the shortcut and display the Essentials workspace again (Figure 2–69).

shortcut redisplays Essentials (Default) workspace

**Figure 2–69**

## To Return to the Default Settings for Keyboard Shortcuts

It is a good idea, especially in a lab situation, to reset the keyboard shortcuts to their default settings. The following steps restore the default shortcut keys.

**1**

- On the Application bar, click Edit, and then click Keyboard Shortcuts to display the Keyboard Shortcuts and Menus dialog box.

- On the Keyboards Shortcuts tab, click the Set box arrow to display the list (Figure 2–70).

Keyboard Shortcuts and Menus dialog box

Set box arrow

Photoshop Defaults command

**Figure 2–70**

**2**

- Click Photoshop Defaults to choose the default settings for shortcuts (Figure 2–71).

**3**

- When Photoshop displays a message asking if you want to save your changes, click the No button so your previous changes are not saved.

- In the Keyboard Shortcuts and Menus dialog box, click the OK button to close the dialog box.

Figure 2–71

## To Quit Photoshop using a Shortcut Key

The following step quits Photoshop and returns control to Windows.

**1** Press CTRL+Q to quit Photoshop.

# Chapter Summary

In this chapter, you learned how to use selection tools, including the marquee tools, the lasso tools, the Quick Selection Tool, and the Magic Wand Tool. You learned about the History panel and its states. You worked with the 'Subtract from selection' command, the Refine Edge dialog box, and the Grow command to edit the selection border. You used the Move Tool to move and copy selections and scaled them. Each of the tools and commands had its own options bar with settings to control how the tool or command worked. You used a guide to help align objects. Finally, you saved the photo as a PDF file, and you learned how to create and test a new keyboard shortcut.

The items listed below include all the new Photoshop skills you have learned in this chapter:

1. Use the Rectangular Marquee Tool (PS 79)
2. Use the Move Tool (PS 80)
3. Duplicate a Selection (PS 82)
4. Use the Quick Selection Tool (PS 83)
5. Display the History Panel (PS 86)
6. Undo Changes using the History Panel (PS 87)
7. Refine Edges (PS 89)
8. Select using the Polygonal Lasso Tool (PS 93)
9. Grow the Selection (PS 94)
10. Display a Grid (PS 96)
11. Create a Guide (PS 97)
12. Snap a Selection to the Guide (PS 98)
13. Select using the Magnetic Lasso Tool (PS 99)
14. Move a Selection using a Shortcut Key (PS 100)

15. Select using the Lasso Tool (PS 100)

16. Subtract from a Selection using the Magic Wand Tool (PS 102)

17. Select using the Elliptical Marquee Tool (PS 105)

18. Subtract Noncontiguous Pixels of the Same Color (PS 106)

19. Duplicate and Scale (PS 107)

20. Reselect (PS 108)

21. Fit Screen (PS 110)

22. Crop a Selection (PS 110)

23. Save a Photo in the PDF Format (PS 112)

24. Create a New Keyboard Shortcut (PS 114)

25. Test a New Keyboard Shortcut (PS 117)

26. Return to the Default Settings for Keyboard Shortcuts (PS 118)

# Apply Your Knowledge

Reinforce the skills and apply the concepts you learned in this chapter.

### Moving and Duplicating Selections

*Instructions:* Start Photoshop and perform the customization steps found on pages PS 6 through PS 10. Open the Apply 2-1 Bread file in the Chapter 02 folder from the Data Files for Students and save it, in the PSD file format, as Apply 2-1 Bread Edited. Visit www.cengage.com/ct/studentdownload for detailed instructions or contact your instructor for information about accessing the required files.

You will create a grocery advertisement featuring bakery items. First, you will select individual items from within the file, and then you will transform and move them so that the finished design looks like Figure 2–72. You will place the rest of the images from back to front.

**Figure 2–72**

*Perform the following tasks:*

1. Because the checkered tablecloth is in the very back of the arrangement, you will start with it. Use the Rectangular Marquee Tool to select the checkered tablecloth.

2. Use the Move Tool to move the tablecloth to the top-center portion of the page. Do not deselect the tablecloth.

3. With the Move Tool still selected, click the Show Transform Controls check box to display a check mark. To distort the tablecloth and make it appear in perspective, CTRL+drag each of the lower corner sizing handles down and outward. Do not overlap any of the bread items. The result should be a trapezoid shape, as shown in Figure 2–72. If you make a mistake, press the ESC key and start again. When you are satisfied with the shape, press the ENTER key to confirm the transformation. Do not deselect.

4. The croissant is the back-most item in the arrangement. Use the Polygonal Lasso Tool to select the croissant. (*Hint:* The croissant is the lower-right item in the Apply 2-1 Bread image.) Right-click the Quick Selection Tool button on the Tools panel, and then click Magic Wand Tool. On the options bar, click the 'Subtract from selection' button, then click the white area around the croissant to remove it.

5. Use the Move Tool to move the croissant to the upper-right portion of the tablecloth. ALT+drag a second croissant to a location below and to the left of the first, as shown in Figure 2–72. (*Hint:* Do not drag the center reference point.) Press CTRL+D to deselect it.

6. Repeat Steps 4 and 5 to select and move the French bread.

7. ALT+drag the French bread to the right to create a duplicate.

8. Select and move the remaining bread items until you are satisfied with the arrangement. For each bread item, use a selection tool that will approximate the shape of the bread. On the options bar, use the 'Add to selection' and 'Subtract from selection' buttons as necessary. Use the Magic Wand Tool to remove white space around the selection before moving it.

9. Right-click the Rectangular Marquee Tool button on the Tools panel, then click Elliptical Marquee Tool. Use the Elliptical Marquee Tool to select the Sale button. (*Hint*: Press and hold the SHIFT key as you select to maintain a perfect circle.)

10. Move the Sale button to the lower-right portion of the advertisement.

11. Use the Crop Tool to select the portion of the image to use for the final advertisement. (*Hint:* The remaining white space is unnecessary.)

12. Save the Apply 2-1 Bread Edited file, and then close Photoshop.

13. Submit the assignment in the format specified by your instructor.

# Extend Your Knowledge

Extend the skills you learned in this chapter and experiment with new skills. You may need to use Help to complete the assignment.

### Separating Objects from the Background

*Instructions:* Start Photoshop and perform the customization steps found on pages PS 6 through PS 10. Open the Extend 2-1 Flowers file in the Chapter 02 folder from the Data Files for Students and save it, in the PSD format, as Extend 2-1 Flowers Edited. Visit www.cengage.com/ct/studentdownload for detailed instructions or contact your instructor for information about accessing the required files.

The original flower image displays the flowers in their natural settings, with various colors in the background. After moving the frame and making a copy, you will select the flowers while preventing background colors from straying into the selection. Finally, you will position each flower in front of a frame, as shown in Figure 2–73.

**Figure 2–73**

*Perform the following tasks:*

1. Use the Elliptical Marquee Tool to select the oval frame. (*Hint:* For more careful placement, while dragging to create the selection, you can press the SPACEBAR key to adjust the location of the drag and then release it to continue drawing the marquee.) Be careful to select only the frame, and eliminate any white around the edge of the selection using the Magic Wand Tool and the 'Subtract from selection' button.

2. Drag the selection to a location below the left side of the word, Flowers. Do not be concerned if you leave a slight shadow behind. On the Move Tool options bar, if necessary, click to display a check mark in the Show Transform Controls check box. SHIFT+drag a corner sizing handle to scale the selection approximately 10 percent bigger. (*Hint:* You also can increase the selection to 110 percent in both the Width and Height boxes.) Press the ENTER key to commit the transformation.

3. With the frame still selected, SHIFT+ALT+drag to create a duplicate and place it to the right of the original. (*Hint:* Recall that using the SHIFT key keeps the duplicate aligned with the original.)

4. Use appropriate selection tools to select the upper flower and its stem. (*Hint:* Use the Magic Wand Tool with a tolerance setting of 50 to select the contiguous pink and then add to the selection using other tools.) Click the 'Intersect with selection' button to combine selected areas, if necessary. Do not include the background.

5. To ensure that the selection does not have any stray pixels around its border, use the Refine Edge dialog box to refine the edge by increasing the radius to 7 px.

6. As you create the selection, if necessary, press CTRL+ALT+Z to step back through the editing history and return the image to an earlier state.

7. Move the selected flower onto the left frame and resize as necessary.

8. Repeat Steps 4 through 7 for the lower flower and the right frame. If you make an error, display the History panel and then click a previous state.

9. Crop the image to include only the word, Flowers, and the two framed flowers. Save the changes.

10. Use the Magic Wand Tool to select the blue color in the word, Flowers. (*Hint:* To select all of the letters, you will have to remove the check mark in the Contiguous box.) If parts of the image other than the word, Flowers, appear within the marquee, use the 'Subtract from selection' button to remove them.

11. Use Photoshop Help to investigate how to soften the edges of selections. Use the Refine Edge dialog box to soften the edges. Expand the selection and feather the edges.

12. Use Photoshop Help to investigate how to stroke a selection or layer with color. With the letters selected, use the Stroke command on the Edit menu to display the Stroke dialog box. Stroke the selection with a white color, 5 pixels wide, on the outside of the selection.

13. Save your changes, close the file, and then quit Photoshop. Send the revised photo to your instructor as an e-mail attachment.

## Make It Right

Analyze a project and correct all errors and/or improve the design.

### Correcting an Error in a Photo

*Instructions:*   Start Photoshop and perform the customization steps found on pages PS 6 through PS 10. Open the Make It Right 2-1 Footballs file in the Chapter 02 folder from the Data Files for Students and save it as Make It Right 2-1 Footballs Edited. Visit www.cengage.com/ct/ studentdownload for detailed instructions or contact your instructor for information about accessing the required files.

A coworker has made an error when trying to make a duplicate of the football (Figure 2–74). The duplicate on the right included some white space around the football, which overlaps the football on the left. In addition, the football on the right should be bigger because it is closer in the picture. Use selection tools as necessary, along with the 'Add to selection' and 'Subtract from selection' buttons, to select only the football (and its shadow) on the right. Refine the edge. ALT+drag with the Move Tool to create a duplicate and place it over the top of the football on the left. Select the football on the right again. Display the transform controls and scale the selection to be approximately 10 percent bigger.

Save the project again. Submit the revised document in the format specified by your instructor.

**Figure 2–74**

# In the Lab

Design and/or create a project using the guidelines, concepts, and skills presented in this chapter. Labs are listed in order of increasing difficulty.

## Lab 1: Using Keyboard Shortcuts to Create a Logo

*Problem:*   You are an intern with the Parks and Recreation department for the city. They are planning to create T-shirts for their summer youth program. Your supervisor has provided a file with some individual graphics about activities in the park. You are to move and place the graphics to form the logo shown in Figure 2–75. He reminds you that the T-shirt manufacturer needs a PDF file.

**Figure 2–75**

*Note:*   To complete this assignment, you will required to use the Data Files for Students. Visit www.cengage.com/ct/studentdownload for detailed instructions or contact your instructor for information about accessing the required files.

*Instructions:*   Perform the following tasks:

1. Start Photoshop. Set the default workspace, and reset all tools and colors.

2. Press CTRL+O to open the Lab 2-1 Park T-shirt file from the Chapter 02 folder of the Data Files for Students, or from a location specified by your instructor.

3. Press SHIFT+CTRL+S to display the Save As dialog box. Save the file on your storage device with the name, Lab 2-1 Park T-shirt Edited.

4. If the photo does not appear at 25% magnification, press CTRL+PLUS SIGN (+) or CTRL+HYPHEN (-) to zoom in or out as necessary.

5. Drag from the horizontal ruler to create a guide at 3.25 inches, which you will use to align the graphics.

6. To select and move the kite:

   a. Press SHIFT+L until the Polygonal Lasso Tool is selected.

   b. On the options bar, click the New selection button, if necessary.

*Continued >*

**In the Lab** *continued*

    c. Click a corner of the kite to start the selection. Continue clicking corners to create straight line segments around the kite. When you are finished, double-click to finish the selection.

    d. On the Select menu, click Grow to expand the selection slightly.

    e. Press the V key to access the Move Tool. Drag the kite to a location in front of the red circle, snapping the bottom of the kite to the ruler guide. It is OK to leave behind a slight shadow, as the logo will be cropped later in the steps.

    f. Press CTRL+D to deselect.

7. To select and move the bat:

    a. Press SHIFT+L until the Lasso Tool is selected.

    b. On the options bar, click the New selection button, if necessary.

    c. Drag to create a selection around the bat.

    d. Press SHIFT+W until the Magic Wand Tool is selected.

    e. ALT+click the white area around the bat, within the selection. Recall that pressing the ALT key while clicking activates the 'Subtract from selection' button on the options bar; the mouse pointer displays a minus sign.

    f. Press the V key to access the Move Tool. Drag the bat to a location in front of the kite, as shown in Figure 2–75 on the previous page, snapping the bottom of the bat to the ruler guide.

    g. Press CTRL+D to deselect.

8. To select and move the ball:

    a. Press SHIFT+M until the Elliptical Marquee Tool is selected.

    b. On the options bar, click the New selection button, if necessary.

    c. SHIFT+drag to create a circular selection around the ball. Avoid including any white space around the ball. If necessary, press the SPACEBAR key while dragging to position the selection marquee.

    d. Press the V key to access the Move Tool. Drag the ball to a location in front of the kite as shown in Figure 2–75, snapping the ball to the ruler guide.

    e. If you make a mistake while selecting or moving the ball, click the History button on the vertical dock of panels to display the History panel. Click a previous state and begin to select or move again.

    f. Press CTRL+D to deselect.

9. To select and move the remote control airplane:

    a. Press the Z key to activate the Zoom Tool, and then click the airplane several times to zoom in.

    b. Press SHIFT+L until the Magnetic Lasso Tool is selected.

    c. On the options bar, click the New selection button, if necessary.

    d. Click a corner of the airplane. Slowly move the mouse pointer around the airplane, creating fasteners along the edge. Click at each corner to create an extra fastener. When you get close to the beginning fastener, move your mouse pointer until a small circle appears, and then click to complete the lasso.

    e. On the options bar, click the Refine Edge button to display the Refine Edge dialog box. Drag the Shift Edge slider to 75%, and then click the OK button to close the dialog box.

    f. Press the z key and then ALT+click to zoom out as necessary. Scroll to display the red circle and the remote control airplane.

    g. Press the v key to access the Move Tool. Drag the airplane to a location in front of the kite as shown in Figure 2–75 on page PS 125.

    h. Deselect.

10. To select and move the tennis racquet:

    a. Press CTRL+PLUS SIGN (+) several times to zoom in on the racquet, scrolling as necessary.

    b. Press SHIFT+W until the Quick Selection Tool is selected.

    c. On the options bar, click the New selection button, if necessary.

    d. Slowly drag from the handle, upward, to create a selection around the racquet. If you make a mistake, deselect and begin again.

    e. Press SHIFT+W until the Magic Wand Tool is selected. On the options bar, select the value in the Tolerance box and then type 10 to replace it. If necessary, click to remove the check mark in the Contiguous check box.

    f. ALT+click a white area within the selection. Be careful not to click the strings of the racquet.

    g. Press CTRL+ HYPHEN (-) to zoom out as necessary.

    h. Press the v key to access the Move Tool. Drag the racquet to a location in front of the kite as shown in Figure 2–75, snapping the bottom of the racquet to the ruler guide.

    i. Deselect.

11. Press CTRL+S to save the file with the same name. If Photoshop displays a Photoshop Format Options dialog box, click the OK button.

12. To crop:

    a. Press SHIFT+M until the Rectangular Marquee Tool is selected.

    b. SHIFT+drag around the red circle to create a square selection.

    c. Press the c key to crop. On the options bar, if necessary, click the Delete Cropped Pixels check box so it displays a check mark. Press the ENTER key twice to crop the selection.

13. To create the PDF file:

    a. Press SHIFT+CTRL+S to open the Save as dialog box.

    b. Click the Format button to display the various formats.

    c. Click Photoshop PDF (*.PDF;*.PDP) in the list to select the PDF format, and then click the Save button to continue the saving process, saving the file with the same name.

    d. When Photoshop displays a dialog box, click the OK button to display the Save Adobe PDF dialog box. Click the Save PDF button to continue the saving process.

    e. When Photoshop displays the Save Adobe PDF dialog box, click the Yes button to finish saving.

14. Quit Photoshop by pressing CTRL+Q.

15. Send the PDF file as an e-mail attachment to your instructor, or submit it in the format specified by your instructor.

*Continued >*

# In the Lab

## Lab 2: Creating a Graphic from Back to Front

*Problem:* A local author has asked for your help in creating a book cover graphic about clock collecting. He has several photos of clocks that he wants placed in specific locations and in varied sizes. The final graphic is shown in Figure 2–76.

*Note:* To complete this assignment, you will required to use the Data Files for Students. Visit www.cengage.com/ct/studentdownload for detailed instructions or contact your instructor for information about accessing the required files.

**Figure 2–76**

*Instructions:* Perform the following tasks:

1. Start Photoshop. Set the default workspace and reset all tools.

2. Open the file, Lab 2-2 Clocks, from the Chapter 02 folder of the Data Files for Students, or from a location specified by your instructor.

3. Use the Save As command to save the file on your storage device with the name Lab 2-2 Clocks Edited.

4. To select and transform the round clock:

    a. Use the Elliptical Marquee Tool to select the round clock (the lower-right clock). If necessary, use the Magic Wand Tool and the Subtract from selection button to remove any white from around the edge of the clock.

    b. Use the Move Tool to move it to a location in the center of the white area.

    c. Show the transform controls and enlarge the selection approximately 500 percent as shown on the options bar. Do not let it overlap any of the other clocks. Drag a side handle to make the clock more round. When you are satisfied with the clock's appearance, deselect it.

5. To select and transform the mantle clock:

    a. Use the Lasso Tool to select the mantle clock (the lower-left clock). Use the Magic Wand Tool and the 'Subtract from selection' button to remove the white areas from around the selection. Grow the selection to avoid leaving a shadow.

    b. Use the Move Tool to move the mantle clock to a location just below the round clock face and slightly to the left.

    c. Display the transform controls and enlarge the selection to match Figure 2–76.

6. To select and resize the grandfather clock:

    a. Use the Rectangular Marquee Tool to select the grandfather clock. Use the Magic Wand Tool and the 'Subtract from selection' button to remove the white areas from around the selection.

    b. Use the Move Tool to move the grandfather clock to a location in front of and on the right side of the round clock face.

    c. Display the transform controls and enlarge the selection to match Figure 2–76. Notice that the clock is not perfectly straight. Move the mouse pointer to a location just outside the selection. When the mouse pointer changes to a curved double-arrow, drag to rotate the clock slightly to make it look like it is standing on a flat surface. (*Hint:* Turning on the grid display will help align the clock.) When you are satisfied with the transformation, deselect it.

7. To select and transform the wall clock:

    a. Use the Lasso Tool to select the wall clock. Use the Magic Wand Tool and the 'Subtract from selection' button to remove any white from around the edge of the clock.

    b. Use the Move Tool to move it to a location in the upper-left corner of the scene, as shown in Figure 2–76.

    c. Display the bounding box and enlarge the selection, and then deselect it.

8. Save the file and then submit the document, shown in Figure 2–76, in the format specified by your instructor.

## In the Lab

### Lab 3: Creating a Money Graphic

*Problem:* Your local bank is starting an initiative to encourage children to open a savings account using their loose change. The bank would like a before and after picture showing how money can grow with interest.

*Note:* To complete this assignment, you will required to use the Data Files for Students. Visit www.cengage.com/ct/studentdownload for detailed instructions or contact your instructor for information about accessing the required files.

*Instructions:* Perform the following tasks:

1. Start Photoshop. Set the default workspace and reset all tools.

2. Open the file, Lab 2-3 Coins, from the Chapter 02 folder of the Data Files for Students, or from a location specified by your instructor.

3. Use the Save As command to save the file on your storage device with the name Lab 2-3 Coins Edited.

4. Use the Elliptical Marquee Tool to select the quarter. (*Hint:* While dragging, if your selection marquee does not match the quarter exactly, press and hold the SPACEBAR key to move the selection.) Once the quarter is selected, ALT+drag to create several duplicate copies. As you create the duplicates, display the transform controls on the options bar, and then right-click the selection to display the context menu. Use the context menu commands to distort, rotate 90° CW, and apply perspective.

5. Use the Magnetic Lasso tool to select the dime. ALT+drag to create several duplicate copies. As you create the duplicates, use the transform control sizing handle to move, scale, and drag a corner to create a slight distortion.

6. Use the Quick Selection Tool to select the nickel. ALT+drag to create several duplicate copies. As you create the duplicates, use the transform controls to change some of the copies.

7. Use the Magic Wand Tool to select the penny. Create several copies. Your document should resemble Figure 2–77.

8. Save the file again, and submit it in the format specified by your instructor.

**Figure 2–77**

# Cases and Places

Apply your creative thinking and problem-solving skills to design and implement a solution.

*Note:*   To complete this assignment, you will required to use the Data Files for Students. Visit www.cengage.com/ct/studentdownload for detailed instructions or contact your instructor for information about accessing the required files.

## 1: Design a Poster for the Computer Lab

**Academic**

The computer lab at your school wants a poster reminding students to save their work often. The department chair has asked you to create a graphic of a computer mouse that seems to be eating data. He has taken a picture of a mouse from the lab and started the poster for you. A file named Case 2-1 Poster is located in the Chapter 02 folder of the Data Files for Students. Start Photoshop and use the selection tools to select the mouse. Flip the mouse horizontally. Then, using the Subtract from selection button, remove the white part around the selection. Also, remove the dark gray bottom portion of the mouse from the selection. With the top portion of the mouse selected, warp the selection up and away from the bottom part of the mouse to simulate an open mouth. Move the selection close to the 0 and 1 data pattern. Save a copy of the poster as a PDF and send it as an e-mail attachment to your instructor.

## 2: Create a New Shortcut

**Personal**

You have decided to create a new keyboard shortcut to reset all tools, rather than having to move the mouse to the options bar, right-click, and then choose to reset all tools. Because other family members work on your computer system, you would like to save the new shortcut in a separate set for your personal use. You also would like to see a complete listing of the Photoshop shortcuts for your system. Access the Keyboard Shortcuts and Menus dialog box. Click the Shortcuts For box arrow, and then click Panel Menus in the list. Scroll down and double-click Tool Presets, and then click Reset All Tools in the list. Enter the shortcut, CTRL+SLASH (/). Click the 'Create a new set based on the current set of shortcuts' button, and save the shortcuts with your name. Click the Summarize button and save the summary as My Shortcut Summary. When the summary displays in the browser, print a copy for your records.

## 3: Create a Grocery Store Flyer

**Professional**

You have been hired to create an advertisement for a grocery store flyer about citrus fruits that are on sale. Search the Web for samples of fruit displays, noting the ones that look most appealing. A file named Case 2-3 Fruits is located in the Chapter 02 folder of the Data Files for Students. Start Photoshop and reset the workspace, tools, and colors. Use selection tools to select the various fruits and move them into an attractive display. Create duplicates of fruits and resize the copies as necessary. Keep in mind the horizon line and perspective.

# 3 | Working with Layers

## Objectives

You will have mastered the material in this chapter when you can:

- Use the Layers panel and change options
- Create a layer via cut
- Rename layers and set identification colors
- Hide, view, and rearrange layers
- Arrange and consolidate document windows
- Create a new layer from another image or selection
- Transform selections and layers

- Use the Eraser, Magic Eraser, and Background Eraser Tools
- Create layer masks
- Make level adjustments and opacity changes
- Apply adjustments using the Adjustments panel
- Add a layer style
- Use the Clone Stamp Tool
- Flatten a composite image

# 3 | Working with Layers

## Introduction

Whether it is adding a new person to a photograph, combining artistic effects from different genres, or creating 3D animation, the concept of layers in Photoshop allows you to work on one element of an image without disturbing the others. You might think of layers as sheets of clear film stacked one on top of another. You can see through transparent areas of a layer to the layers below. The nontransparent, or opaque, areas of a layer are solid and obscure the content of the layers beneath. You can change the composition of an image by changing the order and attributes of layers. In addition, special features, such as adjustment layers, layer masks, fill layers, and layer styles, allow you to create sophisticated effects.

Another tool that graphic designers use when they want to recreate a portion of another photo is the Clone Stamp Tool. As you will learn in this chapter, the Clone Stamp Tool takes a sample of an image and then applies, as you draw, an exact copy of that image to your document.

Graphic designers use layers and clones, along with other tools in Photoshop, to create **composite** images that combine or merge multiple images and drawings to create a new image, also referred to as a **montage**. Composite images illustrate the power of Photoshop to prepare documents for businesses, advertising, marketing, and media artwork. Composite images such as navigation bars can be created in Photoshop and used on the Web along with layered buttons, graphics, and background images.

## Project — Room Furnishing

Chapter 3 uses Photoshop to create a composite image from several photographs by using layers. Specifically, it begins with a photo of an empty room and creates a composite image by inserting layers of furniture, a plant, a painting, and other decorative pieces to create a complete room design (Figure 3–1). The enhancements will show how the room will look when furnished. Wood flooring will replace the carpeting; a sofa, lamp, table, and other decorations will be added. Finally, adjustment layers will give the room eye appeal.

**(a) Original image**

**(b) Edited image**

**Figure 3–1**

## Overview

As you read this chapter, you will learn how to create the composite room shown in Figure 3–1b by performing these general tasks:

- Create a layer via cut.
- Insert layers from new images.
- Use the eraser tools.
- Add a layer mask.
- Create layer adjustments and apply layer styles.
- Clone an image.
- Flatten the image.
- Save the photo with and without layers format.

**General Project Guidelines**

When editing a photo, the actions you perform and decisions you make will affect the appearance and characteristics of the finished product. As you edit a photo, such as the one shown in Figure 3–1 on the previous page, you should follow these general guidelines:

1. **Gather your photos and plan your layers.** The graphics you choose should convey the overall message of your composite image. Choose high-quality photos with similar lighting characteristics. Create an ordered list of the layers you plan to include. Select images that are consistent with the visual effect you want to achieve as well as with customer requirements.

2. **Evaluate the best way to move outside images into the composite.** Sometimes it is easier to create a selection first and move the selection into the composite image as a layer. Other times, you may want to bring in the entire image and then erase or mask portions of the image. Once the layer exists, choose the correct tool for making edits and erasures.

3. **Create layer adjustments.** Fine-tune your layers by creating layer adjustments. Look at each layer and evaluate how it fits into the background scene. Experiment with different adjustment tools until the layer looks just right. Decide whether to use destructive or nondestructive edits. Keep in mind the standard tonal dimensions of brightness, saturation, and hue.

4. **Edit layer styles.** Add variety to your layers by including layer styles such as shadow, glow, emboss, bevel, overlay, and stroke. Make sure the layer style does not overwhelm the overall image or detract from previous layer adjustments.

When necessary, more specific details concerning the above guidelines are presented at appropriate points in the chapter. The chapter also will identify the actions performed and decisions made regarding these guidelines during the creation of the edited photo shown in Figure 3–1.

# Creating a Composite

Creating a composite with visual layers is a powerful effect. Photographers sometimes try to achieve this effect by using a sharp focus on objects in the foreground against an out-of-focus background. Others stage their photos with three layers of visual action. For example, at a baseball game, a person in the stands (foreground) may be observing a close call at first base (middle ground), while outfielders watch from afar (background). When those kinds of photographic techniques cannot be achieved, graphic artists use **composition techniques,** the layering of images and actions. Not only can you make realistic changes to parts of a photo, but you also can add additional images and control their placement, blending, and special effects. In addition, you can make changes to a layer, independent of the layer itself, which is extremely helpful in composite production.

Simple layers may incorporate new objects or new people. Layer effects create adjustments, add blending modes, or edit the coloring, fill, and opacity of the layer. Masks conceal or reveal part of a layer. All of the layering techniques are **nondestructive,** which means that no pixels are changed in the process; the effect is applied over the image or layer to create the change. Adding layers increases the file size of a Photoshop document, but that increase is justified by the value and flexibility layers provide. When you are finished working with layers, you can flatten the Photoshop document to reduce the file size. You will learn about flattening later in this chapter.

When an image duplication is required and layering a new copy does not achieve the required effect, some graphic artists **clone,** or reproduce, an image by painting a copy into the scene. As with masks, cloning allows you to control exactly how much of the image you want to use — even down to the smallest pixel. You also can use cloning to remove minor imperfections in a photo or to clone over intricate elements that do not fit into the picture.

The steps in this chapter create a composite image with layers, layer effects, adjustments, masks, and cloning.

## To Start Photoshop

If you are stepping through this project on a computer and you want your screen to match the figures in this book, then you should change your computer's resolution to 1024 × 768 and reset the panels, tools, and colors. For more information about how to change the resolution on your computer, and other advanced Photoshop settings, read the Changing Screen Resolution appendix.

The following steps, which assume Windows 7 is running, start Photoshop based on a typical installation. You may need to ask your instructor how to start Photoshop for your system.

**1** Click the Start button on the Windows 7 taskbar to display the Start menu, and then type `Photoshop CS6` in the 'Search programs and files' box.

**2** Click Adobe Photoshop CS6 in the list to start Photoshop.

**3** If the Photoshop window is not maximized, click the Maximize button next to the Close button on the Application bar to maximize the window.

## To Reset the Workspace

As discussed in Chapter 1, it is helpful to reset the workspace so that the tools and panels appear in their default positions. The following steps select the Essentials workspace.

**1** Click Window on the Application bar to display the Window menu and then point to Workspace to display the Workspace submenu.

**2** Click Essentials (Default) on the Workspace submenu to select the default workspace panels.

**3** Click Window on the Application bar, and then point to Workspace again to display the list.

**4** Click Reset Essentials to restore the workspace to its default settings and reposition any panels that may have been moved.

## To Reset the Tools and the Options Bar

Recall that the Tools panel and the options bar retain their settings from previous Photoshop sessions. The following steps select the Rectangular Marquee Tool and reset all tool settings in the options bar.

**1** If the tools in the Tools panel appear in two columns, click the double arrow at the top of the Tools panel.

**2** If necessary, click the Rectangular Marquee Tool button on the Tools panel to select it.

**3** Right-click the Rectangular Marquee Tool icon on the options bar to display the context menu, and then click Reset All Tools. When Photoshop displays a confirmation dialog box, click the OK button to restore the tools to their default settings.

## To Set the Interface and Default Colors

Recall that Photoshop retains the interface color scheme, as well as the foreground and background colors, from session to session. The following steps set the interface to Medium Gray and the foreground and background colors to black over white.

**1** Click Edit on the Application bar to display the Edit menu. Point to Preferences and then click Interface on the Preferences submenu to display the Preferences dialog box.

**2** Click the third button, Medium Gray, to change the interface color scheme.

**3** Click the OK button to close the Preferences dialog box.

**4** Press the D key to reset the default foreground and background colors.

## To Open a File

To open a file in Photoshop, it must be stored as a digital file on your computer system or on an external storage device. The photos used in this book are stored in the Data Files for Students. Visit www.cengage.com/ct/studentdownload for detailed instructions or contact your instructor for information about accessing the required files.

The following steps open the Room file from the Data Files for Students.

**1** With the Photoshop window open, click File on the Application bar, and then click Open to display the Open dialog box.

**2** In the Open dialog box, click the Look in box arrow to display the list of available locations, and then navigate to the storage location of the Data Files for Students.

**3** Double-click the Photoshop folder and then double-click the Chapter 03 folder to open it. Double-click the file, Room, to open it.

**4** When Photoshop displays the image in the document window, if the magnification shown on the status bar is not 33.33%, double-click the magnification box on the document window status bar, type 33.33 and then press the ENTER key to change the magnification (Figure 3–2).

**Figure 3–2**

## To View Rulers

The following steps display the rulers in the document window to facilitate making precise measurements.

**1** If the rulers are not shown on the top and left sides of the document window, press CTRL+R to display the rulers in the workspace.

**2** If necessary, right-click the horizontal ruler and then click Inches on the context menu to display the rulers in inches.

## To Save a Photo

Even though you have yet to edit the photo, it is a good practice to save the file on your personal storage device early in the process. The following steps save the photo with the name Room Edited in a new folder named Chapter 03.

**1** With your USB flash drive connected to one of the computer's USB ports, click File on the Application bar to display the File menu and then click Save As to display the Save As dialog box.

**2** In the File name text box, type `Room Edited` to rename the file. Do not press the ENTER key after typing the file name.

**3** Click the Save in box arrow and then click Removable Disk (F:), or the location associated with your USB flash drive, in the list, if necessary.

**Layer Comps**
Graphic artists often create multiple versions, or compositions, of their work. A **layer comp** is a single view of the page layout with specific visible layers and attributes. You can use layer comps to demo versions of your composition to customers or colleagues, or simply to jump back and forth between different views and layers of your document. Similar to the History panel's snapshot, a layer comp takes a picture of the composite, using the Layers panel to show a particular stage of development.

**4** On the Save As dialog box toolbar, click the Create New Folder button to create a new folder on the selected storage device.

**5** When the new folder appears, type Chapter 03 to change the name of the folder, and then press the ENTER key. Double-click the new folder to open it.

**6** Click the Save button in the Save As dialog box to save the file in the new folder.

# Creating a Composite Image using Layers

Photoshop has many tools to help create composite images, photomontages, and collages. A composite, or composite image, is one that combines multiple photographs or images to display in a single combined file. Graphic artists use the newer term, **photomontage**, to refer to both the process and the result of creating a composite from photos.

**Plan Ahead**

**Gather your photos and plan your layers.**
One of the keys to successful image compositions is finding the best source material with similar lighting situations and tonal qualities. Choose high-quality photos and images that convey your overall message. Make sure you have permission to use the images if they are not original photographs taken by you or provided to you by a colleague or client. Obtain several versions of the same photo, if possible, including photos from different angles and with different lighting situations. Make two copies of each photo and store one as a backup. Crop unwanted portions of the photos before adding them as new layers.

**Layer Comps vs. History Snapshots**
Layer comps include the visibility, position, and appearance of layers, not the edited steps. In addition, layer comps are saved with the document, whereas History panel snapshots are not. You can export layer comps to separate graphic or PDF files for easy distribution.

**Layer Comps Panel**
The Layer Comps panel includes a status bar with buttons to move back and forth through the comps, to update comps from the current view, to create them, and to delete them. The Layer Comps menu has some of those same commands, as well as others to duplicate a layer comp and set its properties.

## Layers

One of the most powerful tools in Photoshop is layering. A **layer** is a section within a Photoshop document that you can manipulate independently from the rest of the document. Layers can be stacked one on top of the other, resembling sheets of clear film, to form a composite image.

Layers have been used by business and industry for years. Cartoonists create layers of physical transparencies to help with animation. The medical field uses overlays to illustrate anatomical features. Virtual simulations use layers to display processes. With Photoshop, layers are easy to create and export for these kinds of applications.

Recall that you used selections in Chapter 2 to move, copy, and scale portions of a photo. Layers can perform all of the same functions performed by selecting, while providing added features. The most powerful feature of layers is the ability to revisit a portion of the image to make further changes, even after deselecting. Layers can be created, copied, deleted, displayed, hidden, merged, locked, grouped, repositioned, and flattened. Layers can be composed of images, patterns, text, shapes, colors, or filters. You can use layers to apply special effects, correct or colorize pictures, repair damaged photos, or import text elements. In previous chapters, you worked with images in a flat, single layer called the Background layer. In this chapter, you will create, name, and manipulate multiple layers on top of the Background layer.

Many layer manipulations are performed using the Layers panel, which lists all the layers, groups, and layer effects in an image (Figure 3–3). Each time you insert a layer onto an image, the new layer is added above the current layer, or to the top of the panel. The default display of a layer on the Layers panel includes a visibility

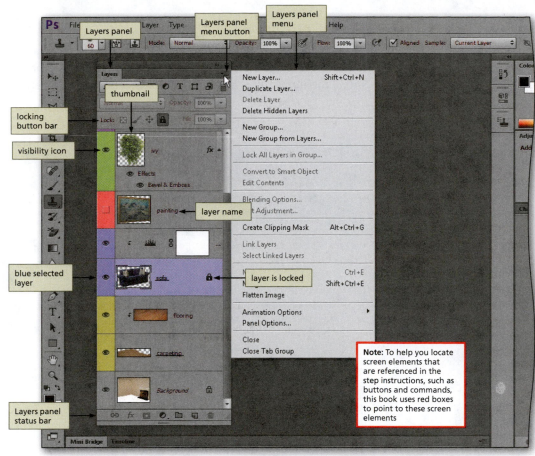

**Figure 3–3**

icon, a thumbnail of the layer, and the layer's name. To the right of the layer's name, a locking icon or other special effect notations might appear.

Photoshop allows you to **lock** three different components of layers. The 'Lock transparent pixels' button confines editing to opaque layer portions. The 'Lock image pixels' button prevents modification of the layer's pixels using paint tools. The Lock position button prevents the layer from being moved. The Lock all button enables all three ways of locking the layer. A lock icon appears to the right of the name on the Layers panel on locked layers.

The Layers panel is used in several different manners: to show and hide layers, create new layers, and work with groups of layers. You can access additional commands and attributes by clicking the Layers panel menu button or by right-clicking a layer. The Layers panel defines how layers interact. As you use the buttons and boxes on the Layers panel, each will be explained.

While Photoshop allows background editing, as you have done in previous chapters, the Background layer cannot be moved, nor can its transparency be changed. In other words, the Background layer fills the document window, and there is no layer behind the background. Partially locked by default, the Background layer displays a hollow lock (Figure 3–3). If you want to convert the Background layer into a fully editable layer, double-click the layer on the Layers panel, and then click the OK button in the New Layer dialog box.

When working with layers, it is important to make sure you know which layer you are editing by looking at the active layer on the Layers panel or by looking at the layer name, appended to the file name on the document window tab. Many other layer commands appear on the Layer menu, including those for making adjustments to the layer, creating layer masks, grouping layers, and other editing and placement commands.

**BTW**

**The Layers Panel Context Menus**
The Layers panel has many ways to work with layers. For example, right-clicking the layer name displays a different context menu from the one you see when right-clicking the thumbnail. Double-clicking the layer name allows you to rename the layer; double-clicking the thumbnail opens the Layer Style dialog box.

**BTW**

**Hiding and Showing Multiple Layers**
To view only one layer in the document window, ALT+click the visibility icon for the layer you want to view. Pressing ALT+click again restores the previous visibility settings. Show or hide all other layers by selecting Show/Hide all other layers from the visibility icon's context menu. To hide or view several contiguous layers, drag through the eye column.

## To Change Layers Panel Options

The Panel Options command, accessible from the Layers panel menu, allows you to change the view and size of the thumbnail related to each layer. A thumbnail displays a small preview of the layer on the Layers panel. The Panel Options dialog box allows you to choose small, medium, large, or no thumbnails. The following steps select a medium-sized thumbnail of each layer.

**1**

• Click the Layers panel menu button to display the Layers panel menu (Figure 3–4).

**Q&A**

Do I have to display thumbnails?

No, but displaying a thumbnail of each layer allows you to see easily what the layer looks like and helps you to be more efficient when editing a layer. To improve performance and save monitor space, however, some Photoshop users choose not to display thumbnails.

Figure 3–4

**2**

• Click Panel Options on the menu to display the Layers Panel Options dialog box.

• Click the medium thumbnail to select it.

• Click the Layer Bounds option button, if necessary, to change the look and feel of the Layers panel (Figure 3–5).

**Q&A**

How does the Layer Bounds option change the interface?

The Layer Bounds option causes the Layers panel to display only the layer, restricting the thumbnail to the object's pixels on the layer.

Figure 3–5

**3**
- Click the OK button to close the Layers Panel Options dialog box (Figure 3–6).

**Q&A** Should I see a difference on the Layers panel?

Yes. Unless a previous user had already changed it, the size of the thumbnail should have changed on the Layers panel. Layer bounds will not appear until you create a layer other than the Background layer.

**Figure 3–6**

# Creating a Layer via Cut

There are several ways to create a new layer. You can:

- Isolate a portion of the image and then cut or make a layer copy
- Create a new layer by copying from a different image
- Duplicate a layer that already exists
- Create a new, blank layer on which you can draw or create text

When you add a layer to an image, a new layer appears above, or on top of, the currently selected layer, creating a **stacking order**. By default, Photoshop names and numbers layers sequentially; however, you can rearrange the stacking order to change the appearance of the image. The final appearance of an edited Photoshop document is a view of the layer stack from the top down. In the document window, the layers at the top of the Layers panel appear in front of the layers at the bottom of the panel.

## To Create a Layer via Cut

The steps on the next page create a new layer that includes only the carpeting on the floor. You will use the Quick Selection Tool to select the area and then use the Layer Via Cut command to isolate the floor from the rest of the photo, creating a new layer. You will manipulate the new layer, later in the chapter.

**BTW**

**Deleting Layers**
To delete a layer permanently, right-click the layer name and then click Delete Layer on the context menu, or activate the layer and press the DELETE key.

**1**

- On the Tools panel, select the Quick Selection Tool button. If the Magic Wand Tool is selected, press SHIFT+W to toggle to the Quick Selection Tool.

- If necessary, click the New selection button on the options bar to start a new selection.

- In the photo, drag slowly from the upper-left corner of the carpeting to the lower-right corner of the photo to select only the carpeting (Figure 3–7).

**Q&A** Why did Photoshop change to the 'Add to selection' button on the options bar?

Once you create a new selection, the most common task is to add more to the selection, so Photoshop selects that button automatically. If you want to start over, you can select the New selection button again.

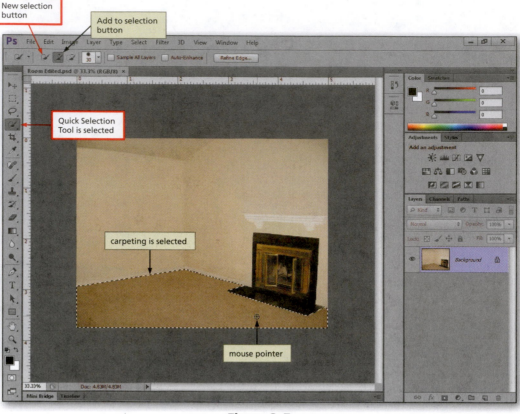

**Figure 3–7**

**2**

- Right-click the selection to display the context menu (Figure 3–8).

**Q&A** Could I use the New Layer command?

No. The New Layer command creates a blank layer.

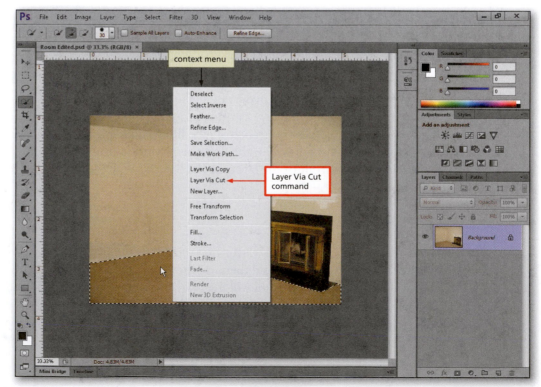

**Figure 3–8**

**3**

- Click Layer Via Cut on the context menu to create the new layer (Figure 3–9).

**Q&A**

What is the difference between Layer Via Cut and Layer Via Copy?

The Layer Via Cut command differs from the Layer Via Copy command in that it removes the selection from the background. Future edits to the Background, such as changing the color or lighting, will not affect the cut layer.

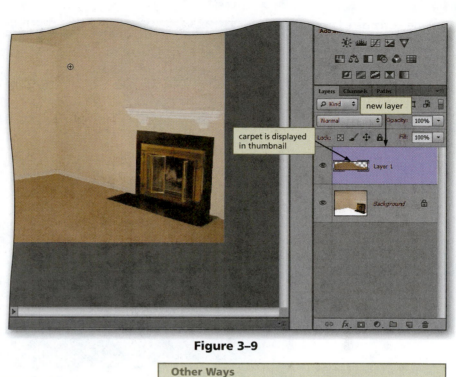

Figure 3–9

| Other Ways | |
|---|---|
| 1. Create selection, on Layer menu, point to New, click Layer Via Cut | 2. Create selection, press SHIFT+CTRL+J |

## To Rename a Layer

It is a good practice to give each layer a unique name so you can identify it more easily. The name of the active layer appears on the Layers panel and on the title bar of the document window. The following steps rename a layer.

**1**

- On the Layers panel, double-click the name of the layer you want to rename, in this case Layer 1 (Figure 3–10).

Figure 3–10

**2**

- Type carpeting to replace the current name of the layer, and then press the ENTER key to rename the layer (Figure 3–11).

**Figure 3–11**

**Other Ways**

1. On Layer menu, click Rename Layer, enter new name, press ENTER key

## To Assign a Color to a Layer

Photoshop allows you to give each layer its own color identification. Assigning a color helps you recognize relationships among layers. For example, if two of your layers display objects in the sky, you might assign those two layers a blue identification color so you quickly could see which layers were related to the sky. The color appears around the visibility icon on the left side of the layer. The following steps assign a color to a layer.

**1**

- Right-click the carpeting layer to display its context menu (Figure 3–12).

**Q&A**

Does it make any difference exactly where I right-click?

No. You can right-click anywhere on the layer. If you click the area around the visibility icon, Photoshop displays a shorter context menu with only color and hide/show options.

**Figure 3–12**

**2**
- Click Yellow in the list to choose a yellow identification color (Figure 3–13).

new layer identification color

**Figure 3–13**

## To Hide and Show a Layer

Sometimes you want to hide a layer to view other layers and make editing decisions. The visibility icon is a button that toggles the visibility of the layer on and off. The following steps hide and show the Background layer.

**1**
- Click the 'Indicates layer visibility' button to the left of the Background layer to hide the layer in the document window and hide the visibility icon (Figure 3–14).

**Q&A**

What is the checkerboard effect in the carpeting layer?

The checkerboard effect represents blank portions of the document window that are transparent.

checkerboard effect indicates transparency

background layer is not visible

visibility icon

Indicates layer visibility button

**Figure 3–14**

**2**

- Click the 'Indicates layer visibility' button again to show the Background layer in the document window and display the visibility icon (Figure 3–15).

**Q&A**

What is the white area on the Background layer thumbnail?

When you cut or delete from a locked layer, such as the Background layer, the default background color shows through; in this case, it is the default white color. Because other layers will eclipse the white, you do not have to remove it.

**Figure 3–15**

---

**Other Ways**

1. Right-click visibility icon, click Hide this layer or Show this layer
2. On Layer menu, click Hide Layers or Show Layers

---

**BTW**

**Layer Selection**
Sometimes a menu or panel will cover the Layers panel, or a layer might be scrolled out of sight. You always can identify which layer you are working with by looking at the document window tab. The name of the current layer appears in parentheses.

# Creating a Layer from Another Image

When you create composite images, you might want to create layers from other images. It is important to choose images that closely match or complement color, lighting, size, and perspective if you want your image to look natural. While you can adjust disparate images to improve how well they match, it is easier to start with as close a match as possible, ideally with similar lighting situations and tonal qualities.

Many sources exist for composite images, and they come in many different file types and sizes. For example, you can use your own digital photos, scanned images, images from royalty-free Web sites, or you can draw your own. If you use a photo or image from the Web, make sure you have legal rights to use the image. Means of obtaining legal rights include getting permission from the photographer or artist to use the image or purchasing the rights, through a contract, from an online store.

**Plan Ahead**

**Evaluate the best way to move outside images into the composite.**
If the desired portion of the outside image is selected easily, such as a rectangle, oval or polygon, then select and copy it. Paste it in the composite image to create a layer. If the desired portion of the outside image is not easy to select, drag the entire image into the composite, creating a layer. Then, use eraser tools to eliminate the unwanted portion of the layer. That way, you have not changed the original image, should you need to return to it later.

The basic process of creating a new layer from another image involves opening a second image, selecting the area you want to use, and then moving it to the original photo in a drag-and-drop, or cut-and-paste, fashion. Once the layer exists in the destination photo, you might need to do some editing to remove portions of the layer, to resize it, or to make tonal adjustments.

## To Open a Second Image

To add a sofa as a layer to the Room Edited image, you will need to open a new file, Sofa, from the Data Files for Students, or from a location specified by your instructor. The following steps open the Sofa file, which is stored in the PSD format.

**①** Press CTRL+O to display the Open dialog box.

**②** In the Open dialog box, if necessary, click the Look in box arrow, and then navigate to the Chapter 03 folder of the Data Files for Students or a location specified by your instructor.

**③** Double-click the file named Sofa to open it (Figure 3–16).

BTW

**Creating Layer Groups**
Layer groups help you manage and organize layers in a logical manner. To create a layer group, click the Create New Group button on the Layers panel. A new layer will appear with a folder icon. You then can drag layers into the folder or use the Layers panel menu to insert a new layer. You can apply attributes and masks to the entire group.

Sofa document window

image of sofa

**Figure 3–16**

## Displaying Multiple Files

Photoshop offers many different ways to arrange and view document windows when more than one file is open. You also can create a custom workspace by moving and manipulating document windows manually.

For example, you might want to display two document windows, horizontally or vertically, in order to drag and drop from one image to another. You might want to compare different versions or views of photos beside each other in the document window. Or, when creating a panorama, you might want to preview how certain photos will look side by side.

When you are finished viewing multiple document windows in the workspace, you can **consolidate** them, or view only one window at a time.

BTW

**2-Up vs. Tile**
When you click Window on the Application bar, the Arrange submenu displays the 2-up Horizontal command, which arranges the more recently opened window on top. The Tile All Horizontally command puts the new window on the bottom.

## To Arrange Document Windows

The following steps display the Room Edited and Sofa windows beside each other using the Arrange submenu on the Window menu.

**1**

- On the Application bar, click Window and then point to Arrange to display the Arrange submenu (Figure 3–17).

**Q&A** Why are some of the arrangements grayed out?

Because you have only two document windows open, the only arrangements enabled are the ones that display two windows.

**Figure 3–17**

**2**

- Click Tile All Vertically in the submenu to display the windows beside each other (Figure 3–18).

**Q&A** What is the difference between Tile All Vertically and 2-up Vertical?

When you have only two document windows open, there is no difference. If you have more than two document windows open, Tile All Vertically will open all the windows; 2-up Vertical will open only the two most recently used document windows.

**Figure 3–18**

## To Create a Layer by Dragging an Entire Image

When you drag a selection from one document window to the other, Photoshop creates a new layer in the destination document window, above the currently selected layer. If you want to include the entire image from the source window, use the Move Tool to drag from any location in the source window to the destination window. Dragging between document windows is an automatic duplication rather than a true move out of one window and into the other. The original, source image remains unchanged.

The following step moves the entire image from the source window, Sofa, to the destination window, Room Edited.

- Press the v key to activate the Move Tool.

- Drag the sofa image into the Room Edited window and drop it in the room (Figure 3–19).

**Q&A**

Why is the sofa so much bigger in its own document window?

The sofa is the same size; the magnification of the windows is different.

**Figure 3–19**

**Other Ways**

1. In source window, on Edit menu click Copy, in destination window on Edit menu click Paste

## To Close the Sofa Document Window

Because you are finished with the Sofa image, the following step closes the Sofa window.

1. Click the Close button on the Sofa document window tab. If Photoshop asks you to save the file again, click the No button.

**BTW**

**Consolidate Windows**
Sometimes, after viewing multiple document windows, you might want to view only one window at a time. In that case, right-click the tab at the top of the Room Edited document window to display the context menu and then click Consolidate All to Here to view that document window alone. The Arrange submenu has a Consolidate All to Tabs command that has the same effect.

## To Move a Layer in the Document Window

If there is no marquee selection, the Move Tool moves the entire current layer when you drag. The following step moves the sofa to a new location.

**1**

- With the new layer still selected on the Layers panel, and the Move Tool still selected on the Tools panel, drag the sofa to a position along the left wall, on the floor (Figure 3–20).

**Q&A**

Is it acceptable for some of the sofa to disappear off the edge of the document window?

Yes. Your goal is to make it look as natural as possible, as if it is sitting on the floor.

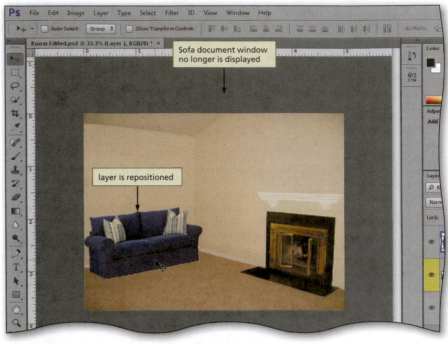

**Figure 3–20**

## To Name and Color the Sofa Layer

The following steps rename the new layer and assign it a color.

**1** On the Layers panel, double-click the name of the layer, Layer 1. Type `sofa` and then press the ENTER key to name the layer.

**2** Right-click the layer to display the context menu, and then click Blue in the list to choose a blue identification color (Figure 3–21).

**Layer Boundaries**
The settings you chose in the Layer Panel Options dialog box appear in Figure 3-21. Only the portion of the layer that contains an image is displayed in the medium-sized thumbnails because of the Layer Bounds setting.

**Figure 3–21**

## To Save the File

Because you have created layers and made changes to the image, it is a good idea to save the file again. The following step saves the file again.

**1** Press CTRL+S to save the Room Edited file with the same name. If Photoshop displays a dialog box about compatibility, click the OK button.

**Break Point:** If you wish to stop working through the chapter at this point, you can quit Photoshop now and then resume the project at a later time by starting Photoshop, opening the file named Room Edited and continuing to follow the steps from this location forward.

# Creating a Layer by Dragging a Selection

Sometimes you do not want to move an entire image from one window to another. When you want to move only a part of an image, you create a selection, as you learned in Chapter 2 and then move the selection to the destination window. Once the selection exists in the destination window, you might need to do some editing, such as scaling, erasing, or adjusting.

**BTW**

**Smart Objects**
You can convert a layer into a smart object, which is a nondestructive layer that does not change the original pixels. Smart Objects are useful for warping, scaling, or rotating both raster and vector graphic layers. To convert a layer into a smart object, right-click the layer, and then click Convert to Smart Object on the context menu.

## To Open the Painting Image

The following steps open a file named Painting.

**1** Press CTRL+O to display the Open dialog box.

**2** Click the Look in box arrow, and then navigate to the Chapter 03 folder of the Data Files for Students, or a location specified by your instructor.

**3** Double-click the file named Painting to open it.

**BTW**

**JPG File Type**
The Painting image is stored as JPG file. Recall that JPG stands for Joint Photographic Experts Group and is the file type typically generated by digital cameras. JPG format supports many different color modes. JPG retains all color information in an RGB image, unlike GIF format.

## To Select the Painting

When adding the painting image to the Room Edited image, you will not need the surrounding wall. The following steps select the painting using the Rectangular Marquee Tool.

**1** If necessary, right-click the current marquee tool and then click Rectangular Marquee Tool on the context menu to select it.

**2** If necessary, click the New selection button on the options bar to start a new selection.

**3** Drag around the painting, including the gold frame and matte. Avoid including the wall in the selection. If you make a mistake while selecting, press the ESC key and then begin again (Figure 3–22 on the next page).

**Figure 3–22**

## To Create a Layer by Dragging a Selection

The following steps move the selection. To facilitate dragging the selection between windows, you will view the windows above and below one another.

**1**

- On the Application bar, click Window, point to Arrange to display the submenu and click the Tile All Horizontally command to display the windows above and below one another (Figure 3–23).

 **Experiment**

- Open a third file and then try some of the other configurations on the Arrange submenu. When you are done, close the third file. Repeat Step 1.

**Figure 3–23**

**②**

- Press the v key to activate the Move Tool.

- Drag the selection and drop it in the Room Edited window (Figure 3–24).

**Figure 3–24**

**Other Ways**

1. In source window, create selection, on Edit menu, click Copy, in destination window, on Edit menu, click Paste

## To Close the Painting Window

The next step closes the Painting window.

**①** Click the Close button on the Painting document window tab. If Photoshop displays a dialog box asking if you want to save the changes, click the No button.

## To Name and Assign a Color to the Painting Layer

The following steps rename the new layer and assign an identification color.

**①** Double-click the name, Layer 1, on the Layers panel and then type `painting` and press the ENTER key to rename the layer.

**②** Right-click the layer and then click Red to assign an identification color.

## To Position the Painting Layer

The following steps move the painting to a location above the sofa.

**①** Press the v key to active the Move Tool, if necessary.

**②** Drag the painting to a location above the sofa, as shown in Figure 3–25 on the next page.

**Figure 3–25**

# The Transformation Commands

In Photoshop, the word **transform** refers to changing the appearance of a selection by altering its shape, size, or other physical characteristics. To choose a transformation command, click the Edit menu, point to Transform, and then click the desired transformation. Alternatively, you can click Transform Selection on the context menu that is displayed when you right-click a selection.

Table 3–1 lists the types of transformations you can perform on a selection, the techniques used to perform a particular transformation, and the result of the transformation. Many of the commands also appear on the context menu when you right-click the bounding box. If you choose free transform, you must use the mouse techniques to perform the transformation.

**Table 3–1 Transformation Commands**

| Using the Menu | Using the Mouse (Free Transform) | Using the Transform Options Bar | Result |
|---|---|---|---|
| Scale | Drag a sizing handle on the bounding box. SHIFT+drag to scale proportionately. ALT+drag to scale opposite sides at the same time. | To scale numerically, enter percentages in the Width and Height boxes, shown as W and H, on the options bar. Click the Link icon to maintain the aspect ratio. | Selection is displayed at a different size. |
| Rotate 180° Rotate 90° CW Rotate 90° CCW (CW stands for clockwise. CCW stands for counterclockwise.) | Move the mouse pointer outside the bounding box border. It becomes a curved, two-headed arrow. Drag in the direction you want to rotate. SHIFT+drag to constrain the rotation to 15° increments. | In the Set Rotation box, shown as a compass on the options bar, type a positive number for clockwise rotation or a negative number for counterclockwise rotation. | Selection is rotated or revolved around the reference point. |

**Table 3–1 Transformation Commands** *(continued)*

| Using the Menu | Using the Mouse (Free Transform) | Using the Transform Options Bar | Result |
|---|---|---|---|
| Skew | Right-click selection and then click Skew. Drag a side of the bounding box. ALT+drag to skew both vertically and horizontally. | To skew numerically, enter decimal values in the horizontal skew and vertical skew boxes, shown as H and V on the options bar. | Selection is tilted or slanted either horizontally or vertically. |
| Distort | Right-click selection and then click Distort. Drag a corner sizing handle to stretch the bounding box. | Enter new numbers in the location, size, rotation, and skew boxes. | Selection is larger on one edge than on the others. |
| Perspective | Right-click selection and then click Perspective. Drag a corner sizing handle to apply perspective to the bounding box. | Enter new numbers in the size, rotation, and skew boxes. | The selection appears larger on one edge than on the others, giving the larger edge the appearance of being closer to the viewer. |
| Warp | When the warp mesh is displayed, drag any line or point. | Click the Custom box arrow. Click a custom warp. | Selection is reshaped with a bulge, arch, warped corner, or twist. |
| Flip Horizontal Flip Vertical | Flipping is available only on the menu. | Flipping is available only on the menu. | Selection is turned upside down or mirrored. |

Figure 3–26 displays a painting in its original state and with various transformation effects applied (Figure 3–26).

(a) original   (b) scale   (c) skew

(d) distort   (e) rotate   (f) perspective

(g) warp   (h) flip horizontal   (i) flip vertical

**Figure 3–26**

Transform is not a tool on the Tools panel; however, Photoshop displays a Transform options bar that contains boxes and buttons to help you with your transformation (Figure 3–27). To display the Transform options bar, create a selection and then do one of the following things: click Free Transform on the Edit menu, click a sizing handle, or press CTRL+T. Recall that if you are using the Move Tool, you also can click the Show Transform Controls check box. As you start to transform, Photoshop displays the Transform options bar.

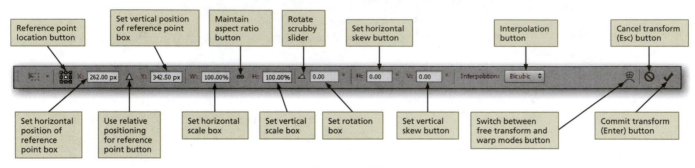

**Figure 3–27**

BTW

**Rotating**

When the bounding box is displayed, you can rotate the selection by dragging just outside of the corner. The mouse pointer changes to a double-headed, curved arrow as shown in Figure 3-28.

When you choose to transform, Photoshop displays a **bounding box**, or border with eight sizing handles around the selection. A small reference point appears in the center of the selection as a small circle with a crosshair symbol. A **reference point** is a fixed pivot point around which transformations are performed (Figure 3–28). You can move a reference point by dragging it.

**Figure 3–28**

On the left side of the Transform options bar, Photoshop displays the 'Reference point location' button. Each of the nine squares on the button corresponds to a point on the bounding box. The default middle square represents the center reference point. To select a different reference point, click a different square on the 'Reference point location' button. By selecting one of the nine preset locations, any transformation, such as rotating, is applied in relation to that reference point.

The X and Y boxes allow you to place the reference point at an exact pixel location in the document window by entering horizontal and vertical values. When you enter a value in one of those boxes, Photoshop moves the entire selection. If you click the 'Use relative positioning for reference point' button, located between the X and Y boxes, the movement of the selection is relative to the current location.

The W and H boxes allow you to scale the width and height of the selection. When you click the 'Maintain aspect ratio' button between the W and H boxes, the aspect ratio of the selection is maintained.

To the right of the scale boxes is a Set rotation box. Entering a positive number rotates, or turns, the selection clockwise; a negative number rotates the selection counterclockwise.

The H and V boxes, to the right of the Set rotation box, set the horizontal and vertical skews of the selection, measured in degrees. A positive number skews the selection to the right; a negative number skews it to the left.

A unique feature is the ability to drag labels to change the box values. For example, if you drag the H, Y, W, or other labels, the values in the text boxes change. The interactive labels, called **scrubby sliders,** appear when you position the mouse pointer over the label. When you point to any of the scrubby sliders on the Transform options bar, the mouse pointer changes to a hand with a double-headed arrow, indicating the ability to drag. Dragging to the right increases the value; dragging to the left decreases the value. Holding the SHIFT key while dragging the scrubby slider accelerates the change by a factor of 10. Many options bars use scrubby sliders.

On the far right of the Transform options bar are three buttons. The first one switches between the Transform options bar and the Warp options bar. After you are finished making transformations, you commit changes, or apply the transformations by pressing the ENTER key or by clicking the Commit transform (Enter) button. **Committing** the transformation is the same as saving it. If you do not want to make the transformation, press the ESC key or click the Cancel transform (Esc) button.

After transforming a selection, you either must commit or cancel the transformation before you can perform any other action in Photoshop.

## To Transform by Skewing

The following steps display the transformation controls and make the painting appear more natural in the setting by skewing the layer.

**1**

- Press CTRL+T to display the bounding box and the Transform options bar (Figure 3–29).

**Q&A**

Should I make a selection before pressing CTRL+T?

In this case, you are transforming the entire layer, so no selection is necessary. Photoshop displays the bounding box around the edges of the layer itself.

**Figure 3–29**

**2**

- Right-click the selection to display the context menu with the list of transformations (Figure 3–30).

**Q&A**

When should I use skew rather than perspective?

You should use skew when the selection or layer is titled or slanted either horizontally or vertically. Use perspective when you want the selection or layer to appear closer or further away in the setting.

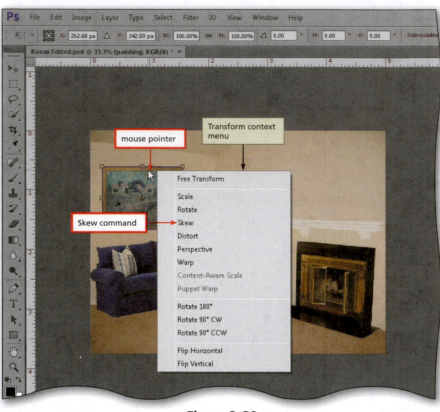

**Figure 3–30**

**3**

- Click Skew on the context menu to activate skewing.

- Drag the upper-left sizing handle up until the top of the painting is parallel with the top of the wall.

- Drag the lower-right sizing handle up until the bottom of the painting is parallel with the top of the sofa (Figure 3–31).

**4**

- Press the ENTER key to commit the transformation.

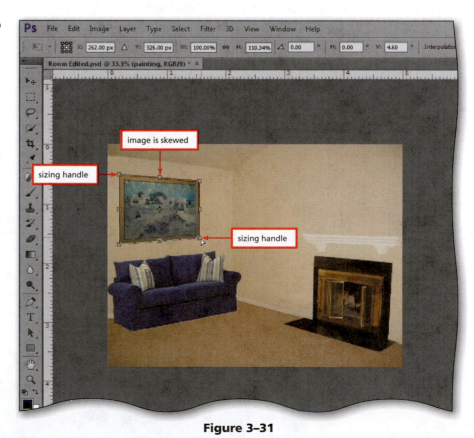

**Figure 3–31**

**Other Ways**

1. On Edit menu, point to Transform, click Skew, drag bounding box sizing handle

## To Open the Coffee Table Image

The following step opens a file named Coffee Table in preparation for the next series of steps.

**1** Open the Coffee Table file from the Chapter 03 folder of the Data Files for Students, or a location specified by your instructor.

## To Create the Coffee Table Layer

The following steps create the coffee table layer.

**1** On the Application bar, click Window, point to Arrange, and then click Tile All Horizontally to display the windows above and below one another.

**2** With the Coffee Table window still active, click the Move Tool button on the Tools panel, if necessary.

**3** Drag the entire coffee table image and drop it in the Room Edited window (Figure 3–32).

**4** Close the Coffee Table document window. If Photoshop displays a dialog box asking if you want to save the changes, click the No button.

**BTW**

**PNG File Type**
The Coffee Table image is stored as PNG file. Recall that PNG stands for Portable Network Graphics and is a cross-platform file type similar to GIF. It differs in that you can control the opacity of transparent colors. PNG files **interlace**, or fill in, faster on Web pages.

**Figure 3–32**

## To Rename and Color the Coffee Table Layer

The following steps rename the new layer and assign an identification color.

**1** Rename the layer `coffee table`.

**2** Assign a Gray identification color to the layer.

**3** With the Move Tool still selected, drag the layer to a location in front of the sofa (Figure 3–33).

**Figure 3–33**

## To Save the File

The following step saves the file again.

**1** Press CTRL+S to save the Room Edited file with the same name. If Photoshop displays a dialog box about compatibility, click the OK button.

---

**Break Point:** If you wish to stop working through the chapter at this point, you can quit Photoshop now and then resume the project at a later time by starting Photoshop, opening the file named Room Edited and continuing to follow the steps from this location forward.

# The Eraser Tools

In the painting layer, you eliminated the painting's background before moving it by using a selection technique. At other times, however, a new layer still might have extra color or objects that are not appropriate for the composite image. The image might be shaped oddly, making selecting tedious, or there might be other images in the background that come along with the selection and are not easily eliminated using the marquee selection technique you used previously. In those cases, dragging the image into a layer and then erasing part of that layer gives you more freedom and control in how the layer appears.

On the Tools panel, when you right-click the Eraser Tool button, Photoshop displays the three eraser tools. To alternate among the three eraser tools, press SHIFT+E. To access the eraser tools after using a different tool, press the E key.

The eraser tools are described in Table 3–2.

| Table 3–2 Eraser Tools | | | |
|---|---|---|---|
| **Tool** | **Purpose** | **Shortcut** | **Button** |
| Eraser Tool | Erases pixels beneath the cursor or brush tip | E<br>SHIFT+E toggles through all three eraser tools | |
| Background Eraser Tool | Erases sample color from the center of the brush | E<br>SHIFT+E toggles through all three eraser tools | |
| Magic Eraser Tool | Erases all similarly colored pixels | E<br>SHIFT+E toggles through all three eraser tools | |

When using the eraser tools, it is best to erase small portions at a time. That way each erasure is a separate state on the History panel. If you make mistakes, you can click earlier states on the panel. Small erasures also can be undone. To undo an erasure, press CTRL+Z, or click Edit on the Application bar, and then click Undo Eraser.

## Using the Magic Eraser Tool

The Magic Eraser Tool erases all similarly colored pixels with one click. The Magic Eraser Tool options bar (Figure 3–34) gives you the choice of erasing contiguous or noncontiguous pixels and allows you to enter a tolerance value to define the range of erasable color. A lower tolerance erases pixels within a range of color values very similar to the pixel you click. A higher tolerance erases pixels within a broader range. Recall that the Anti-alias check box creates a smooth edge that can apply to both selecting and erasing. **Opacity** refers to the level at which you can see through a color to reveal the layer beneath it. When using the eraser tools, an opacity setting of 100% completely erases pixels. A lower opacity partially erases pixels.

**Figure 3–34**

# To Display Only the Current Layer

Some users find it easier to erase in a layer when only that layer appears in the document window. The following step hides all but the current layer by ALT+clicking the visibility icon.

**1**

- On the Layers panel, ALT+click the coffee table layer visibility icon, so only the coffee table is displayed.

- Press the z key to activate the Zoom Tool, and then click the coffee table several times to zoom in (Figure 3–35).

- If necessary, scroll the document window so that the entire coffee table is visible.

**Figure 3–35**

# To Erase using the Magic Eraser Tool

The following steps use the Magic Eraser Tool to remove the blue wallpaper background from the coffee table image layer.

**1**

- Right-click the Eraser Tool button on the Tools panel to display the context menu (Figure 3–36).

**Figure 3–36**

**2**

- Click Magic Eraser Tool to select it.

- If necessary, click the Anti-alias check box so it displays a check mark.

- Click the Contiguous check box so it does not display a check mark (Figure 3–37).

**Q&A** Why do I need to remove the Contiguous check mark?

You want to erase all occurrences of the wallpaper color, even those that are not connected continuously, such as those in between the slats of the coffee table.

**Figure 3–37**

**3**

- Click the wallpaper to delete all of the blue color.

- If some blue remains in your layer, click it (Figure 3–38).

**Q&A** How should I position the Magic Eraser Tool mouse pointer?

Position the lower-left tip of the eraser over the pixel color to erase.

**Figure 3–38**

**Other Ways**

1. Press SHIFT+E until Magic Eraser Tool is selected, click photo

## Using the Eraser Tool

The Eraser Tool changes pixels in the image as you drag through them. On most layers, the Eraser Tool simply erases the pixels or changes them to transparent, revealing the layer beneath. On a locked layer, such as the Background layer, the Eraser Tool changes the pixels to the current background color.

The Eraser Tool options bar (Figure 3–39 on the next page) displays a Mode box in which you can choose one of three shapes for erasure: brush, block, and pen. The brush shape gives you the most flexibility in size, and many different brush tips are available. The default brush tip is a circle. Block mode is a hard-edged, fixed-sized square with no options for changing the opacity or flow; however, it does give you quick access to a square to erase straight lines and corners. The pencil mode is similar to the brush mode, except that the pencil does not spread as much into adjacent pixels.

**Pressure Buttons**
If you have a tablet and stylus connected to your computer system, the pressure you apply to the stylus can indicate the opacity or size of your brush stroke. For example, when using the eraser tools, if you click the Always use Pressure for Opacity button, applying a light pressure creates a lighter erasure. Applying more pressure erases the color more deeply.

Figure 3–39

As with the Magic Eraser Tool options bar, an Opacity box allows you to specify the depth of the erasure. The Flow box specifies how quickly the erasure is performed. In addition, you can erase to a saved state or snapshot in the History panel.

As you erase with the brush shape, the RIGHT BRACKET (]) and LEFT BRACKET ([) keys increase and decrease the size of the eraser, respectively.

## To Select the Eraser Tool and Resize the Mouse Pointer

The following steps select the Eraser Tool in preparation for erasing more of the layer.

**1** Right-click the Magic Eraser Tool button on the Tools panel, and then click Eraser Tool on the context menu.

**2** Move the mouse pointer into the document window.

**3** If the mouse pointer is extremely small, press the RIGHT BRACKET (]) key several times to resize the eraser until the mouse pointer changes from a dot to a small circle (Figure 3–40).

Figure 3–40

## To Erase using the Eraser Tool

The following steps erase the floor using the Eraser Tool.

**1**

- Drag the mouse across a portion of the floor to erase it. Do not drag across the coffee table (Figure 3–41).

**Q&A**

How should I position the Eraser Tool mouse pointer?

By default, the Eraser Tool mouse pointer appears as a circle. When you click or drag, Photoshop erases everything within the circle. You can change the size of the mouse pointer using the bracket keys.

**Figure 3–41**

**2**

- Continue dragging to erase more of the floor and the molding, using the LEFT BRACKET ([) and RIGHT BRACKET (]) keys to change the size of your eraser. Do not erase completely along the very edge of the coffee table (Figure 3–42).

**Experiment**

- Drag a short erasure over the coffee table that creates an error. Then press CTRL+Z to undo the erasure.

**Figure 3–42**

## To Erase using the Block Mouse Pointer

The following steps delete flooring and shadows that are very close to the coffee table using a block mouse pointer.

● Click the Mode button on the options bar to display its list (Figure 3–43).

Figure 3–43

**2**

● Click Block to choose a block mouse pointer.

● Drag close to the coffee table to erase the rest of the flooring and shadows (Figure 3–44).

**Q&A**

I cannot get close enough to the edge to erase. What should I do?

You can zoom in to erase more closely, or use the Magic Eraser Tool, contiguously, with a high tolerance level. When you get close, you can press and hold the SHIFT key while dragging to create a straight line of erasure.

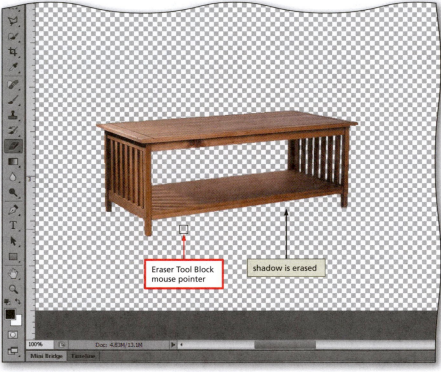

Figure 3–44

**Other Ways**

1. Press SHIFT+E until Eraser Tool is selected, click document

## To View All Layers

The following steps show all of the layers.

**1** ALT+click the visibility icon on the visible layer, in this case the coffee table, to show all of the layers.

**2** If you see pixels that need to be erased, click them, zooming and scrolling as necessary.

## To Transform by Changing the Perspective

The following steps transform the coffee table layer to make it fit the perspective of the room.

**1**

- With the coffee table layer still selected, press CTRL+T to turn on the bounding box.

- Right-click within the bounding box to display the context menu and then select Perspective.

- Drag the left-center sizing handle down to change the perspective so that the horizontal lines of the coffee table parallel the lines of the sofa (Figure 3–45).

**2**

- Press the ENTER key to confirm the transformation.

- If necessary, use the Move Tool to drag the coffee table to a location centered in front of the sofa.

coffee table is repositioned and appears in perspective

all layers are displayed

left-center sizing handle

**Figure 3–45**

---

**Other Ways**

1. On Edit menu, point to Transform, click Perspective, drag bounding box sizing handle

## To Create the Ivy Layer

To create the ivy layer, you will open the file and then move the entire image into the Room Edited document window.

**1** Open the Ivy file from the Chapter 03 folder of the Data Files for Students, or from a location specified by your instructor.

**2** On the Application bar, click Window, point to Arrange, and then click Tile All Vertically to display the windows beside each other.

**3** With the Ivy window still active, click the Move Tool button on the Tools panel, if necessary.

**4** Drag the entire ivy image and drop it in the Room Edited window.

**5** Close the Ivy document window. If Photoshop displays a dialog box asking if you want to save the changes, click the No button.

**BTW**

**TIFF File Type**
The Ivy file is stored as a TIF file. The TIF, or TIFF, is a flexible raster image format. A raster image is a digital image represented by a matrix of pixels. TIFF stands for Tagged Image File Format and is a common file format for images acquired from scanners and screen capture programs. Because TIF files are supported by virtually all paint, image-editing, and page-layout applications, it also is a versatile format for cross-platform applications.

## To Rename and Color the Ivy Layer

The following steps rename the new layer and assign an identification color.

**1** Rename the layer `ivy`.

**2** Assign a Green identification color to the layer.

**3** Zoom to 50 percent magnification and scroll to display the entire layer (Figure 3–46).

**Figure 3–46**

## Using the Background Eraser Tool

The Background Eraser Tool erases the background while maintaining the edges of an object in the foreground, based on a set color that you choose for the background. The Background Eraser Tool samples the color in the center of the mouse pointer, called the **hot spot**. As you drag, the tool erases that color, leaving the rest of the layer intact. You release the mouse button and drag again to sample a different color. On the Background Eraser Tool options bar (Figure 3–47), you can use the tolerance setting to control the range of colors that will be erased, sample the color selections, and adjust the sharpness of the boundaries by setting limits. The three sampling buttons on the Background Eraser Tool options bar sample in different ways. When you use the Sampling: Continuous button, it samples colors and erases continuously as you drag, the Sampling: Once button erases only the areas containing the color you first click, and the Sampling: Background Swatch button erases only areas containing the current color on the Tools panel, Color panel, or Swatches panel.

**Figure 3–47**

## To Erase using the Background Eraser Tool

The following steps use the Background Eraser Tool to remove the paneling from behind the ivy plant. If you make a mistake while erasing, click the previous state on the History panel or press CTRL+Z and begin erasing again.

**1**

• With the ivy layer still selected, right-click the Eraser Tool button on the Tools panel and then click Background Eraser Tool on the context menu to select the tool.

• On the options bar, click the Sampling: Once button to erase only the areas containing the color you first click.

• Click the Limits button to display its list (Figure 3–48).

**Figure 3–48**

**2**

- Click Discontiguous to choose the setting.

- Enter 25 in the Tolerance box, and then press the ENTER key to lower the Tolerance setting, which will erase a more narrow range of color.

- Move the mouse pointer to the document window, and then press the RIGHT BRACKET (]) key several times to increase the size of the eraser, if necessary (Figure 3–49)

**Q&A**

What does discontiguous mean?

Discontiguous refers to noncontiguous pixels, or pixels of the same color that are not physically located together. In the ivy layer, parts of the brown panel appear behind the ivy and are not adjacent to the other brown paneling.

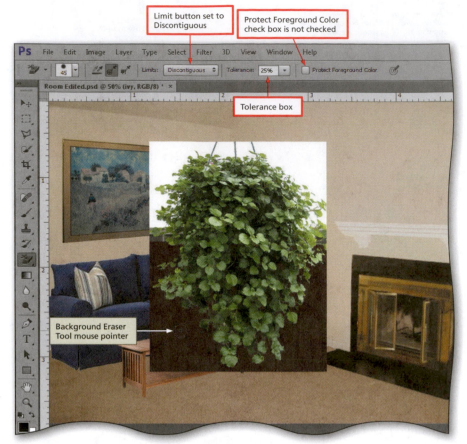

**Figure 3–49**

**3**

- Position the center of the mouse pointer directly over a portion of the paneling.

- Click and hold the mouse button. Drag across the layer, including the ivy, to erase some of the paneling (Figure 3–50).

**Q&A**

What is the purpose of the Protect Foreground Color check box?

When checked, the Protect Foreground Color check box gives you even more control of the background erasing. When colors are very similar, you can ALT+click the color you want to keep, then drag the color you want to erase.

**Figure 3–50**

**4**

- Position the mouse pointer directly over a portion of the paneling.

- Click and hold the mouse button. Drag to erase the rest of the paneling.

- If some color remains, zoom as necessary to position your mouse directly over any remaining shadow or color of the paneling. Click and drag to erase the rest of the color (Figure 3–51).

all paneling is erased

**Figure 3–51**

**Other Ways**

1. Press SHIFT+E until Background Eraser Tool is selected, set options bar, click document

## To Finish the Ivy Layer

The following steps erase the rest of the background and resize the ivy layer.

**1** With the ivy layer still selected on the Layers panel, use a combination of eraser tools and techniques in the document window to erase the white portion of the layer and the chair rail molding.

**2** Press CTRL+T to display the Transform bounding box, and then SHIFT+drag a corner sizing handle to scale the size of the selection down to approximately 35 percent. Press the ENTER key to commit the transformation.

**3** Move the layer to a location on the left side of the fireplace mantel (Figure 3–52).

background is removed and layer is scaled and repositioned

**Figure 3–52**

## To Add a Pole Lamp to the Room

The following steps add a pole lamp layer to the room.

**1** Open the file named Pole Lamp from the Chapter 03 folder of the Data Files for Students or from a location specified by your instructor.

**2** Use the techniques you have learned to create a new layer and place the pole lamp in the Room Edited document window.

**3** Name the new layer `pole lamp` and color the layer orange.

**4** Close the Pole Lamp document window.

## To Rearrange Layers

The following steps rearrange the layers on the Layers panel, moving the pole lamp layer below the sofa layer, so the pole lamp appears behind the end of the sofa.

**1**

• Select the pole lamp layer on the Layers panel, if necessary.

• Press CTRL+LEFT BRACKET ([) several times to move the layer down and place it below the sofa layer on the Layers panel.

• In the document window, move the pole lamp to the right end of the sofa, in the corner of the room (Figure 3–53).

🔍 **Experiment**

• Drag individual layers on the Layers panel to new locations in the stack, and watch how that changes the document window. When you are finished, rearrange the layers to appear as shown in Figure 3–53.

Figure 3–53

**2**

• Reposition the pole lamp layer as necessary.

| Other Ways |  |
|---|---|
| 1. To move a layer up, press CTRL+RIGHT BRACKET (]) | 2. Drag layer on Layers panel, drop between other layers |

BTW

**Arranging Layers**
To rearrange layers, change their visibility, or better organize them, drag the layer up or down on the Layers panel. The top layer on the Layers panel appears in front of any other layers in the document window. The Layer menu also contains an Arrange submenu to help you organize your layers.

## To Add Mantel Decorations to the Room

The following steps add a mantel decoration layer to the room.

**1** On the Layers panel, click the top layer to select it, so the new layer will appear on top.

**2** Open the file named Mantel Decorations from the Chapter 03 folder of the Data Files for Students, or from a location specified by your instructor.

**3** Use the techniques you have learned to create a new layer and edit it as necessary; you may want to scale to 50% and adjust the perspective.

**4** Place the mantel decorations on the mantel in the Room Edited document window.

**5** Name the new layer `mantel decorations` and color the layer violet.

**6** Close the Mantel Decorations document window, and zoom to 33.33% magnification (Figure 3–54).

**Figure 3–54**

**BTW**

**Saving Files**
Photoshop displays an asterisk (*) on the document window tab to denote changes have been made to the file (Figure 3–54). Once you save the file, the asterisk no longer is displayed.

## To Save the File

Many layers have been added to the composite image. The following step saves the file.

**1** Save the Room Edited file with the same name.

**Break Point:** If you wish to stop working through the chapter at this point, you can quit Photoshop now and then resume the project at a later time by starting Photoshop, opening the file named Room Edited and continuing to follow the steps from this location forward.

# Layer Masks

Another way to edit layers is by creating a mask. A **mask** is an overlay that hides portions of a layer; it also can protect areas of the layer from inadvertent editing. For example, in a graphic of an exotic animal, you might want to mask all of the area except the animal, rather than permanently delete the background. Or, if you wanted to layer a musical score over the top of a piano graphic, you might mask the edges of the paper so the notes look like they blend into the piano. A mask does not alter the layer as the Eraser Tool does; it merely overlays a template to conceal a portion of the layer. That way, if you change your mind and need to display more of the layer, you can. Nothing has been erased permanently. With the Eraser Tool, you would have to delete the layer, open a backup copy, recreate the layer, and then begin to edit again. With masks, you simply edit the mask.

Photoshop provides two types of masks. **Layer masks** or **pixel masks** are resolution-dependent bitmap images, created with the painting or selection tools. **Vector masks** are resolution independent, created with a pen or shape tool. In this chapter, you will create a layer mask.

When you add a mask, a layer mask thumbnail appears on the Layers panel in **grayscale**, which means each pixel in the mask uses a single shade of gray on a scale from black to white. When selecting the layer mask thumbnail, the default colors change to white over black and the eraser tools are inactive. To mask, you paint on the layer with black. If you change your mind and want to unmask, you paint with white. Painting with gray displays various levels of transparency in the layer.

## To Open the Potted Plant File

The following steps open the Potted Plant file in preparation for creating a layer mask, and uses a copy and paste process to place the plant in the room.

**1** Open the file named Potted Plant from the Chapter 03 folder of the Data Files for Students or from a location specified by your instructor.

**2** With the Potted Plant window active, press CTRL+A to select all, and then press CTRL+C to copy the entire image.

**3** Click the Room Edited document window tab to make the window active. Press CTRL+V to paste the copied image from the Windows clipboard.

**4** Name the new layer potted plant and color the layer green.

**5** Close the Potted Plant document window.

## To Create a Layer Mask

The following steps mask the plant in the potted plant layer to reveal only the pot. That way, potential decorators can see what the room would look like with and without the plant. As you create the layer mask, you will use the Brush Tool to brush over the parts of the image to mask.

**1**

- With the potted plant layer selected, zoom to 100 percent.

- Click the 'Add layer mask' button on the Layers panel status bar to create a layer mask (Figure 3–55).

**Q&A** What is the new notation on the Layers panel?

Photoshop adds a layer mask thumbnail to the selected layer on the panel. The link icon **links**, or connects, the mask to the layer. A link icon appears between the layer thumbnail and the mask thumbnail. Also, notice that the default color swatches on the Tools panel are reversed.

**Figure 3–55**

**2**

- Press the x key to choose black over white, which creates a mask.

- Press the B key to activate the brush and then move the mouse pointer into the document window.

- Press the RIGHT BRACKET (]) key to increase the size of the brush's circle, as necessary.

- Drag the mouse across the plant itself. Do not drag the pot (Figure 3–56).

**Q&A** Did I erase the plant?

No, you still can see the plant in the layer thumbnail on the Layers panel. You only masked the plant out of view.

**Figure 3–56**

**3**

● Continue dragging through the layer to remove everything except the pot. Zoom the magnification and adjust the size of the brush mouse pointer, as necessary (Figure 3–57).

**Q&A**

Why does the layer mask use a brush tip mouse pointer?

Layer masks use painting techniques to mask out portions of the image.

**Figure 3–57**

## To Correct a Masking Error

The following steps create a masking error and then unmask the area by painting with white.

**1**

● Drag across the pot to mask a portion of the pot (Figure 3–58).

**Figure 3–58**

**2**

● Press the X key to switch the foreground and background colors so you are painting with white, which restores the image.

● Drag across the same portion of the pot to unmask it (Figure 3–59).

🔍 **Experiment**

● On the Layers panel, right-click the mask and then click Disable Layer Mask. Notice the entire potted plan appears and the mask has an X through it. Right-click the mask again and then click Enable Layer Mask.

**Figure 3–59**

## To Move the Potted Plant

The following step moves the potted plant to the right side of the fireplace.

**1** Select the Move Tool and drag the potted plant to the floor on the right side of the fireplace. Scroll as necessary.

# Fine-Tuning Layers

Sometimes layers need special adjustments to better fit into their new surroundings in the document window. This fine-tuning usually involves **tonal adjustments** that affect the color, lighting, opacity, level, or fill; **style adjustments** such as special effects or blends; or **filter adjustments** that let you apply pictures, tiles, or patterns. With the correct adjustment, a layer can be made to look like it was an original part of the image, maintaining a consistency of appearance for the overall composite image.

<table>
<tr>
<td>

**Create layer adjustments.**
Layer adjustments allow you to fine-tune your layers. Evaluate layers to see if a change in levels, brightness, saturation, or hue would help them to fit more naturally into the background scene. Use nondestructive edits when possible, so that if you are not satisfied with the adjustment, you can remove it.

</td>
<td>

**Plan Ahead**

</td>
</tr>
</table>

When you do not want to alter the pixels in an image permanently, you can create an extra layer in which to make changes while preserving the original pixels. An **adjustment layer** is a new layer added to the image to affect a large-scale tonal change. You can create adjustment layers for the entire composite image or just a specific layer.

Adjustment layers have several advantages. They are nondestructive, which means you can experiment with various settings and reedit the adjustment layer at any time. Adjustment layers reduce the amount of damage you do to an image by making direct edits. You can copy adjustments to other layers and images, saving time and maintaining consistency.

If you want to make permanent tonal, style, or filter changes to the pixels themselves, you can edit the layer directly. Features such as opacity, fill, and blending modes can be changed on the Layers panel. These changes can be undone using the History panel, but they become permanent when you save the image.

## Making an Opacity Change to a Layer

Some adjustment tools specific to layers are located on the Layers panel. (See Figure 3-60 on the next page.) The Opacity box allows you to change the opacity or transparency of a layer. You can control exactly how solid the objects on a specific layer appear. For example, if you wanted to display an American flag superimposed over a memorial or monument, you might change the flag layer's opacity to 50 percent. The monument easily would be visible through the flag.

The Fill box changes the fill of a layer's opacity as well, but it only changes the pixels in the layer rather than changing any applied layer styles or blending modes. Adjusting the fill percentage sometimes is called changing the **interior opacity**. If you have no layer styles or blending modes, you can use either the Opacity or Fill box.

The Blending mode button displays a list of blending modes for the selected layer or layers. **Blending modes** define how an object interacts with other objects, such as the Background layer.

**BTW**

**Pop-Up Sliders**
If there is a triangle next to a text box in the Photoshop interface, you can click it to display a **pop-up slider**. Drag the slider to the desired value. Click outside the slider or press the ENTER key to close the slider box. To cancel the changes, press the ESC key.

**BTW**

**Panel Boxes**
The Opacity and Fill boxes can be changed in one of three ways. You can drag the scrubby slider label. When you click the box arrow, a pop-up slider is displayed to adjust the percentage. You also can type a percentage in either box.

## To Make an Opacity Change to a Layer

The following step lightens the mantel decorations by lowering the opacity, to make them fit better into the room design.

**1**

- Zoom to display the mantel decorations in the document window at 100% magnification.

- On the Layers panel, click to select the mantel decorations layer.

- On the Layers panel, point to the word, Opacity, and then drag the scrubby slider to the left until the Opacity box displays 85% to lower the opacity (Figure 3–60).

**Experiment**

- Click the Blending mode button and choose a blending mode such as Hard Light or Linear Burn. Experiment with other blending modes. When you are done, click the Blending mode button and then click Normal in the list.

**Figure 3–60**

# Adjustments and Properties

Tools that nondestructively adjust image lighting and shading are located on the Adjustments panel (Figure 3–61).

**Figure 3–61**

Clicking an **adjustment icon**, or preset, also displays the Properties panel and its settings for the specific adjustment, including channel selectors, eyedroppers, sliders, and input boxes, among others. Buttons on the Properties panel status bar allow you to specify visibility, delete the adjustment, or create a **clip** that applies the adjustment to a layer rather than the entire image.

Some adjustments also can display their settings using a dialog box, if accessed from outside the Adjustments panel with a shortcut key or a menu command. Table 3–3 displays a list of the Adjustments available on the Adjustments panel. Many of the adjustments also are available through the Adjustments panel menu (Figure 3–61), through the Layers menu on the application bar, or through a button on the Layers panel.

### Table 3–3 Adjustments Panel Icons

| Adjustment | Description | Shortcut (if available) | Icon |
|---|---|---|---|
| Brightness/ Contrast | Changes general brightness (shadows and highlights) and overall contrast (tonal range) | | |
| Levels | Adjusts color balance for shadows, midtones, highlights, and color channels | CTRL+L | |
| Curves | Adjusts individual points in the tonal range of black to white | CTRL+M | |
| Exposure | Changes exposure, which adjusts the highlights; changes offset, which darkens the shadows and midtones; changes gamma, which adjusts the midtones | | |
| Vibrance | Adjusts vibrance and color saturation settings so shifting to primary colors, or clipping, is minimized | | |
| Hue/Saturation | Changes hue, saturation, and lightness of entire image or specific colors | CTRL+U | |
| Color Balance | Adjusts the overall midtone of colors in an image | CTRL+B | |
| Black & White | Converts a color image to grayscale | ALT+SHIFT+CTRL+B | |
| Photo Filter | Simulates effects of using a filter in front of a camera lens | | |
| Channel Mixer | Modifies and adjusts individual color channels | | |
| Color Lookup | Remaps every color using a lookup table or predetermined style | | |
| Invert | Converts every color to its inverse or opposite | CTRL+I | |
| Posterize | Specifies the number of tonal levels in each channel | | |
| Threshold | Converts images to high-contrast black and white | | |
| Selective Color | Changes the mixture of colors in each of the primary color components | | |
| Gradient Map | Maps colors to a specified gradient fill | | |

**Level Sliders**
In the Levels dialog box, the Input Level sliders on each end map the black point (on the left) and white point (on the right) to the settings of the Output sliders. The middle Input slider adjusts the gamma or midtone in the image, changing the intensity values of the middle range of gray tones without dramatically altering the highlights and shadows. As you move any of the Input Level sliders, the black point, midtone, and white point change in the Output sliders; all the remaining levels are redistributed.

# Level Adjustments

A **level adjustment** is one way to make tonal changes to shadows, midtones, and highlights. A **shadow** is a darkened shade in an image. A **midtone**, also called **gamma**, is the midpoint gray between shadows and highlights. A **highlight** is a portion of an image that is strongly illuminated and may appear as the lightest or whitest part of the image. To change levels, Photoshop uses black, gray, and white sliders to adjust any or all of the three tonal input levels. A **histogram**, or frequency distribution bar chart, indicates the amount of color in the tonal ranges. When adjusting levels using the histogram, a general guideline is to drag the black-and-white sliders to the first indication, or outlier, of strong tonal change in the histogram. Then, experiment with the gray slider to change the intensity value of the middle range of gray tones without dramatically altering the highlights and shadows. Becoming proficient at adjusting levels takes practice. Furthermore, adjustments are subjective; the impact of some effects is a matter of opinion.

## To Make a Levels Adjustment

In the sofa layer of the image, you will adjust the levels to make the layer better fit into the picture. The following steps make level adjustments to the sofa.

**1**

- Select the sofa layer on the Layers panel and scroll the document window to display the sofa.

- Click the Levels icon on the Adjustments panel to display the level settings and options on the Properties panel.

- Click the Clip to Layer button on the Properties panel status bar to adjust only the sofa layer (Figure 3–62).

🔍 **Experiment**

- Drag the three Levels Input sliders below the histogram to see how they affect the appearance of the sofa layer.

**Figure 3–62**

**2**

- Click the 'Calculate a more accurate histogram' button to make the level change more visible.

- Below the histogram display, drag the white Levels Input slider to approximately 223, aligning it with the first visible increase on the right side of the histogram to adjust the highlights.

- Drag the black Levels Input slider to approximately 30, aligning it with the first visible increase on the left side of the histogram to adjust the shadows.

**Figure 3–63**

- Drag the gray Levels Input slider to 1.20 to adjust the midtone colors (Figure 3–63).

**Q&A** | My visible changes were at different levels. Did I do something wrong?

No, your histogram might differ, depending on your previous erasures.

**3**

- Click the Properties button on the vertical dock to collapse the Properties panel and complete the adjustment.

**Q&A** | Did the Layers panel change?

Yes, you will see an extra layer created just above the sofa layer, with a clipping symbol to imply the relationship (Figure 3-64 on the next page).

🔍 **Experiment**

- Click the visibility icon of the new levels layer to notice the change in the sofa. Click it again to redisplay the level adjustment.

**Other Ways**

1. Press CTRL+L, adjust levels, click OK button

2. On Image menu, point to Adjustments, click Levels, adjust levels, click OK button

## Hue and Saturation

Another way to adjust a layer or image is to change the hue or saturation. **Hue** is the shade of a color in an image. **Saturation** is the intensity of a hue and is highly dependent upon the chosen color model, but in general, pastels have low saturation, and bright colors have high saturation. You will learn more about color models and the color wheel in later chapters and by reading Appendix B, the Graphic Design Overview appendix.

**BTW**

**Other Level Adjustments**
The three eyedroppers in the Levels area allow you to select the values for shadow, midtone, and highlight from the image itself. To do so, click the eyedropper and then click the location in the image that you want use. Once selected, that color becomes the slider value.

## To Adjust the Hue and Saturation

The following steps adjust the hue and saturation of the coffee table layer.

**1**

- Select the coffee table layer and scroll to display the coffee table in the document window, if necessary.

- Click the Hue/Saturation icon on the Adjustments panel.

- Click the Clip to Layer button on the Properties panel status bar to adjust only the selected layer.

- Drag the Hue slider to +5. Drag the Saturation slider to –5. Drag the Lightness slider to –10 (Figure 3–64).

**Figure 3–64**

🔍 **Experiment**

- Drag the sliders to view the effect of hue and saturation settings to the layer. When you are done experimenting, drag the sliders to the settings listed in the step.

**2**

- Click the Properties button on the vertical dock to collapse the Properties panel and complete the adjustment.

| Other Ways |
|---|
| 1. Select layer, press CTRL+U, drag sliders, click OK button.   2. On Layer menu, point to New Adjustment Layer, click Hue/Saturation, edit settings |

## To Fit the Image on Screen

In previous chapters, you changed the magnification by using a box on the status bar and by using the Navigator panel. The View menu also offers several settings to change the magnification. The following steps use a command to change the magnification, to display the picture as large as possible while still fitting on the screen, in preparation for adjusting the Background layer.

**1**

- Click View on the Application bar to display the View menu (Figure 3–65).

**Q&A** What does the Actual Pixels command do?

The Actual Pixels command displays the document window so that one image pixel equals exactly one monitor pixel, allowing you to see the maximum amount of detail available in your image.

**Figure 3–65**

**2**

- Click Fit on Screen to display the entire photo at the largest magnification (Figure 3–66).

**Figure 3–66**

| Other Ways |
| --- |
| 1. Press CTRL+0 (zero) |

## Brightness and Contrast

**Brightness** refers to color luminance or intensity of a light source, perceived as lightness or darkness in an image. Photoshop measures brightness on a sliding scale from –150 to +150. Negative numbers move the brightness toward black. Positive numbers compress the highlights and expand the shadows. For example, the layer might be an image photographed on a cloudy day; conversely, the image might appear overexposed by having been too close to a photographer's flash. Either way, editing the brightness might enhance the image.

**Contrast** is the difference between the lightest and darkest tones in an image, involving mainly the midtones. When you increase contrast, the middle-to-dark areas become darker, and the middle-to-light areas become lighter. High-contrast images contain few color variations between the lightest and darkest parts of the image; low-contrast images contain more tonal gradations.

## To Adjust the Brightness and Contrast

The following steps edit the brightness and contrast of the Background layer, this time creating the adjustment layer using the Layers panel.

**1**

- Scroll in the Layers panel as necessary to select the Background layer.

- On the Layers panel status bar, click the 'Create new fill or adjustment layer' button to display the list of adjustments (Figure 3–67).

**Q&A**

What is the difference between clicking the Brightness/Contrast button on the Adjustments panel and clicking the 'Create new fill or adjustment layer' button?

There is no difference when adjusting the brightness or contrast. The list of adjustments accessed from the Layers panel includes a few more settings than the Adjustments panel.

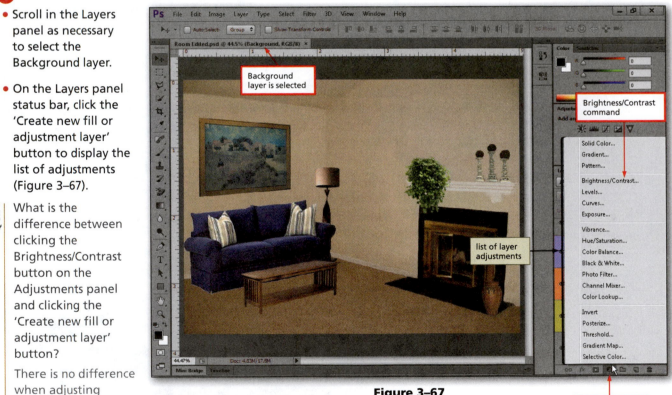

**Figure 3–67**

**2**

- Click Brightness/ Contrast in the list to display the settings on the Properties panel.

- Click the Clip to Layer button on the Properties panel status bar to adjust only the Background layer.

- Drag the Brightness slider to 10 and the Contrast slider to –10 to brighten the room (Figure 3–68).

🔍 **Experiment**

Drag the sliders to various locations and note how the document window changes. When you are finished, drag the Brightness slider to +10 and the Contrast slider to –10.

**Figure 3–68**

**2**

- Collapse the Properties panel.

| Other Ways |  |
|---|---|
| 1. On Adjustments panel, click Brightness/ Contrast icon, adjust settings | 2. On Layer menu, point to New Adjustment Layer, click Brightness/Contrast, click OK, adjust settings |

# Layer Styles

Similar to a layer adjustment, a **layer style** is applied to a layer rather than changing the layer's actual pixels. Layer styles, or layer effects, alter the appearance of the layer by adding depth, shadow, shading, texture, or overlay. A layer can display multiple styles or effects.

**Edit layer styles.**
Layer styles add dimension, texture, and definition to your layers. Styles such as shadow, glow, emboss, bevel, overlay, and stroke commonly distinguish the layer rather than making it fit in. Choose the settings carefully and think about direction, angle, distance, and spread. Make sure the layer style does not overwhelm the overall image or detract from previous layer adjustments.

**Plan Ahead**

**BTW**

**Copying and Moving Layer Styles**
To copy a layer style, right-click the source layer and then click Copy Layer Style on the context menu. Right-click the destination layer and then click Paste Layer Style. To move a layer style, drag the fx icon from one layer to another on the Layers panel.

BTW

**Styles vs. Adjustments**
Layer styles are special effects such as shadows, glows, and overlays. Styles appear attached to a layer on the Layers panel. An adjustment applies color, level, and tonal changes on its on layer.

**Bevels**
A bevel adds depth to an image by creating an angle between an edge and a shadow that softens the look. A bevel increases the 3D look of an image.

Table 3–4 lists the layer styles.

### Table 3–4 Layer Styles

| Style | Description |
|---|---|
| Drop Shadow | Creates a shadow behind the layer |
| Inner Shadow | Creates a shadow inside the edges of the layer |
| Inner Glow | Adds a glow around the inside edge of the layer |
| Outer Glow | Adds a glow around the outside edge of the layer |
| Bevel and Emboss | Adds highlights and shading to a layer |
| Satin | Applies interior shading to create a satin finish |
| Color Overlay | Adds a color over the layer |
| Gradient Overlay | Inserts a gradient in front of the layer |
| Pattern Overlay | Fills the layer with a pattern |
| Stroke | Outlines the layer with a color, gradient, or pattern |

Each of the layer styles has its own set of options and properties. Table 3–5 describes some of the layer style options. The options apply to many of the styles.

### Table 3–5 Layer Style Options

| Option | Description |
|---|---|
| Angle | Sets a degree value for the lighting angle at which the effect is applied |
| Anti-alias | Blends the edge pixels of a contour or gloss contour |
| Blend Mode | Determines how a layer style blends with its underlying layers |
| Color | Assigns the color of a shadow, glow, or highlight |
| Contour | Allows you to create rings of transparency such as gradients, fades, beveling and embossing, and sculpting |
| Depth | Sets the depth of a bevel or pattern |
| Distance | Specifies the offset distance for a shadow or satin effect |
| Fill Type | Sets the content of a stroke |
| Global Light | Allows you to set an angle to simulate the direction of the light |
| Gloss Contour | Creates a glossy, metallic appearance on a bevel or emboss effect |
| Gradient | Indicates the gradient of a layer effect |
| Highlight or Shadow Mode | Specifies the blending mode of a bevel or emboss highlight or shadow |
| Jitter | Varies the color and opacity of a gradient |
| Layer Knocks Out Drop Shadow | Controls the drop shadow's visibility in a semitransparent layer |
| Noise | Assigns the number of random elements in the opacity of a glow or shadow |
| Opacity | Sets the opacity or transparency |
| Pattern | Specifies the pattern |
| Position | Sets the position of a stroke |
| Range | Controls which portion or range of the glow is targeted for the contour |
| Size | Specifies the amount of blur or the size of the shadow |
| Soften | Blurs the results of shading to reduce unwanted artifacts |
| Source | Specifies the source for an inner glow |
| Style | Specifies the style of a bevel or emboss |

**Hide Layer Styles**
If you want to hide the notation of the Layer styles on the Layers panel, click the 'Reveals layer effects in the panel' button. To redisplay the style, click the button again.

**Delete Layer Styles**
If you want to delete a layer style, right-click the layer style, and then click Clear Layer Style on the context menu.

When a layer has a style applied to it, an fx icon appears to the right of the layer's name on the Layers panel. You can expand the icon on the Layers panel to view all of the applied effects and edit them when changing the style.

As you can tell from Table 3–4 and Table 3–5, there are a large number of layer styles and settings in Photoshop.

# To Apply a Layer Style

The following steps apply a layer style to the ivy. You will create an inner bevel to give the ivy more depth.

**1**

- On the Layers panel, select the ivy layer.

- Click the 'Add a layer style' button on the Layers panel status bar to display the menu (Figure 3–69).

**Q&A**

Will I see much change in the document window?

It depends on the magnification — at larger magnifications, you will see more change. The printed image will display more depth in the ivy.

**Figure 3–69**

**2**

- Click Bevel & Emboss to display the Layer Style dialog box.

- In the Layer Style dialog box, enter 50 in the Depth box to decrease the strength of the shading.

- Enter 10 in the Size box and 5 in the Soften box to edit the bevel (Figure 3–70).

**3**

- Click the OK button to close the Layer Style dialog box.

### 🔍 Experiment

- To view the difference that the adjustment has made, press CTRL+Z to undo the step and then press CTRL+Z again to redo the step.

**Figure 3–70**

**Other Ways**

1. On Layer menu, point to Layer Style, click desired style, edit settings in Layer Style dialog box, click OK button

# The Clone Stamp Tool

The Clone Stamp Tool reproduces portions of an image, changing the pixels in a specific area. After clicking the Clone Stamp Tool button on the Tools panel, you press and hold the ALT key while clicking the portion of the picture that you want to copy. Photoshop takes a **sample** of the image, remembering where you clicked. You then move the mouse pointer to the position where you want to create the copy. As you drag with the brush, the image is applied. Each stroke of the tool applies more of the sample. The Clone Stamp Tool is useful for duplicating specific parts of an object or correcting defects in an image. You can clone from image to image, or clone locations within the same document window.

The Clone Source panel (Figure 3–71) appears when you click Clone Source on the Window menu. The panel has options to rotate or scale the sample, or specify the size and orientation. The Clone Source panel makes it easy to create variegated patterns using multiple sources. You can create up to five different clone sources to select the one you need quickly, without resampling each time. For example, if you are using the Clone Stamp Tool to repair several minor imperfections in an old photo, you can select your various samples first, and then use the sources as needed. The Clone Source panel also helps you create unique clones positioned at different angles and perspectives from the original.

**Figure 3–71**

The Clone Stamp Tool options bar (Figure 3–71) displays some of the same settings that you used with layer masks, along with an Aligned check box and Sample box. When you align, the sample point is not reset if you start dragging in a new location; in other words, the sampling moves to a relative point in the original image. Otherwise, the sample point begins again as you start a new clone. The default value is to sample only the current layer or background. When you select All Layers in the Sample box, the clone displays all layers. One restriction when using the Clone Stamp Tool from one image to another is that both images have to be in the same color mode, such as RGB or CMYK. The color mode of an image appears on the document window tab. You will learn more about color modes in a later chapter.

Grouped with the Clone Stamp Tool, a second kind of stamp, the Pattern Stamp Tool, allows you to paint with a pattern chosen from Photoshop's pattern library. A **pattern** is a repeated or tiled image, used to fill a layer or selection. On the Pattern Stamp Tool options bar, a Pattern Picker box arrow displays installed patterns. You can import additional patterns into the Pattern Picker box.

## To Open the Flooring File and Arrange the Windows

To finish the composite image of the room, you will replace the carpeting with wood flooring. The following steps open the Flooring file.

**1** Open the Flooring file from the Chapter 03 folder of the Data Files for Students or from a location specified by your instructor.

**2** Tile All Horizontally to arrange the windows above and below one another.

**3** Drag the border between the two document windows so more of the Room Edited window is displayed. Scroll in the Room Edited window to display the carpeting.

**4** Select the carpeting layer.

## To Create a New Blank Layer

The following steps create a new blank layer that clips the carpeting layer, in preparation for cloning.

**1**

- ALT+click the visibility icon on the carpeting layer to display only the carpeting.

- Press SHIFT+CTRL+N to display the New Layer dialog box.

- Name the layer, flooring.

- Click to display a check mark in the Use Previous Layer to Create Clipping Mask check box.

- Choose a yellow identification color. Do not change the mode or opacity (Figure 3–72).

**2**

- Click the OK button to close the New Layer dialog box.

**Figure 3–72**

## To Create a Clone

Using the Clone Stamp Tool, you will sample the Flooring image and then clone it to the carpeted area in the Room Edited image, as shown in the following steps. As you clone the flooring, adjust the magnification of the image to view the corners and small areas clearly. If you make a mistake while cloning, press CTRL+Z to undo the most recent clone stroke or access the History panel and click a previous state, then begin cloning again.

**1**

- Click the Flooring document window tab to make the window active.

- Click Window on the Application bar, and then click Clone Source to display the Clone Source panel.

- On the Clone Source panel, click the Invert check box to remove its check mark, if necessary.

- On the Tools panel, right-click the Clone Stamp Tool button to display its context menu (Figure 3–73).

**2**

- Click Clone Stamp Tool to select it.

- On the options bar, click the Aligned check box so it displays a check mark, if necessary.

- Click the Clone Source button on the vertical dock to collapse the panel.

- Move the mouse pointer to the Flooring document window and ALT+click the left-middle edge of the flooring to select the sampling point (Figure 3–74).

**Q&A** How do I know if I indicated the clone source correctly?

As you ALT+click, the Clone Stamp Tool displays a crosshair mouse pointer and the Clone Source panel displays the source of the clone.

**Figure 3–73**

**Figure 3–74**

**3**

- Click the Room Edited document window tab to make it active.

- With the flooring layer still selected, and the carpeting layer visible, move the mouse pointer into the document window. Adjust the size of the mouse pointer as necessary.

- Drag from the upper-left corner of the carpeting down to the lower-left corner to create the first stroke of the clone (Figure 3–75).

**Figure 3–75**

**4**

- Working from left to right, drag to replace the carpeting. Zoom, scroll, and adjust the pointer size as necessary to fill in corners. Use short strokes, so if you make a mistake, you can press CTRL+Z to undo the error. Do not resample (Figure 3–76).

**Q&A**

What is the purpose of the Aligned check box?

When checked, the Aligned check box allows you to use short strokes as you clone. The clone will not start over if you lift the mouse button to drag in another location. Aligning is good for cloning areas with a pattern.

**Figure 3–76**

| **Other Ways** | |
|---|---|
| 1. From another tool, press S key, ALT+click sample, drag clone | 2. From Pattern Stamp Tool, press SHIFT+S, ALT+click sample, drag clone |

### To Close the Flooring Window

The following steps close the Flooring window and redisplay all the layers.

**1** Close the Flooring document window. If Photoshop asks if you want to save changes to the document, click the No button.

**2** Display all of the layers.

# Flattening a Composite Image

When you **flatten** a composite image, Photoshop reduces the file size by merging all visible layers into the background, discarding hidden layers, and applying masks. A flattened file is easier to print, export, and display on the Web. It is a good practice, however, to save the layered version in PSD format before flattening in case you want to make further changes to the file. It is very important to remember that once a file is flattened and saved, no changes can be made to individual layers. If you flatten an image and then change your mind, if the file still is open, you can click the previous state on the History panel to restore all of the layers.

If you want to save each layer as a separate file, click File on the Application bar, point to Scripts, and then click Export Layers to Files. This script is useful if you think you might want to use your layers in other composite images.

The Layer menu displays a Flatten Image command and has many of the same choices as the Layers panel menu. The choice of which to use is a matter of personal preference and the location of your mouse pointer at the time. After saving the composite image, you will use the Layer menu to flatten the visible layers. Finally, you will save the flattened file in TIFF format with the name, Room TIFF.

### To Save the Composite Image

The following steps save the Room Edited image with its layers.

**1** With your USB flash drive connected to one of the computer's USB ports, click File on the Application bar and then click Save As.

**2** When the Save As dialog box is displayed, type `Room Composite` in the File name text box. Do not press the ENTER key after typing the file name.

**3** If necessary, click the Format box arrow and then choose Photoshop (*.PSD, *.PDD) in the list.

**4** If necessary, click the Save in box arrow and then click Removable Disk (F:), or the location associated with your USB flash drive, in the list.

**5** Click the Save button in the Save As dialog box. If Photoshop displays an options dialog box, click the OK button.

# To Flatten a Composite Image

The following steps use the Layer menu to flatten the composite image.

**1**

- Click Layer on the Application bar to display the Layer menu (Figure 3–77).

**Figure 3–77**

**2**

- Click Flatten Image on the Layer menu to combine all of the layers (Figure 3–78).

**Q&A**

What is the difference between flatten and merge?

The Merge command flattens specific layers together. The Flatten command uses all of the layers and merges into a Background layer.

**Figure 3–78**

| Other Ways |
|---|
| 1. Right-click any layer, click  Flatten Image | 2. Click Layers panel menu  button, click Flatten Image |

## To Save a File in the TIFF Format

The following steps save the flattened image as a TIFF file.

**1** With your USB flash drive connected to one of the computer's USB ports, click File on the Application bar and then click Save As.

**2** When the Save As dialog box is displayed, type `Room TIFF` in the File name text box. Do not press the ENTER key after typing the file name.

**3** Click the Format box arrow and then click TIFF (*.TIF, *TIFF) in the list.

**4** If necessary, click the Save in box arrow and then click Removable Disk (F:), or the location associated with your USB flash drive, in the list.

**5** Click the Save button in the Save As dialog box.

**6** When Photoshop displays the TIFF Options dialog box, click the OK button to finish saving the file (Figure 3–79).

**Figure 3–79**

## To Print the Room TIFF Image

The following steps print a copy of the Room TIFF image on the default printer. If you are unsure which printer is set as your default, use the Print command rather than the Print one Copy command so you can choose your printer.

**1** Ready the printer according to the printer instructions.

**2** Click File on the Application bar and then click Print One Copy on the File menu to print the image on the default printer.

## To Close the Document Window and Quit Photoshop

The final steps close the document window and quit Photoshop.

**1** Click the Close button in the document window.

**2** If Photoshop displays a dialog box, click the No button to ignore the changes since the last time you saved the photo.

**3** Quit Photoshop.

# Chapter Summary

In virtually decorating a room, you gained a broad knowledge of Photoshop's layering capabilities. First, you were introduced to the concept of layers. You created a layer via cut, a layer from another image, and a layer from a selection, using the Layers panel to set options, select, rename, color, view, and hide layers. You then used the eraser tools to erase unneeded portions of a layer. You learned how to hide portions of layers and fine-tuned layers with layer masks, adjustments, and styles. Finally, you used the Clone Stamp Tool to add wood flooring into the composite image. The file was flattened and saved in the TIF format.

The items listed below include all the new Photoshop skills you have learned in this chapter:

1. Change Layers Panel Options (PS 142)
2. Create a Layer via Cut (PS 143)
3. Rename a Layer (PS 145)
4. Assign a Color to a Layer (PS 146)
5. Hide and Show a Layer (PS 147)
6. Arrange Document Windows (PS 150)
7. Create a Layer by Dragging an Entire Image (PS 151)
8. Move a Layer in the Document Window (PS 152)
9. Create a Layer by Dragging a Selection (PS 154)
10. Transform by Skewing (PS 159)
11. Display Only the Current Layer (PS 164)
12. Erase using the Magic Eraser Tool (PS 164)
13. Erase using the Eraser Tool (PS 167)
14. Erase using the Block Mouse Pointer (PS 168)
15. Transform by Changing the Perspective (PS 169)
16. Erase using the Background Eraser Tool (PS 171)
17. Rearrange Layers (PS 174)
18. Create a Layer Mask (PS 176)
19. Correct a Masking Error (PS 178)
20. Make an Opacity Change to a Layer (PS 180)
21. Make a Levels Adjustment (PS 182)
22. Adjust the Hue and Saturation (PS 184)
23. Fit the Image on Screen (PS 184)
24. Adjust the Brightness and Contrast (PS 186)
25. Apply a Layer Style (PS 189)
26. Create a New Blank Layer (PS 191)
27. Create a Clone (PS 192)
28. Flatten a Composite Image (PS 195)

# Apply Your Knowledge

Reinforce the skills and apply the concepts you learned in this chapter.

### Creating Layers in a Poster

*Instructions:*   Start Photoshop and perform the customization steps found on pages PS 6 through PS 10. Open the file named Apply 3-1 Storage History from the Data Files for Students. Visit www.cengage.com/ct/studentdownload for detailed instructions or contact your instructor for information about accessing the required files.

The purpose of this exercise is to create a composite poster showing the history of external storage devices by creating layers. The edited photo is displayed in Figure 3–80.

*Perform the following tasks:*

1. Press SHIFT+CTRL+S to open the Save As dialog box. Enter the name, `Apply 3-1 Storage History Composite`. Do not press the ENTER key. Click the Format box arrow and then select the Photoshop PSD format, if necessary. Click the Save in box arrow and then select your USB flash drive location. Click the Save button to save the file in the PSD format. If Photoshop displays an Options dialog box, click the OK button.

**Figure 3–80**

Table 3–6 lists the other files, layer names, identification colors, and manipulations that you will use in this assignment.

| Table 3–6 Storage Device Layers | | | |
| --- | --- | --- | --- |
| **File Name** | **Layer Name** | **Layer Color** | **Layer Manipulations** |
| Apply 3-1 CD | CD | Violet | Layer Style \| Outer Glow |
| Apply 3-1 Flash Drive | flash drive | Green | Layer Style \| Inner Glow<br>Mask lid |
| Apply 3-1 Zip Disk | zip disk | Orange | Layer Style \| Bevel and Emboss |
| Apply 3-1 Tape | tape | Yellow | Adjustments \| Hue 10, –10, 0 |
| Apply 3-1 Cassette Tape | cassette tape | Yellow | Adjustments \| Brightness/Contrast |
| Apply 3-1 Small Floppy | small floppy | Blue | erase background and rotate |
| Apply 3-1 Medium Floppy | medium floppy | Blue | erase background and rotate |
| Apply 3-1 Large Floppy | large floppy | Blue | erase background and rotate |
| Apply 3-1 Punched Card | punched card | Red | clone |

2. To create the CD layer:

   a. Press CTRL+O to display the Open dialog box. Navigate to the Data Files for Students and then double-click the file named Apply 3-1 CD to open it.

   b. On the Application bar, click Window, point to Arrange to display the Arrange submenu, and then click Tile All Horizontally to arrange the document windows. Press the V key to activate the Move Tool. Drag the image from the Apply 3-1 CD document window into the Apply 3-1 Storage History Composite document window. Close the Apply 3-1 CD file.

    c. Name and color the layer as directed in Table 3–6.

    d. Click the 'Add a layer style' button on the Layers panel status bar, and then click Outer Glow. Change the Opacity to 75% and the Size to 150 px. Use the default values for all other settings.

    e. Resize the CD, if necessary, and position it as shown in Figure 3–80.

3. To create the flash drive layer:

    a. Press CTRL+O to display the Open dialog box. Navigate to the Data Files for Students and then open the file named Apply 3-1 Flash Drive.

    b. On the Application bar, click Window, point to Arrange and then click Tile All Horizontally to arrange the document windows.

    c. Drag the flash drive image into the Apply 3-1 Storage History Composite document window. Close the Apply 3-1 Flash Drive file.

    d. Name and color the layer.

    e. Click the 'Add a layer style' button on the Layers panel status bar, and then click Inner Glow. Change the Opacity to 75% and the Size to 25 px. Use the default values for all other settings.

    f. Resize the flash drive and position it as shown in Figure 3–80.

    g. Click the 'Add a layer mask' button. Press the X key to switch the default colors to black over white, if necessary. Press the B key to access the brush and then paint over the lid to mask it.

4. To create the zip disk layer:

    a. Open the file, Apply 3-1 Zip Disk.

    b. Arrange the document windows side by side.

    c. Drag the image from the new window into the Storage History Composite document window. Close the Apply 3-1 Zip Disk file.

    d. Name and color the layer.

    e. Click the 'Add a layer style' button on the Layers panel status bar, and then click Bevel & Emboss. Click the Style button and then click Inner Bevel, if necessary. Change the Size to 90 px. Use the default values for all other settings.

    f. Resize the zip disk, if necessary, and position it as shown in Figure 3–80.

5. To create the tape layer:

    a. Open the file, Apply 3-1 Tape. Press CTRL+A to select the entire image. Press CTRL+C to copy the image to the clipboard.

    b. Paste the image into the Apply 3-1 Storage History Composite document window. Close the Apply 3-1 Tape file.

    c. Name and color the layer.

    d. Click the Hue/Saturation icon on the Adjustments panel to display the settings. On the panel's status bar, click the Clip to Layer button. Adjust the Hue to 10, the Saturation to –10 and the Lightness to 0. Click the Adjustments button in the vertical dock to collapse the Adjustments panel.

    e. Resize the tape, if necessary, and position it as shown in Figure 3–80.

*Continued >*

6. To create the cassette tape layer:

   a. Open the file, Apply 3-1 Cassette Tape.

   b. Arrange the document windows and drag the image from the new window into the Apply 3-1 Storage History Composite document window. Close the Apply 3-1 Cassette Tape file.

   c. Name and color the layer.

   d. On the Adjustments panel, click the Brightness/Contrast icon and then click the Clip to Layer button. Adjust the Brightness to 35.

   e. Click the Adjustments button in the vertical dock to collapse the Adjustments panel.

7. To create the floppy disk layers:

   a. One at a time open each of the floppy disk files listed in Table 3–6 on page PS 198.

   b. Copy and paste each image into the Storage History Composite document window.

   c. Name and color each layer.

   d. Use the eraser tools to erase extraneous background.

   e. Position and rotate the images as shown in Figure 3–80 on page PS 198.

8. To clone the punched card:

   a. Select the Background layer. Create a new layer by pressing CTRL+SHIFT+N. Name the layer, punched card. Do not check the Use previous Layer to Create Clipping Mask check box. Choose a red identification color. Do not change the mode or opacity. Click the OK button to close the New Layer dialog box. Press CTRL+LEFT BRACKET ([) to move the punched card layer below the Background layer. ALT+click the visibility icon on the punched card layer to display only that layer.

   b. Open the file, Apply 3-1 Punched Card.

   c. Arrange the document windows above and below one another.

   d. Press the S key to activate the Clone Stamp Tool. On the options bar, click to display the Aligned check mark, if necessary.

   e. ALT+click in the punched card document window, close to the upper-left corner.

   f. Drag in the Apply 3-1 Storage History Composite document window to create a clone.

   g. Repeat Steps e and f to create four more clones at various locations in the window. (*Hint:* in this montage, it is okay for part of a cloned image to run off the edge of the document window.)

9. Close the Apply 3-1 Punched Card window.

10. On the Layers panel of the Apply 3-1 Storage History Composite window, click the 'Indicates layer visibility' button beside each layer to display the layers.

11. Save the file again by pressing CTRL+S.

12. On the Layers panel, click the Layers panel menu button to display the menu. Click Flatten Image on the menu to flatten all of the layers.

13. Press SHIFT+CTRL+S to open the Save As dialog box. Type Apply 3-1 Storage History Complete in the Name box. Click the Format box arrow and then click TIFF in the list. Click the Save button. If Photoshop displays a dialog box, click the OK button.

14. Turn in a hard copy of the photo to your instructor.

15. Quit Photoshop.

# Extend Your Knowledge

Extend the skills you learned in this chapter and experiment with new skills. You may need to use Help to complete the assignment.

## Exploring Layer Comps

*Instructions:* Start Photoshop. Set the default workspace, default colors, and reset all tools. To complete this assignment, you will be required to use the Data Files for Students. Visit www.cengage.com/ct/studentdownload for detailed instructions or contact your instructor for information about accessing the required files. Open the file Extend 3-1 Marketing Graphic from the Chapter 03 folder of the Data Files for Students.

The purpose of this exercise to create layer comps of a product box for client evaluation. The current graphic has layers for the background, inside, and outside of the box. You are to insert the trophy graphic and scale it to fit the box, then create layer comps showing the inside and the outside. The edited photo is shown in Figure 3–81.

**Figure 3–81**

*Perform the following tasks:*

1. Save the file with the name, Extend 3-1 Marketing Graphic Composite. If necessary, click the Format box arrow and then select the Photoshop PSD format. Click the Save in box arrow and then select your USB flash drive location. Click the Save button. If Photoshop displays a Format Options dialog box, click the OK button.

2. Show and hide the various layers using the visibility icon to gain familiarity with the graphic.

3. Make the Background layer and inside layer visible; hide all other layers. Select the inside layer.

4. Open the Extend 3-1 Trophy file from the Chapter 03 folder of the Data Files for Students. Use the Arrange Documents button to display the windows side by side.

5. Use the Move Tool to drag the trophy from its own window into the Extend 3-1 Marketing Graphic Composite document window. Scale the trophy to fit in the box. Make the outside

*Continued >*

**Extend Your Knowledge** *continued*

layer visible and make sure the trophy can be seen through the opening in the outer box. Name the layer, trophy.

6. Make the front panel layer visible and select it. At the top of the Layers panel, adjust the Fill setting so the layer looks more transparent, as if it were plastic.

7. Make the gleam layer visible. Adjust the Opacity and Fill settings as necessary. Save the file.

8. Use Photoshop Help to learn about Layer Comps. Also read the BTW boxes on page PS 140. Open the Layer Comps panel and create the layer comps described in Table 3–7.

| Table 3–7 Marketing Graphic Layer Comps | |
|---|---|
| **Layer Comp Name** | **Visible Layers** |
| Empty Box | Background, inside |
| Inner Box with Trophy | Background, inside, trophy |
| Outer Box with Trophy | Background, inside, trophy, outside, shadow |
| Complete Graphic | All layers |

9. Save the file again.

10. For extra credit, copy the trophy layer and scale it to approximately 30 percent of its original size. In the Layers panel, move the layer above the outside layer. Position the trophy in the lower-middle portion of the box. Warp the layer to make it wrap around the corner of the box. Create a layer comp named Complete with Wrapped Logo and include all layers.

11. Submit this assignment in the format specified by your instructor.

# Make It Right

Analyze a project and correct all errors and/or improve the design.

## Correcting Layer Errors

*Instructions:* Start Photoshop and perform the customization steps found on pages PS 6 through PS 10. To complete this assignment, you will be required to use the Data Files for Students. Visit www.cengage.com/ct/studentdownload for detailed instructions or contact your instructor for information about accessing the required files. Open the Make It Right 3-1 Park file from the Chapter 03 folder of the Data Files for Students.

The photo has layers that are invisible, layers that need transformation, and layers that need to be moved, trimmed, and adjusted for levels (Figure 3–82).

*Perform the following tasks:*

Save the file on your storage device in the PSD format with the name, Make It Right 3-1 Park Composite. For each invisible layer, reveal the layer, correct any order problem by dragging the layer to an appropriate position on the Layers panel, erase or mask parts of the layer as necessary, and move the layer to a logical position.

Use the Adjustments panel and tools such as Levels, Brightness/Contrast, and Hue/Saturation to create adjustment layers. (*Hint:* Be sure to click the Clip to Layer button on the Adjustments panel status bar, so the adjustment will apply to that layer only.) Make any other adjustments or layer style changes that you deem necessary. Save the file again and submit it in the format specified by your instructor.

**Figure 3–82**

# In the Lab

Design and/or create a project using the guidelines, concepts, and skills presented in this chapter. Labs are listed in order of increasing difficulty.

### Lab 1: Using the Clone Stamp Tool and Creating a Layer with Outer Glow

*Problem*:   The marketing agency that you work for has asked you to edit the latest advertisement for Qintara perfume. You decide to use Photoshop's layering capabilities to insert the image of the perfume bottle. You also decide to clone the Q of the logo multiple times to create a stylistic band of color across the advertisement. A sample of the advertisement is displayed in Figure 3–83.

*Note*:   To complete this assignment, you will be required to use the Data Files for Students. Visit www.cengage.com/ct/studentdownload for detailed instructions or contact your instructor for information about accessing the required files.

*Continued >*

**Figure 3–83**

**In the Lab** *continued*

*Instructions*: Perform the following tasks:

1. Start Photoshop. Set the default workspace, default colors, and reset all tools.

2. Open the file Lab 3-1 Perfume from the Chapter 03 folder of the Data Files for Students.

3. Click View on the Application bar and then click Fit on Screen to view the entire image at the largest possible magnification.

4. Click the Save As command on the File menu. Type `Lab 3-1 Perfume Edited` as the file name. If necessary, click the Format box arrow and then click PSD in the list. Browse to your USB flash drive storage device. Click the Save button. If Photoshop displays a Format Options dialog box, click the OK button.

5. On the Layers panel, select the layer named, slogan. In the document window, use the Move Tool to move the layer to the lower portion of the image.

6. Open the Lab 3-1 Bottle file from the Chapter 03 folder from the Data Files for Students. Arrange the files horizontally. Select the entire bottle image and then drag a copy to the Lab 3-1 Perfume Edited window.

7. In the Lab 3-1 Perfume Edited window, name the new layer and set an identification color. Close the Lab 3-1 Bottle document window.

8. On the Layers panel status bar, use the 'Add layer mask' button to create a layer mask in the bottle layer. (*Hint:* Make sure you have black over white for the foreground and background colors.) Use the Brush Tool with black to mask the area around the bottle.

9. Click the 'Add a layer style' button on the Layers panel status bar, and then click Outer Glow. When the Layer Style dialog box is displayed, type `25` in the Size box, and then click the OK button.

10. Select the Background layer. Click the Clone Stamp Tool on the Tools panel. ALT+click the top of the letter Q in the logo. Move the mouse pointer down and to the right. Drag to create a clone of the Q.

11. Repeat Step 10, creating multiple, overlapped clones of the letter Q as shown in Figure 3–83 on the previous page. Use short strokes. If you make a mistake, press CTRL+Z and drag again.

12. When you are satisfied with your clones, flatten the image.

13. Save the file again and submit the assignment in the format specified by your instructor.

## In the Lab

### Lab 2: Creating a Toy Company Advertisement

*Problem:* You are to create a composite photo for a toy company by adding and adjusting layers, as shown in Figure 3–84.

*Note:* To complete this assignment, you will be required to use the Data Files for Students. Visit www.cengage.com/ct/studentdownload for detailed instructions or contact your instructor for information about accessing the required files.

**Figure 3–84**

*Instructions*:    Perform the following tasks:

1. Start Photoshop. Perform the customization steps found on pages PS 6 through PS 10.

2. Open the Lab 3-2 Robot Background file from the Chapter 03 folder of the Data Files for Students and save it on your USB flash storage device with the file name Lab 3-2 Robot Composite.

3. To clone over the shadow on the right side of the image:

   a. Select the Clone Stamp Tool. On the options bar, click the Aligned check box so it does not display a check mark.

   b. ALT+click the ground approximately one inch below the shadow to create the sample for the clone. Drag over the shadowed area, including any rocks, to create a cloned area and hide the shadow. (*Hint*: Use the LEFT BRACKET ([) and RIGHT BRACKET (]) keys to adjust the size of the mouse pointer as needed.)

4. To create a sky layer:

   a. Use the Magic Wand Tool and the 'Add to selection' button to select all of the sky.

   b. On the Layer menu, point to New, and then click Layer Via Cut.

   c. On the Layers panel, double-click the new layer name and type  sky  to rename the layer. Right-click the visibility icon and select Blue in the list.

5. To add the robot body:

   a. Open the Lab 3-2 Robot Body file from the Chapter 03 folder of the Data Files for Students.

   b. Using the Window menu, arrange the windows side by side.

   c. Use the Move Tool to drag the robot body from the Lab 3-2 Robot Body document window to the Lab 3-2 Robot Composite document window. (*Hint:* Holding down the SHIFT key as you drag automatically centers the image and creates a new layer.) After creating the layer, close the Lab 3-2 Robot Body document window.

   d. Name the layer, robot, and use a violet identification color.

6. Repeat Step 4 to add the shadow graphic using the file, Lab 3-2 Robot Shadow file. Position it behind the robot near the feet, as shown in Figure 3–84. Name the layer, shadow, and use a gray identification color. Close the Lab 3-2 Robot Shadow document window.

*Continued >*

**In the Lab** *continued*

7. To move the shadow behind the robot, on the Layers panel, drag the shadow layer just below the robot layer.

8. Repeat Step 4 to add the earth graphic using the file, Lab 3-2 Robot Earth file. Position it in the upper-right corner of the scene. Name the layer, earth, and use a green identification color.

9. Repeat Step 4 to add the title graphic using the file, Lab 3-2 Robot Title file. Position the words centered above the robot's head. Name the layer, title, and use a yellow identification color.

10. To create an adjustment layer and make the background appear more like a moonscape:

    a. On the Layers panel, select the Background layer.

    b. On the Adjustments panel, click the Hue/Saturation icon to display the settings on the Properties panel.

    c. On the Properties panel status bar, click the Clip to Layer button to create a new adjustment layer for the background.

    d. Change the Hue to +20 and the Saturation to –80.

    e. Click the Properties button on the vertical dock of panels to collapse the panel.

11. To create an adjustment layer and make the sky layer appear black:

    a. Select the sky layer.

    b. On the Adjustments panel, click the Brightness/Contrast icon to display the settings on the Properties panel. Click the Clip to Layer button. Click the Use Legacy check box so it displays a check mark.

    c. Drag both the Brightness and Contrast sliders to the left to create a black sky.

    d. Click the Properties button on the vertical dock of panels to collapse the panel.

12. To add a layer effect to the title layer:

    a. Select the title layer.

    b. Click the 'Add a layer style' button on the Layers panel status bar, and then click Stroke to display the Layer Style dialog box. (*Hint:* You can read about the Stroke command in Photoshop Help.) Reposition the Layer Style dialog box title bar so you can view title in the document window.

    c. In the Layer Style dialog box, click the Color box to display the Color Picker (Stroke Color) dialog box. Reposition the dialog box so you can view the robot in the document window, if necessary.

    d. Click one of the yellow eyes of the robot to select the yellow color. (*Hint:* The mouse pointer looks like an eyedropper when selecting a color.)

    e. Click the OK button to close the dialog box and then click the OK button to close the Layer Style dialog box.

13. Save the composite file again with all the layers.

14. Right-click any layer on the Layers panel and then click Flatten Image.

15. Press SHIFT+CTRL+S to open the Save As dialog box. Type Lab 3-2 Robot Complete in the Name box. Click the Format box arrow and then click TIFF in the list. Click the Save in box arrow, and then click Removable Disk (F:) or the location associated with your USB flash drive, in the list. Click the Save button. If Photoshop displays a dialog box, click the OK button.

16. Quit Photoshop.

# In the Lab

## Lab 3: Creating a Contest Entry with Layers

*Problem:* You would like to enter your hamster in a creative pet photo contest. You decide to use Photoshop's layering capabilities to dress up your hamster, as shown in Figure 3–85.

*Note:* To complete this assignment, you will be required to use the Data Files for Students. Visit www.cengage.com/ct/studentdownload for detailed instructions or contact your instructor for information about accessing the required files.

**Figure 3–85**

*Instructions:* Perform the following tasks:

Start Photoshop. Set the default workspace, default colors, and reset all tools. Open the file Lab 3-3 Hamster from the Chapter 03 folder of the Data Files for Students. Rename the file, Lab 3-3 Hamster Composite and save it as a PSD file on your file storage device.

Open the Lab 3-3 Pipe file, arrange the windows, and then drag a copy to the Lab 3-3 Hamster Composite window. Set the layer properties. Close the Lab 3-3 Pipe document window. Remove the background around the pipe. Scale and position the layer as necessary. Adjust the perspective. Repeat the process for the Lab 3-3 Magnifying Glass file. Reposition the layers as necessary.

Repeat the process for the Lab 3-3 Hat file, scaling the layer as necessary, and place it on top of the hamster's head. Select the right third (back) of the hat and create a layer via cut. On the Layers panel, set the properties and move the back of hat layer, below the hamster layer, so that part of the hat appears behind the hamster's ear.

Make any other adjustments to the layers that you feel would enhance the photo. When you are satisfied with your layers, save the image again. Flatten the image, save it as a TIFF file, and submit a copy to your instructor.

## Cases and Places

Apply your creative thinking and problem-solving skills to design and implement a solution.

*Note*:   To complete this assignment, you will be required to use the Data Files for Students. Visit www.cengage.com/ct/studentdownload for detailed instructions or contact your instructor for information about accessing the required files.

### 1: Clone within the Same Document

**Academic**

Earlier in this chapter, a suggestion was made to create a flag with 50 percent opacity superimposed over a memorial. Open the files named Case 3-1 Memorial and Case 3-1 Flag, located in the Chapter 03 folder of the Data Files for Students. (Alternatively, locate or take a photo of a memorial in your city or a building on your campus. If necessary, obtain permission to use a digital photo or scan the image.) Arrange the windows. Select only the flag and then drag it as a new layer into the memorial photo. Resize the layer to fit across the memorial. Change the opacity to 50 percent. Make other corrections as necessary. Save the composite photo and print a copy.

### 2: Create a Graphic with Opacity Changes

**Personal**

You recently took a photo of a deer at the local forest preserve. To make the picture more interesting, you decide to create a layer and clone the deer. Open the photo named Case 3-1 Deer, located in the Chapter 03 folder of the Data Files for Students. Click the Layer command on the Application bar, point to New, and then click Layer. Click the Background layer, choose the Clone Stamp Tool, and take a sample of the middle of the deer. Click the new layer and clone the deer. On the Edit menu, click Free Transform and resize the cloned deer so it appears to be farther away. Flip the clone horizontally. Save the file as Case 3-2 Deer Cloned on your storage device.

### 3: Create a Greeting Card Graphic with Masking

**Professional**

You have been hired as an intern with a greeting card company. You were given several photos to use in preparing holiday cards. The file named Case 3-3 Santa Scene is located in the Chapter 03 folder of the Data Files for Students. You want to use only the figure of Santa Claus on the front of a card. Save the photo in the PSD format on your USB flash drive storage device as Case 3-3 Santa Layered. Create a rectangular marquee selection around the figure. Use the Layer Via Cut command and name the new layer, Santa. Hide the background. Create a layer mask, painting with black to display only the figure. Print the photo with the background hidden.

# Project Planning Guidelines

## Using Project Planning Guidelines

The process of communicating specific information to others is a learned, rational skill. Computers and software, especially Adobe Photoshop CS6, can help you develop ideas and present detailed information to a particular audience.

Using Adobe Photoshop CS6, you can edit photos and create original graphics. Computer hardware and image-editing software, such as Adobe Photoshop CS6, reduces much of the laborious work of drafting and revising projects. Some design professionals use sketch pads or storyboards, others compose directly on the computer, and others have developed unique strategies that work for their own particular thinking and artistic styles.

No matter what method you use to plan a project, follow specific guidelines to arrive at a final product that presents an image or images clearly and effectively (Figure A–1). Use some aspects of these guidelines every time you undertake a project and others as needed in specific instances. For example, in determining content for a project, you may decide an original graphic would communicate the idea more effectively than an existing photo. If so, you would create this graphical element from scratch.

## Determine the Project's Purpose

Begin by clearly defining why you are undertaking this assignment. For example, you may want to correct camera errors and adjust image flaws. Or you might want to create a graphic for a specific publishing or marketing purpose. Once you clearly understand the purpose of your task, begin to draft ideas of how best to communicate this information.

## Analyze Your Audience

Learn about the people who will use, analyze, or view your work. Where are they employed? What are their educational backgrounds? What are their expectations? What questions do they have? How will they interact with your product? What kind of computer system and Internet connection will they have? Design experts suggest drawing a

---

**PROJECT PLANNING GUIDELINES**

**1. DETERMINE THE PROJECT'S PURPOSE**
*Why are you undertaking the project?*

**2. ANALYZE YOUR AUDIENCE**
*Who are the people who will use your work?*

**3. GATHER POSSIBLE CONTENT**
*What graphics exist, and in what forms?*

**4. DETERMINE WHAT CONTENT TO PRESENT TO YOUR AUDIENCE**
*What image will communicate the project's purpose to your audience in the most effective manner?*

**Figure A–1**

mental picture of these people or finding photographs of people who fit this profile so that you can develop a project with the audience in mind.

By knowing your audience members, you can tailor a project to meet their interests and needs. You will not present them with information they already possess, and you will not omit the information they need to know.

Example: Your assignment is to raise the profile of your college's nursing program in the community. Your project should address questions such as the following: How much does the audience know about your college and the nursing curriculum? What are the admission requirements? How many of the applicants admitted complete the program? What percent of participants pass the state nursing boards?

## Gather Possible Content

Rarely are you in a position to develop all the material for a project. Typically, you would begin by gathering existing images and photos, or designing new graphics based on  information that may reside in spreadsheets or databases. Design work for clients often must align with and adhere to existing marketing campaigns or publicity materials. Web sites, pamphlets, magazine and newspaper articles, and books could provide insights of how others have approached your topic. Personal interviews often provide perspectives not available by any other means. Consider video and audio clips as potential sources for material that might complement or support the factual data you uncover. Make sure you have all legal rights to any photographs you plan to use.

## Determine What Content to Present to Your Audience

Experienced designers recommend identifying three or four major ideas you want an audience member to remember after viewing your project. It also is helpful to envision your project's endpoint, the key fact or universal theme that you want to emphasize. All project elements should lead to this ending point.

As you make content decisions, you also need to think about other factors. Presentation of the project content is an important consideration. For example, will the content of your brochure look good when printed on thick, colored paper or transparencies? Will the format in which you save the content affect how your photo be viewed in a classroom with excellent lighting and a bright projector? How will the content look when viewed on a notebook computer monitor? Determine relevant time factors, such as the length of time to develop the project, how long editors will spend reviewing your project, or the amount of time allocated for presenting your designs to the customer. Your project will need to accommodate all of these constraints.

Decide whether a graphic, photograph, or artistic element can express or emphasize a particular concept. The right hemisphere of the brain processes images by attaching an emotion to them, so in the long run, audience members are more apt to recall themes from graphics rather than those from the text.

Finally, review your project to make sure the theme still easily is identifiable and has been emphasized successfully. Is the focal point clear and presented without distraction? Does the project satisfy the requirements?

## Summary

When creating a project, it is beneficial to follow some basic guidelines from the outset. By taking some time at the beginning of the process to determine the project's purpose, analyze the audience, gather possible content, and determine what content to present to the audience, you can produce a project that is informative, relevant, and effective.

# Appendix B

# Graphic Design Overview

## Understanding Design Principles

Understanding a few basic design principles can catapult you to the next level of digital artistry. Beyond knowing how to use software, a graphic designer must know how to create effective and readable layouts no matter what the product type. In this Appendix, you will learn the design principles, color theory, typography, and other technical knowledge required to create usable and successful graphic designs.

A major goal in graphic design work, whether for print or Web page layout, is to guide the viewer's eyes toward some key point. Another major goal of design work is to convey a certain emotion — a project can have the effect of making the viewer feel relaxed, energetic, hungry, hopeful, or even anxious. By implementing a few basic principles of design, you can control your viewers' physical focus so they look where you want them to look as you steer them toward a desired emotion. Design principles typically include the following:

- Balance
- Contrast
- Dominance
- Proximity
- Repetition
- Closure
- Continuance
- Negative space
- Unity

# Balance

Visual elements can be **balanced** within a design, with visual elements distributed in a horizontal or vertical arrangement. Unbalanced designs can cause viewers to feel anxious or uncomfortable, or even as if they are falling sideways out of their seats. Balance may be achieved symmetrically or asymmetrically. Symmetrical balance mirrors a visual element to achieve equilibrium (Figure B–1). Asymmetrical balance can be achieved by balancing a small, dark element with a large, light element (Figure B–2) or balancing one large element with several smaller elements (Figure B–3).

with symmetrical balance, the left and right halves are mirror reflections, and the two trees, which are identical in size and shape, balance the composition

**Figure B–1**

left-heavy design with sparse right sidebar that is too white to add much weight

balanced design with a darker right sidebar adding weight to the right side

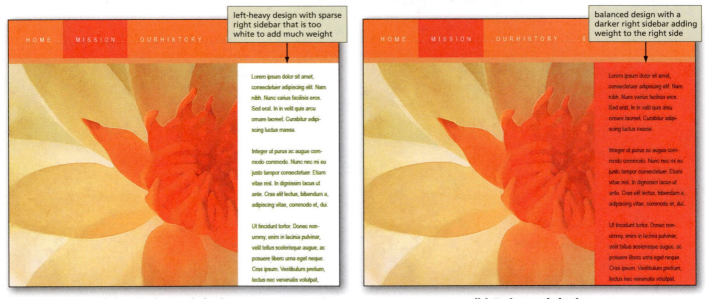

**(a) Unbalanced design** **Figure B–2** **(b) Balanced design**

large photo at right is asymmetrically balanced by the multiple small thumbnails on left

**Figure B–3**

## Contrast

Contrast describes the visual differences between elements; it adds variety to a design and helps to draw the viewer's focus. Differences in color, scale, quantity, or other characteristics of visual elements help to achieve contrast. The element that is different from the others draws the viewer's attention. In Figure B–4, the words in white contrast against the other words on the page, and the viewer's eye is drawn to the contrasting sentence.

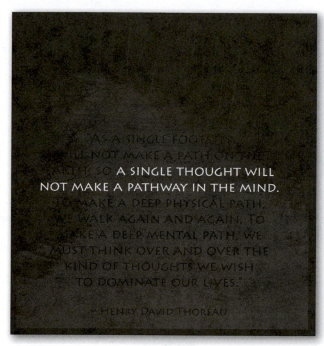

**Figure B–4**

## Dominance

**Dominance** is a critical principle in controlling viewer focus. The dominant element in a design is the one to which a viewer's eyes and attention usually move first. An element's position within a design or its contrast to other elements can establish dominance. If you want your viewer to focus on a certain area of your design or on a specific design element, make it dominant, like the yellow V.I.P. banner in the discount card shown in Figure B–5, which grabs your attention with its contrasting color, even though it is not the largest element in the design.

**Figure B–5**

BTW

**Dominant Object Placement**
Placing an object at a certain location within a grid, such as the intersection of thirds or slightly above and to the right of center, helps to establish dominance.

## Proximity

**Proximity** describes the relative space between elements. Related elements should be close to each other. Headings should be close to their related paragraph text, and product names should be close to their photos and prices. As shown in Figure B–6, when related items are not within close proximity of each other (Figure B–6a), the viewer might not know the items are related. When elements are too close, the design looks cluttered and text can become difficult to read. Strive for balance in your proximity, as in Figure B–6b.

**(a) Items without proximity are not clearly related**

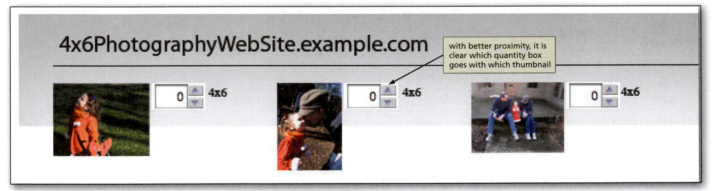

**(b) Items with close proximity are clearly related**

**Figure B–6**

## Repetition

Repeating a visual element helps to tie a design together. **Repetition** of color, shape, texture, and other characteristics can help to unify your design (Figure B–7), create patterns, or impart a sense of movement. Most Web sites repeat a design theme across all the pages so users know they are on the same site as they navigate from page to page. Repeated colors and layouts help to unify the overall Web site design.

logo is repeated throughout the design

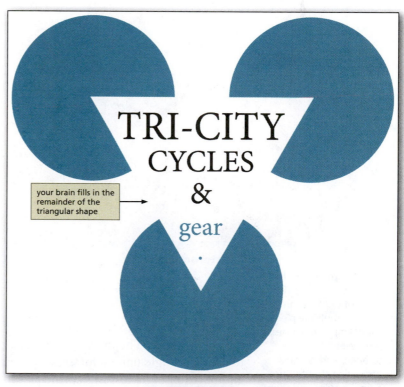

orange and reddish colors are repeated throughout the design

# Lorem Ipsum Dolor.

Lorem ipsum dolor sit amet, consectetuer adipiscing elit. Nam nibh. Nunc varius facilisis eros. Sed erat. In in velit quis arcu ornare laoreet. Curabitur adipiscing luctus massa.

- ● Vestibulum.
- ● Vestibulum Vestibulum.

Integer ut purus ac augue commodo commodo. Nunc nec mi eu justo tempor consectetuer. Etiam vitae nisl. In dignissim lacus ut ante. Cras elit lectus, bibendum a, adipiscing vitae, commodo et, dui.

Ut tincidunt tortor. Donec nonummy, enim in lacinia pulvinar, velit tellus scelerisque augue, ac posuere libero urna eget neque. Cras ipsum. Vestibulum pretium, lectus nec venenatis volutpat, purus lectus ultrices risus, a condimentum risus mi et quam. Pellentesque auctor fringilla neque. Duis eu massa ut lorem iaculis vestibulum.

# Call Us Today.
Toll Free 800.123.4567

Lorem ipsum dolor sit amet, consectetuer adipiscing elit. Nam nibh. Nunc varius facilisis eros. Sed erat. In in velit quis arcu ornare laoreet. Curabitur adipiscing luctus massa.

Integer ut purus ac augue commodo commodo. Nunc nec mi eu justo tempor onsectetuer. Etiam vitae nisl. In dignissim lacus ut ante. Cras elit lectus, bibendum a, adipiscing vitae, commodo et, dui.

Ut tincidunt tortor. Donec nonummy, enim in lacinia pulvinar, velit tellus scelerisque augue, ac posuere libero urna eget neque. Cras ipsum. Vestibulum pretium, lectus nec venenatis volutpat, purus lectus ultrices risus, a condimentum risus mi et quam. Pellentesque auctor fringilla neque.

HOME | SERVICES | PARTNERS | CONTACT

**Figure B–7**

# Closure

Not everything in a design must be composed of solid lines. Composing objects from small parts and spaces allows a design to breathe and creates visual interest. Under the concept of **closure**, the human brain will fill in the blanks to close or complete the object (Figure B–8).

TRI-CITY CYCLES & gear

your brain fills in the remainder of the triangular shape

**Figure B–8**

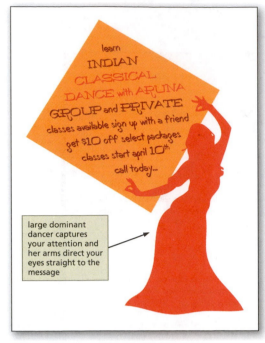

large dominant dancer captures your attention and her arms direct your eyes straight to the message

**Figure B–9**

## Continuance

Once a viewer's eyes start to move across a page, they tend to keep moving — and you can exploit this **continuance** to guide the viewer's eyes exactly where you want them to go. A dominant object can capture the viewer's initial focus, and diagonal lines within that dominant object can guide the viewer's eyes toward the focal point of your design (Figure B–9).

## Negative Space

**Negative space** refers to the space in your design that does not contain information, or the space between elements. For example, the space between the vertical heading and descriptive text or the space between a logo and the vertical heading, as shown in Figure B–10, is negative space. Without negative space, your design will feel cluttered, and viewers will have difficulty identifying on the focal point. Note that negative space, also called **white space**, literally does not translate to "white space," as negative space does not have to be white (Figure B–10).

elements are cramped

moving the shoe adds white space and relieves visual tension

**(a) Cluttered design**     **(b) Uncluttered design**

**Figure B–10**

BTW

**Unity**
Unity is not limited to elements in a specific piece of work; it can apply to multiple pieces. For example, a business card, Web site, letterhead, and product packaging that feature a similar color and style can help unify a business's identity.

## Unity

**Unity** refers to the concept that all elements within a design work well together to form a whole. The individual images, textures, text, and negative space join together to create a single unified message or meaning. Unity can be created by applying a combination of basic design principles. Balanced elements alone do not produce a visually appealing design. The same is true for elements with appropriate proximity and negative space, good contrast, or clear dominance. No single design principle is responsible for a pleasing design. Instead, the combination of these principles creates a single unified design. Without unity, a design degrades into chaos and loses meaning. Of course, that is not a bad thing if chaos is the intentional message.

## Layout Grids

A graphic designer needs to know where to place elements within a document or Web page. The use of grids makes it easy to align objects to each other and can help with balance and proximity. You can apply any of the many standard grids to Web page layouts or print layouts for standard paper sizes. One very popular grid system uses thirds, a method that is derived from the golden ratio.

**Rule of Thirds and Golden Ratio**    The rule of thirds specifies that splitting a segment into thirds produces an aesthetically pleasing ratio. The rule of thirds is derived from a more complex mathematical concept called the golden ratio, which specifies segment ratios of long segment divided by short segment equal to about 1.618 — which is close enough to the rule of thirds that designers typically apply the rule of thirds rather than break out their calculators (Figure B–11).

Figure B–11

## Color Theory

Color can have a profound effect on the overall message a design conveys. Certain colors evoke specific emotions, and the way colors are combined can make the difference between readable copy and copy that is unable to be read.

## Color Properties

Before you begin to work with color, it is important to understand the properties of color, which include hue, saturation, shade, tint, and value.

**Hue** refers to the tone, or actual color, such as red, yellow, or blue. Many color theorists interpret hue to mean pure color. A pure color, or hue, can be modified to create color variations. A basic color wheel, shown in Figure B–12, displays hue.

**Saturation** refers to the intensity of a color. As hues become less saturated, they create muted tones and pastels as they approach gray. As hues become more saturated, they appear very bright (Figure B–13).

Figure B–12

Figure B–13

desaturated hues can have calming effect

**Figure B–14**

oversaturated hues can be hard on the eyes

**Figure B–15**

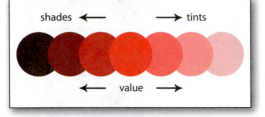

shades ← → tints

← value →

**Figure B–16**

Desaturated colors can produce mellow tones and evoke calm feelings (Figure B–14). Oversaturated colors can produce neon-like colors and cause excitement (Figure B–15). Sometimes it is appropriate to use very bright colors, such as in a picture book for children or a high-energy advertisement for a sports drink. Other times, bright, saturated colors produce the wrong feeling for your work.

A **shade** is a mixture of a hue and black, producing a darker color. A **tint** is a mixture of a hue and white, producing a lighter color. A color's **value** describes its overall lightness or darkness. A tint has a higher value, while a shade has a lower value (Figure B–16). Mixing a hue with its shades, tints, and variations of saturation can lead to very harmonious color combinations.

## Color Modes

A color mode describes the way in which colors combine to create other colors. The most commonly used color modes are RGB, CMYK, and LAB. Each mode has its strengths and weaknesses, and each is appropriate for a specific type of work.

The **RGB** color mode mixes red, green, and blue light to create other colors. Computer monitors and TV screens use the RGB color mode. All images used on a Web site must use the RGB color mode because few Web browsers can display CMYK images. RGB is an additive color mode, meaning colored light combines (light waves are added) to create other colors. The absence of all color in the RGB mode results in black. As colored light is added, white is created, as shown in Figure B–17. RGB is also device dependent, because the colors you see depend on the viewing device. Different computer screens will display colors in the same photograph differently because of variances in the manufacturing process and component wear over time. Do not waste your time trying to get your Web site to display the same exact colors consistently from computer to computer. It is not possible.

The **CMYK** color mode mixes physical cyan, magenta, yellow, and black pigments (such as ink) to create other colors, and is used in color printing. CMYK is a subtractive color mode. The absence of all color in the CMYK mode results in white light, and, as colored pigment is added, light wavelengths are absorbed or subtracted, creating color (Figure B–18).

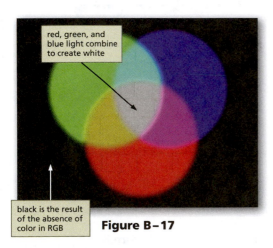

red, green, and blue light combine to create white

black is the result of the absence of color in RGB

**Figure B–17**

cyan, magenta, and yellow combine to create a dark color but cannot create black

white is the result of the absence of color in CMYK

**Figure B–18**

Cyan, magenta, and yellow alone cannot create black; thus, the need for pure black in the CMYK mode.

Unlike RGB and CMYK, which combine individual well-defined colors, the **LAB** color mode combines levels of lightness with two color channels, a and b. One color channel ranges from green to magenta, while the other includes blue through yellow. By combining color ranges with lightness values, LAB is able to closely approximate the true human perception of color and thus is able to produce more colors than either RGB or CMYK. This makes it an ideal color mode for photographers wanting to have access to every possible color in a photograph. LAB typically is used during photographic retouching and color correction. The image then is converted to RGB or CMYK for use with electronic media or print.

**BTW**

**LAB**
LAB is sometimes written as L*a*b for lightness, color channel a, and color channel b.

## Psychological Considerations of Color

Colors can evoke both positive and negative emotions in people, and the influence of a color can differ among individuals and cultures. While the effect of color on people is not an exact science, there are some generalities.

White often is associated with cleanliness, purity, and hope. Doctors and brides in most Western cultures wear white. However, white is associated with death and mourning attire in some Eastern cultures. White is the most popular background color and offers great contrast for highly readable dark text.

Black often is used to represent evil, death, or mourning, but also mystery, intelligence, elegance, and power. Black text on a white background is the easiest to read.

Red is used in Western cultures to signify love, passion, and comfort — but also is used to represent sin, anger, hell, and danger. Use dark reds to imply indulgence or fine living and brownish reds for designs dealing with Thanksgiving, harvest, or the fall season in general.

Green symbolizes many positives such as growth, tranquility, luck, money, ecology, environmentalism, and health, but it also symbolizes jealousy. Green can have a calming effect.

Blue often is cited as the favorite color by men. Like green, it evokes feelings of calmness and serenity. Blue implies authority, stability, loyalty, and confidence. However, it is one of the least appetizing colors, as there are few naturally blue foods. It also is associated with sadness and bad luck, as evidenced in blues music or phrases like "I've got the blues."

Yellow generally makes people happy. It is a highly visible and active color. However, too much yellow can lead to frustration and eye fatigue. Babies cry more in yellow rooms. Avoid using yellow as a page background and use it instead in smaller areas to draw attention.

## Print Considerations for Color

The printing process cannot reproduce every color. Gamut refers to the range of printable colors, and colors that cannot be printed are said to be *out of gamut*. If an out of gamut color exists in your document, the printer you are using simply will get as close to it as it can — but it will not be exact. Depending on the printer you have installed, the actual color produced can vary. Photoshop identifies out of gamut colors in the Color Picker with a small icon. If your document contains out of gamut colors, you have two options: change or replace the out of gamut color with one that is in gamut, or accept that the final print may not be exactly what you expected.

## Web Considerations for Color

When working with color for the Web, the most important thing to remember is that colors will appear differently on different computers. Web sites look similar, but not exactly the same, from computer to computer. Years ago, Web designers used only the **Web-safe colors**, which were a set of 216 colors that supposedly appear the same on all monitors. This was the result of the limitations of video subsystems at the time, as computer monitors could display only 256 specific colors. Microsoft Windows supported 256 specific colors, and Apple Macintosh supported a different 256 colors. Of the two sets, 216 were the same across both platforms; these 216 became the **Web-safe palette**. However, designers soon realized that only 22 of those 216 were truly the same between Windows and Macintosh; this subset was called the **really Web-safe colors**.

Photoshop displays a warning in the Color Picker for non-Web-safe colors. Modern computers (as well as cell phone browsers) can display millions of distinct colors, so limiting yourself to 216 Web-safe colors is no longer a necessity. In fact, it is extremely limiting, because the 216 Web-safe colors are generally very bright or very dark with few choices for pastels or saturation and value variances. Most designers do not use Web-safe colors for their designs.

**BTW**

**Using Web-Safe Colors**
Use Web-safe colors if you know the site will be viewed on ancient computer systems; otherwise, allow yourself the full spectrum with the understanding the colors will vary slightly from computer to computer.

gray looks lighter against brown background

gray looks darker against pale yellow background

**Figure B–19**

## Relativity

A color's relative lightness/darkness value can appear different depending on what other color neighbors it. The gray block in Figure B–19 looks lighter against the brown background and darker against the light yellow background. Keep this in mind as you choose background/foreground relationships. A certain hue (or tint or shade) might look great when it is by itself, but you may not be so fond of it when it is used in close proximity to another certain color.

## Color Schemes and Matching

Choosing colors that work well together and enforce the design's message can be challenging but worth the effort. Successful color matching requires an understanding of **color schemes**, which simply describes an organized method of matching colors based on their positions on a color wheel. The color scheme can make or break a design.

Figure B–12 on page APP 9 displayed a color wheel. While there are various color wheel models, the most popular uses the primary colors red, blue, and yellow (Figure B–20a). Primary colors combine to create the secondary colors green, orange, and purple (Figure B–20b). A primary and a secondary color combine to create a tertiary (third level) color (Figure B–20c). More complex color wheels can include gradients to show varying saturation, tints, and shades (Figure B–21).

**(a) Primary colors**

**(b) Secondary colors**

**(c) Tertiary colors**

**Figure B–20**

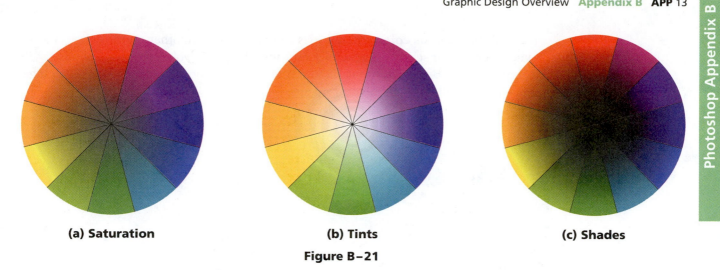

(a) **Saturation**          (b) **Tints**          (c) **Shades**

**Figure B–21**

**Color Schemes**   A **monochromatic color scheme** is one that uses a single hue with a variety of shades and tints (Figure B–22). This is an easy color scheme to create. While a monochromatic color scheme can appear soothing, the lack of hue variance can leave it looking a bit boring.

**BTW**

**Color Scheme Web Sites**
Stand-alone color scheme software programs are available for purchase, but Adobe offers a free online service at kuler.adobe.com that lets you browse color schemes created by other users, modify them, and create and save your own.

you are invited...

**Figure B–22**

A **complementary color scheme** uses colors directly across from each other on the color wheel. Their high contrast can look vibrant but also can be hard on the eyes. Avoid using complementary pairs in a foreground/background relationship, as shown in Figure B–23. Adjusting the saturation or substituting tints and shades makes this color scheme more workable.

bright complementary colors do not work well in a foreground/background relationship

adjusting the arrangement of the colors or using a variety of values or saturation can help

you are invited...          you are invited...

**Figure B–23**

An **analogous color scheme** uses colors next to each other on the color wheel. This color scheme is generally very appealing and evokes positive feelings (Figure B–24). Be careful not to choose colors that are too far apart. A very wide range of analogous colors can appear mismatched.

**Figure B–24**

The **split-complementary scheme** uses a base color and, instead of its direct complement, the two colors on either side of its complement (Figure B–25). This scheme offers a lot of hue variance, and therefore excitement. However, if all the hues are overly saturated, split-complementary colors can be very harsh. Try keeping one hue saturated and use tints, shades, or desaturated colors for the rest of the scheme.

**Figure B–25**

Other color schemes such as triadic, tetradic, neutral, and an infinite number of custom schemes also exist. Using a color-matching resource such as software or a Web site is a good way to help you get started choosing colors and allows you to experiment to see what you and your client like.

# Typography

**Typography** is the art of working with text. Perhaps the two most important factors for graphic designers to address when working with text are visual appeal and readability. A dull text heading will not entice viewers to read the rest of the advertisement, but a text heading that looks beautiful can be useless if it is not readable (Figure B–26).

## Readability

    **Readability** is the measurement of how comfortable or easy it is for readers to read the text. Many factors contribute to overall readability. Commonly accepted readability factors include the following:

- Large text passages written in lowercase are easier to read than long text passages in uppercase.

- Regular text is easier to read than italicized text.

- Black text on a white background is easier to read than white text on a black background.

- Legibility affects readability.

- Line length, letterforms, and appearance all influence readability.

    Before learning the details of readability, you must understand some type basics. A **font** is a set of characters of a specific family, size, and style. For example, the description Times New Roman, 11 points, italic is a font. What most people consider a font is actually a **typeface** (Times New Roman, in this example). A font represents only a single specific size and style within a family, while a typeface is a set or family of one or more fonts.

    **Legibility** refers to the ease with which a reader can determine what a letter actually is. If readers cannot figure out the letter, they cannot read the text, resulting in low readability and failed message delivery. The difference between legibility and readability is subtle. Figure B–27 shows an exit sign — something that needs to be legible.

    **Line length** refers to the physical length of a line of text. When lines are too long, the reader's eyes can get lost trying to go all the way back to the left side of the page to find the next line. There is no conclusive magic number for how long a line of text should be. Optimal line lengths differ for adults and children, and for people with dyslexia and without. The best choices for line length differ based on the media of the message; printed newspapers, books, text on a Web site, and the subject lines in an e-mail message all require different line lengths. Some studies recommend line lengths based on physical lengths in inches, while other studies recommend a maximum number of characters per line. However, many designers follow the guideline that line lengths should not exceed 70 characters (about two-and-a-half alphabets' worth of characters).

**Figure B–26**

flat and unappealing

visually appealing and easy to read

elegant, but difficult to read

letters are difficult to discern

letters are easy to read

**Figure B–27**

BTW

**PLEASE DO NOT YELL**
Not only is typing in all uppercase difficult to read, but it connotes yelling at your reader.

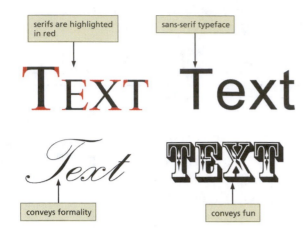

serifs are highlighted in red

sans-serif typeface

conveys formality

conveys fun

**Figure B–28**

## Typeface Categories

Typefaces are organized into several categories, including serif, sans-serif, script, and display. Serif typefaces include additional appendages, while sans-serif typefaces do not (Figure B–28). It is generally accepted that large passages of serif text in print are easy to read, while sans-serif text is easier to read on a Web page. Because headlines are typically small, either serif or sans-serif is appropriate. Varying the headline typeface style from the body copy typeface style is an effective method of adding some visual excitement to an otherwise dull page of text. Script typefaces look like handwriting, and display typefaces are decorative.

In addition to differences in readability, the choice of a serif, sans-serif, or other typeface can help to create an emotion much like the selection of a color scheme. Wedding invitations often use a script typeface to signify elegance, while headlines using display typefaces can grab a reader's attention. The same phrase written in different typefaces can have different implications (Figure B–29). Similarly, differences in the size, weight (boldness), or spacing of a typeface also can influence emotion or meaning (Figure B–30).

typeface implies a fancy party or elegant gathering

typeface implies the event will be fun, zany, or whimsical

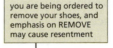

**Figure B–29**

you are asked to remove your shoes, but you are still made to feel welcome

you are being ordered to remove your shoes, and emphasis on REMOVE may cause resentment

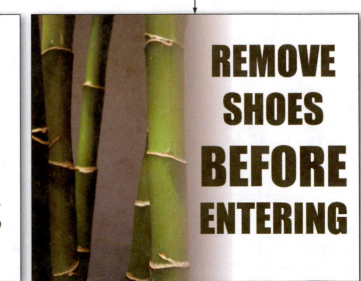

**Figure B–30**

# Designing for Web versus Print

Graphic designers must be aware of subtle differences in how print and Web projects are created and perceived when designing for these media. While many design principles are common to both, it takes a different mindset to successfully create a design for either medium. Print designs are static, as the layout never varies from print to print (though differences in color may appear because of inconsistencies with the printer or printing press). The appearance of Web designs can vary, depending on the device used to view them. Some print designers struggle with the device dependency and fluidity of Web page designs. Some Web designers unnecessarily concern themselves about accommodating fluid or shifting content when designing a print advertisement.

## Device Dependency and Fluidity

The main differences between print and Web design are related to device dependency and fluidity. Web pages are **device dependent**, meaning that the appearance of the page varies depending on the device (computer, cell phone, or PDA) on which they are viewed (Figure B–31). Discrepancies in monitor color calibration, screen resolution, and browser window size can affect how a Web page appears to the viewer. Colors can change, objects can shift, and text can wrap to a new line on different words from one device to another. In comparison, a newspaper or magazine looks the same no matter where it is purchased or where it is read. Designers can work with Web programmers to design pages for different devices.

Web browser version of recording studio site

cell phone browser version of the same page with relocated page elements

**Figure B–31**

## Pixels, Dimensions, and Resolution

A pixel is the smallest element of a digital image. Magnifying an image reveals the individual pixels (Figure B–32). A pixel, unlike an inch or centimeter, is not an absolute measurement. The physical size of a pixel can change depending on device resolution.

enlarged image shows pixels

**Figure B–32**

As you learned in Chapter 1, resolution refers to the number of pixels displayed on a computer screen. More pixels gives greater detail. When referring to an image file, the phrase, document dimensions, is used to describe the number of pixels in the file. For example, a document might have the dimensions of 450 × 337, meaning it contains 450 pixels across and 337 pixels vertically, for a total of 151,650 pixels. File size is directly related to document dimension. The more pixels there are in a document, the larger the file size.

When used to describe an image file, the word, resolution, also is used to describe the printed output. The print resolution is given in pixels per inch (PPI); for example, 72 PPI or 300 PPI. PPI is a linear measurement: 72 PPI means that, when printed, the output will contain 72 pixels across every linear inch. If the document dimensions were 450 × 337, those 450 horizontal pixels would print in groups of 72 PPI, resulting in a printout just over 6 inches wide (Figure B–33). If the resolution,

**Note:** The rulers are not to scale

300 ppi version will be better quality, though smaller, because the pixels are smaller and able to produce more detail

**Figure B–33**

but not the dimensions, were increased to 300 PPI, then those same 450 pixels would print in groups of 300 per inch, producing a final output about 1.5 inches wide.

Key points to remember when working with resolution are:

- A pixel is not a static measurement. Pixels change in size. They get smaller or larger to fill an inch as defined in the PPI setting.
- Changing the resolution of an image file has no effect on the file size. It affects the physical size of the printed output.
- Changing the document dimensions does affect the file size.

When printing documents, printers create each individual pixel with a group of microscopic dots of ink (or toner or other pigment). The number of dots a printer can generate is measured in dots per inch (DPI). People sometimes incorrectly use the term DPI when they really mean PPI. A printer with a resolution of 2400 DPI means it can squeeze 2400 dots of ink (not pixels) into a single inch. The more dots used to create a pixel, the truer color each pixel can have — resulting in a higher-quality print.

A common misconception related to creating image files is that all graphics for use on the Web should be created at a resolution of 72 PPI. However, because PPI affects the output of printing only, the PPI setting has no effect on the screen display of an image.

It is common practice to save Web images at 72 PPI, not because it optimizes images for the Web, but because the 72 PPI myth so widely is believed.

# Working as a Graphic Designer

The business world offers many opportunities for people with creativity and an eye for design. From automotive design to fashion to advertising, the need for talented graphic artists is vast. Many industry experts believe there are generally three levels of professionals working in the graphics field: graphic artists, graphic designers, and people who own graphics editing/design software.

**Graphic artists** typically receive extensive schooling as art majors and know a lot about design principles and art history. However, schooling does not necessarily mean formal education in a school environment. A graphic artist can be self-educated. The key to the "artist" designation revolves around a personal need to creatively express oneself beyond that of producing commercial work for hire. While graphic artists work with software, they typically also produce art with more traditional media such as paints, pencils, fiber, metals, or other physical materials. Graphic artists may hold the same job as a graphic designer, but very often graphic artists will create and sell their own original artwork. This personal drive to create and the resulting independent production of original artwork is what distinguishes graphic artists from graphic designers.

The line separating graphic artists from graphic designers is a fine one. A **graphic designer** often is knowledgeable about design principles and may possess a wealth of information about art history, but not all graphic designers are graphic artists. They usually create design products for others, such as brochures, advertisements, or Web sites, using software, but do not create their own original works.

The third category of graphic designers includes people who own and use graphics design software for various purposes. This category, **software owners**, is not a true graphic design designation. Simply owning a copy of Photoshop or knowing how to use a certain software program does not make you a graphic artist/designer. Whereas artists and designers understand principles of design and effective use of color, and possess a certain degree of artistic ability or raw talent, design amateurs rely on the power of the software to help them create projects. Of course, it is possible for an amateur to become a professional designer or artist — but doing so requires education and training, not just purchasing a software suite.

---

**BTW**

**Resolution and Print Quality**
The higher the resolution, the smaller the pixels and the printout, and the better the quality.

**BTW**

**PPI and Printing**
An image with the dimensions of 800 x 600 at 72 PPI will look exactly the same on screen as the same image at 300 PPI. In fact, the file sizes will be identical. There only will be a difference when printed. For Web images, you can save them at 0 PPI, and they would work just as well, and have the same file size, as if you saved them at 1200 PPI. However, when printed, they will differ.

**BTW**

**PPI on the Web**
You cannot make an image appear larger on screen by resizing its pixels. Every pixel on the same screen will always be the same size.

## Jobs in Graphic Design

An understanding of design principles and software skills opens the door to many opportunities in the professional graphics industry. Jobs for graphic designers range from freelance work and self-employment to full-time careers with advertising agencies, Web design firms, print houses, software companies, or the marketing team within an organization such as a school or commercial or nonprofit business. Perhaps the most important questions to ask yourself when considering a job in this field are:

- Do I want to work for myself or for someone else?
- Am I truly an artist? Am I creative? Or do I simply follow direction well, understand basic design principles, and know how to use graphics software?
- What is my preferred medium — physical (print) or electronic (Web, software interface)?

Once you have secured a position in the graphics field, you will be assigned projects that will call on your design skills and other abilities.

# Design Projects

A successful project always begins with solid planning. Proper planning helps you to stay focused and reduces the potential for wasted time and money — both yours and your client's. A project plan must specify the following aspects of the project:

- Scope of design work
- Roles and responsibilities of designer and client
- Expectations and specifications for final product, including time frame

When you and your client agree on the scope of the work and are clear on what the final product should look like, you as the designer know exactly what it is you need to produce. It is better to take the time to plan a project before sitting down with Photoshop, so you have a good idea of what to do once you start the software.

## Client and Designer Roles

Both the client and the designer have specific jobs. Defining and agreeing on these roles is crucial for the success of the collaboration.

Simply put, the client must clearly communicate his or her expectations. Clients often need help articulating their wants and needs, and the designer must be able to help draw this information from the client. Additionally, the client must be available to provide feedback when the designer offers a draft for feedback or proofing. A client's responsibilities include the following:

- Clearly communicate the needs of the project
- Provide timely and constructive feedback
- Trust the designer's expertise
- Pay the bills on time

Aside from the obvious (creating the product), the designer also is responsible for making sure the client knows their own responsibilities and avoids poor design choices. Sometimes, a client will request something that is just bad — like certain colors that do not work well together or make text unreadable. The designer is responsible for respectfully steering the client away from the bad options and toward a better alternative.

In a highly competitive job market, you must determine what sets you apart from your competition. A potential client might choose one designer over another not because one is a better or more creative artist, but simply because they like the other designer more.

Customer service is part of your job, as well. Treat your client and your client's time and money with respect, be personable, and appreciate your client, and you will have more to offer than your competitors will. In addition to meeting the responsibilities previously defined, you should do the following:

- Be on time to meetings
- Meet or beat your deadlines so you do not submit work late
- Be able to explain your design choices
- Ensure adherence to copyright law

## Defining the Project

As a designer, you must understand you are acting in the role of a hired hand — not an artist with complete creative control. You are being hired to create what your client wants, not what you necessarily prefer. While you need to educate your client as to best practices in design, ultimately the client is paying the bill, so he or she has the final word when it comes to making decisions.

## Specifying Project Details

Project details should be discussed with the client and agreed upon before any design work begins. One detail to consider is what the client needs for files. For example, does the client require a 300 PPI TIF file or a layered Photoshop file? How will the files be delivered? Will they be sent by e-mail, burned to a CD and mailed, or downloaded from a Web site or FTP server? Additionally, a timeline of deliverables should be stated. A first draft of the design should be sent to the client for approval by a certain date, and pending timely client feedback, the final version should be delivered by the project deadline. The client may have a desired time frame, and the designer must be able to deliver the work within that time frame. Sometimes a compromise must be reached.

## Collecting Materials

Existing materials help to speed up the design process. If you are hired to create a Web site or brochure, ask your client for copies of their existing promotional materials, such as a business card, letterhead, or logo. Ask your client what they like and dislike about these materials and if the product you are creating should be stylistically similar. This approach can prevent you from going down the wrong path, inadvertently creating something the client does not like or need. Additionally, you will need to collect any photographs your client has earmarked for the project.

Next, you must gather other assets for the project; specifically, high-quality artwork and photographs.

**Original Artwork**   If you have the raw artistic ability or own high-quality camera equipment, you can create your own original artwork or take your own photographs if you are a professional-level photographer. You can outsource some of this work to professional artists or photographers — just be sure to get your client's approval for the cost. Your other option is to use stock art.

**Stock Art**   **Stock art** includes existing artwork and photographs that can be licensed for use. The cost of a single picture can range from zero to several thousand dollars, depending on the source and license restrictions. Realistically, you should expect to pay between $5 and $40 for each print-quality digital file if you cannot find free sources.

BTW

**Photos on CD or DVD**
If possible, get photos and images on a CD or DVD. Many times a collection of photographs and other materials are too large to send by e-mail, and even if they are successfully sent, e-mails accidentally get deleted. Having all the materials on CD or DVD also guarantees you always have a backup of the original files as you modify copies with Photoshop or other software.

**Public Domain vs. Commercial Stock Art**
Public domain stock art sites can be difficult to use because they do not have the funding for the more intuitive style of interface found on the commercial sites. You often can find exactly what you want in the public domain. However, sometimes it is worth the $5 to more easily find exactly what you want on a commercial Web site.

Stock art is commercially available from many companies, most with a Web presence — meaning you can download images or purchase whole collections of stock art on CD or DVD from a Web site. Thousands of companies sell commercial stock art online. Some of the most popular resources are fotosearch.com, corbis.com, and gettyimages.com.

When searching for stock art, be sure to seek out **royalty-free images**. Images that are royalty free can be reused without paying additional fees. For example, you could spend $100 to purchase an image that is not royalty free and use it on a Web site. If you want to use the same image in a brochure or another client's Web site, you might have to pay another fee to reuse the image. Royalty free means that once the initial payment is made, there are no re-usage fees.

If you do not want to pay anything for your images, look into finding **public domain** artwork or photographs. Images in the public domain are completely free to use. The only trick is finding quality artwork in the public domain. Whereas commercial stock art Web sites typically have millions of high-quality images from which to choose, public domain stock art Web sites often have far fewer choices. Public domain stock art sites include Flickr, Morgue File, and Uncle Sam's Photos.

**Other Licenses**   There are usage licenses allowing free unrestricted use of images, audio, video, text, and other content similar to that of the public domain. These licenses include Copyleft, Creative Commons, education use, fair use, GNU general public license, and open source. The definitions of these alternative licenses read like a law book, but it is helpful to recognize the names. Laws related to these licenses allow for limited use of copyright-protected material without requiring the permission of the copyright owner. If you find images or other content offered as one of these alternatives, there is a good chance it will be completely free to use.

Whatever the source for your images, be sure to read the license and usage rights and restrictions carefully. No matter your source for artwork, you need to document its origin. The documentation serves two important purposes. First, it provides a record of the image's origin in case you need to get additional similar artwork. Second, it provides peace of mind should you or your client ever face legal action for copyright infringement. The documentation does not have to be fancy; it can simply be a list of where an image is used in a project and where that image was acquired.

# Summary

Successful design uses the principles of balance, contrast, dominance, proximity, repetition, closure, continuance, negative space, and unity. The properties of color include hue, saturation, shade, tint, and value. Color modes include RGB for Web images, CMYK for images you intend to print, and LAB for access to the largest color space possible when working with digital photographs. Adherence to Web-safe colors is unnecessary. Colors can have emotional implications and should be used in harmony with neighboring colors. Color schemes include monochrome, complementary, analogous, and split-complementary.

Typeface selections can affect text readability, as can line lengths. Typefaces are organized into several categories, including serif, sans-serif, script, and display. The same Web site can look different from one monitor or computer to another.

Pixels per inch (PPI) determines the number of pixels printed per inch and affects the printed size of an image only, not how it appears onscreen or its file size. Higher PPI settings produce better quality printouts but have no effect on how an image appears onscreen. Dots per inch (DPI) refers to printer capabilities and defines how many dots of ink a printer can print in a linear inch. Pixel dimensions, not image resolution, affect how large an image appears on-screen and the size of a file.

Working in graphic design can incorporate a range of creative roles; working with clients in a design role requires specifying project expectations and the responsibilities of both designer and client.

# Appendix C

# Publishing to a Web Server

## Publishing a Web Site

Once you have created a Web site, you need to make it available to its intended audience. The discussion in this appendix is generally appropriate for small business and personal Web sites. Keep in mind that midsize and larger businesses typically publish their sites using their own dedicated Web servers; however, the concepts are the same. Publishing a Web site, also called going live, involves four general steps:

1. Select a Web hosting company
2. Choose and register a domain name
3. Publish your Web site files to a Web server
4. Associate your domain name with your nameserver

## Web Hosting Companies

In order for your Web site to be available to users or visitors, it must reside on a special computer called a Web server. A Web server is a computer connected to the Internet, with Web server software installed. It is the Web server software that makes files stored on a computer available as a Web site. While anyone with a computer can download and install Web server software at no cost, configuring Web server software is a complex process best left to experts. A **Web hosting company**, or **Web host**, is a company that offers Web hosting services. Web hosting companies rent space on their Web servers for you to store your Web site.

## How to Choose a Web Host

Choosing a Web host begins with research. Read about Web hosts online and in technology publications. Keep in mind, however, that online reviews of Web hosting companies often are biased or sponsored. Reviews are biased negatively as it is human nature to complain when you do not like something, but fewer people take the time and energy to write a review when they are pleased with a product or service. A review is biased positively when the review is sponsored by the Web hosting company itself — meaning either the Web host owns the review Web site or it purchases advertising on the review Web site, potentially influencing the display of positive reviews.

Once you have identified a few potential Web hosts, you should compare their features and test their tech support policies, as described later in this appendix. Recommendations from friends or colleagues are also important to consider when choosing a Web host. Choosing a host is an important consideration that should not be rushed.

Before choosing a Web hosting company, you should decide whether you need shared hosting or dedicated hosting and review the services and features outlined in the section that follows.

## Dedicated and Shared Hosting

When a single Web server hosts a single Web site, the arrangement is called **dedicated hosting**. Dedicated hosting allows the client and the Web site full access to all of the server's resources, such as the processor, memory, and hard drive space (Figure C–1a). Unfortunately, dedicated hosting is expensive, sometimes costing several hundred dollars or more per month.

**(a) Dedicated hosting**       **(b) Shared hosting**

**Figure C–1**

© 2013 Cengage Learning

**Shared hosting** refers to multiple Web sites sharing a single Web server or a bank of Web servers (Figure C–1b). Shared Web servers host many, sometimes thousands of individual Web sites that reside on the same server. Those Web sites share the server's processor, memory, hard drive space, and other computer resources. A reputable Web host has powerful Web server computers that can handle this kind of load, as well as the expert staff to configure the computers and Web server software. The disadvantage to shared hosting is that you do not get all the power of the server to yourself, as you do with dedicated hosting. The advantage is that shared hosting is very inexpensive, often just a few dollars a month. Most small business and personal Web sites use shared hosting.

## Hosting Services and Features

The following paragraphs outline some of the more important features to consider when choosing a Web host (Figure C–2).

**Disk Space**   Web site pages (HTML documents) are small files that do not take up much storage space, but other files, such as images, Flash movies, or other video and audio files, used on your site may be quite large. A typical image file used on a Web site may be as large as 50 kilobytes. A Flash movie file might be several thousand kilobytes. If your Web site files are larger than the disk space available to you, your Web site will not fit on the server. Choose a Web hosting plan that offers unlimited disk space.

© 2013 Cengage Learning

**Figure C–2**

**Bandwidth**    Every time a user connects to your Web site, your files are transferred across the Internet to the user. **Bandwidth** refers to the number of bytes your Web site is sending across the Internet. A **byte** is approximately equivalent to one character — a **kilobyte** is 1,024 bytes. The more users that connect to your site, or the larger your files are, the more bandwidth you use. Some Web hosts disable your Web site if you exceed the allotted bandwidth for your account, while other Web hosts charge you additional fees for overages. Choose a Web hosting plan that offers unlimited bandwidth.

**E-Mail Accounts**    To maintain professionalism, it is best to have an e-mail address that uses the same name as your Web site. For example, if your Web site is www.MyWebSite.com, it is best to have e-mail addresses such as info@MyWebSite.com or contact@MyWebSite.com rather than MyWebSite@hotmail.com or MyWebSite@gmail.com. Having an e-mail address that uses the same name as your Web site increases brand and name recognition, and is more likely to drive people to your site. Some hosting plans offer fewer than five e-mail accounts, which can be problematic if you need e-mail addresses for more many employees, for example. Choose a Web hosting plan that offers an adequate number of e-mail accounts for your site's needs.

**FTP Accounts**    To copy your Web site to a Web server, you must connect to the Web server using software called an FTP client. **FTP** stands for **file transfer protocol**, which is a method of copying files between computers across the Internet. Because multiple people may be working on the Web site and updating files, each person should have his or her own FTP account for security purposes. If several people use the same FTP account, passwords might be changed inadvertently, making it impossible for the others to log on. Individual FTP accounts also help track who added, updated, or deleted files from the Web site. Choose a Web hosting plan that offers an unlimited number of FTP accounts.

**Other Hosting Considerations**
You might want to ask potential Web hosting companies about their financial strength, their physical security, their disaster recovery plan, and how long they have been in business.

**Cost**   Shared hosting plans typically cost anywhere from $0.99 to $15 per month. The most expensive plans are not necessarily the best, nor are the least expensive always the best value. You can find excellent features from a reputable Web host such as webhostinghub.com or hostgator.com for about $6 per month. Choose a Web hosting company whose costs offer the best value for the services offered.

**Setup Fee**   Some Web hosting companies charge a setup fee of $20 or more just to set up a new account. Choose a Web host that does not charge a setup fee.

**Uptime Guarantee**   **Uptime** is the amount of time your Web site is available. Ideally, you want your site available 100 percent of the time; however sometimes computers crash, hard drives become damaged, or other components in a computer cause it to stop working. When this happens on a Web server, Web sites residing on that server are not available. The reliability of the service is an important consideration. Choose a Web host that offers at least a 99.9 percent uptime guarantee to ensure that your Web site always is available.

**Tech Support**   Tech support can be offered in a variety of ways. Make sure you choose a Web host that offers e-mail, phone, and online chat support 24 hours a day, 7 days a week. It is a good idea to test the tech support service of a hosting company before signing up for an account. Sales and billing departments are usually excellent about taking phone calls and responding to e-mails, but you are not likely to need to reach those people once your account is active. Call tech support and see how long it takes them to answer. E-mail tech support and see how long it is until you receive a response. Ask a basic question such as, "What is the typical wait time before receiving a response from your tech support?" Some $0.99 per month hosting plans seem like a good deal until you encounter a problem. If you cannot reach tech support or they reply with a generic programmed response as if they are reading from a script, that $0.99 per month cost may not be such a great deal after all. Choose a Web hosting company that offers 24-hour support, short wait times, and quick turnaround for e-mail questions.

# Domain Names

Every computer connected to the Internet is assigned a unique number, called an **Internet Protocol (IP) address**, which identifies the computer. An IP address is used when one computer needs to contact another computer. For example, when a user opens a Web browser and types the name of a Web site, such as cengage.com, his or her computer actually connects to the Web server by using the IP address of the Web server. Because IP addresses are difficult to remember, most sites use a domain name such as cengage.com. A **domain name** is a combination of letters and numbers that names a Web site for locating purposes; it is the part of the URL that follows the **protocol designation** such as http:// and any **subdomain** listing such as www (Figure C–3). The user's computer automatically matches the domain name with the IP address in order to connect to the Web server. You need to choose a domain name carefully, and purchase, or register, your domain name to work in conjunction with your Web hosting company. You will learn how to register a domain name later in this appendix.

**IP Addresses**
An IP address typically is four decimal numbers separated by periods. However, as these numbers are being exhausted rapidly, a new eight-number IP address, using a hexadecimal notation, is being advocated by the Internet Assigned Numbers Authority (IANA).

protocol designation    subdomain        domain name    top-level domain

**Figure C–3**

## Choosing a Domain Name

Choose a domain name that is easy to spell, easy to type, and easy to remember. Your domain name might have to fit on a business card, and some users will need to type it into their Web browser's Address bar. Avoiding domain names that are lengthy or complicated is a good approach. A **top-level domain** (**TLD**) is the last part of a Web site's name. For example, .com, .org, .net, and .edu are all top-level domains. When choosing a domain name, you need to decide which top-level domain is best for your site. Table C–1 describes a few of the more popular top-level domains that you are likely to use.

| Table C–1 Top-Level Domains | | |
| --- | --- | --- |
| **Top-Level Domain** | **Eligibility** | **Description** |
| .biz | Anyone can register | Intended for businesses as an alternative to .com |
| .com | Anyone can register | Originally intended for for-profit businesses, .com has become the most popular top-level domain |
| .edu | Only educational institutions may register | Used by educational institutions |
| .info | Anyone can register | No prescribed theme or orientation |
| .org | Anyone can register | Originally intended for nonprofit organizations |

In most cases, you should choose to use .com if possible, because it is the most familiar to people.

**BTW**

**Domain Availability**

After you choose a domain name, you need to make sure that no one has chosen that domain name already. You can use a Web site that will check for you, such as godaddy.com or checkdomain.com, or you can type the domain name with its subdomain and top-level domain into a browser's URL text box and see similar Web sites. Keep in mind that some sites may be registered but are not up and running yet.

# Registering a Domain Name

You **register**, or purchase, a domain name through a company called a domain name registrar service. Many registrars can be found online. Some of the most popular registrar services include register.com, godaddy.com, and networksolutions.com. By registering a domain name, you become the registrant, or official owner of the site name (Figure C–4).

© www.godaddy.com

**Figure C–4**

Expect to pay anywhere from $10 to $30 per year for domain name registration. After the domain name is registered, you must renew it yearly. If your domain name registration expires, your Web site no longer will be available to the public.

Many registrars also offer Web hosting, and conversely most Web hosting companies offer free domain name registration. However, avoid this temptation to consolidate services. It is best to keep them separate. Register your domain through one company, and host your Web site with a different company. For any number of reasons, you might want to change Web hosting companies. By registering the domain name with a company other than your Web host, you easily can associate your domain name with any current hosting company.

# DNS

The **Domain Name System** (**DNS**) is a system that associates or connects a domain name with a Web server (Figure C–5). Computers on the Internet called DNS servers, or **nameservers**, store these associations in a database. The final step in making your Web site available is associating your domain name with the Web server so that when someone opens their browser and types www.YourWebSite.com, that user's computer can find the Web server that hosts your site.

**Domain Name System**

**Figure C–5**

© 2013 Cengage Learning

Some hosting companies associate your domain name for you; others require you to do it yourself. To associate your domain name with your Web server, obtain the name of your nameserver from your Web hosting company. Then go into your domain name registrar service account and update your domain name with the name of the nameserver. As every registrar's Web site is different, you might need to contact the registrar's tech support to learn where to make the nameserver change. Once you have updated your domain name to use a specific nameserver, your domain name will be **associated** with your Web server. This allows the user's Web browser to link to your Web site when a visitor types your domain name in his or her Web browser.

## DNS Propagation

There are thousands of nameservers all over the world, and when one is updated, all of the other nameservers receive an update with the new information. The updating process of the nameserver database, across all DNS servers on the Web, is called **DNS propagation**. After you make a change to your nameserver setting, it can take up to 72 hours for that change to propagate, meaning that your Web site might not be available during those three days. Several companies, including whatsmydns.net and viewdns.info, offer instant checking of DNS propagation (Figure C–6 on the next page). DNS propagation is a feature to consider when evaluating potential Web hosts.

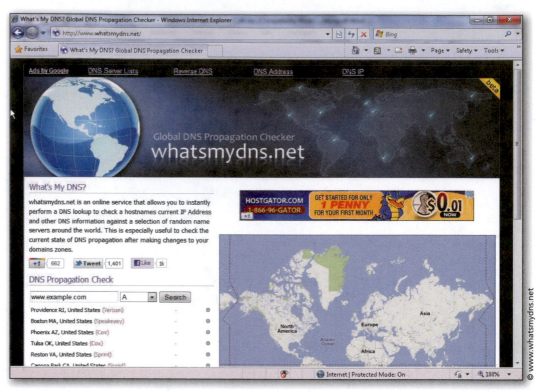

**Figure C–6**

# Copying Files using FTP

Once you have contracted with a Web host, registered your domain name, and associated your domain name with a nameserver, you need to copy your files to the Web server using FTP client software. Some Web design software, such as Dreamweaver, includes a built-in FTP client (Figure C–7). You also can purchase FTP client software, or use free software such as FileZilla or SmartFTP.

**Figure C–7**

## Copying Files

The process of copying files to the Web server is straightforward, but first you must have four pieces of information from the Web hosting company. Although all FTP clients have slightly different interfaces, they all allow you to specify these four pieces of information:

1. Host name: the name of the Web server. This is usually the same as your domain name, but your Web host should provide an alternate name to use until DNS propagation is complete.
2. Username: the name you use to log on to the Web server.
3. Password: the password you use in conjunction with the username.
4. Remote folder: the name of the folder on the Web server to which you copy your files.

The Web hosting company should provide all this information in an e-mail message. If this information is not provided to you by e-mail, you should contact the hosting company's tech support.

Once the information is entered, you can connect to the Web server and copy your files from your computer to the Web server, either by dragging and dropping or by clicking a Move button. The process of copying files from your computer to another computer, such as a Web server, is called **uploading**. Copying files from another computer to your computer is called **downloading**. With FTP software and the proper user permissions, you can upload your Web files to publish them and download your Web files to edit them as necessary.

BTW

**Viewing Server Files**
Your Web hosting service may allow Windows Explorer-based copy and paste techniques for copying files to your Web server. With the correct FTP URL, you can use a browser to log into your files. Your browser may display a message such as, "On the menu, click View, and then click Open FTP Site in Windows Explorer."

## Summary

Publishing a Web site to a Web server requires research and preparation. Prior to publishing you must select and hire a Web hosting company. Consider both technical and support offerings provided by the Web host before you decide on a company. You must acquire a domain name through a domain name registrar, and associate it with a Web server for DNS propagation. Finally, publishing the Web files involves uploading files to your Web server using FTP.

## Publishing to a Web Server

### 1: Choosing a Web Hosting Company

*Instructions*: This appendix recommends several features and characteristics to measure when choosing a Web hosting company. Research Web hosts — online at reputable sources and in technology publications. Find at least four different Web Hosting companies and create a table similar to the following, using the criteria described in the appendix.

| Company name | | | | |
|---|---|---|---|---|
| Web site | | | | |
| Dedicated or shared? | | | | |
| Disk space | | | | |
| Bandwidth | | | | |
| E-mail accounts | | | | |
| FTP accounts | | | | |
| Cost | | | | |
| Setup fee | | | | |
| Uptime guarantee | | | | |
| Tech support | | | | |

## Publishing to a Web Server

### 2: Choosing a Domain Name

*Instructions*: You have taken a job as an intern with a consulting firm that helps start-up businesses create a Web presence. Your boss has asked you to recommend three appropriate domain names for a small hobby store named Hobby Express. Their specialty is model railroading, but they also sell puzzles, craft kits, art supplies, and strategy games.

Using the recommendations in this appendix, research domain names that are not currently used. Choose an appropriate top-level domain and an effective domain name that is easy to spell, easy to type, and easy to remember. Write a paragraph for each of the three recommendations explaining why you chose the domain.

## Appendix D
# Using Photoshop Help

This appendix shows you how to use Photoshop Help. At anytime, whether you are accessing Photoshop currently or not, there are ways to interact with Photoshop Help and display information on any Photoshop topic. The help system is a complete reference manual at your fingertips.

## Photoshop Help

Photoshop Help documentation for Photoshop CS6 is available in several formats, as shown in Figure D–1 on the next page. The first format is a Web-based help system that was introduced in Chapter 1. If you press the F1 key or choose Photoshop Online Help on the Help menu, Adobe Community Help appears in your default browser. You then can use the Web page to search for help topics. The Adobe Community Help page also contains many other kinds of assistance, including tutorials and videos. Your computer must be connected to the Web to use this form of Photoshop Help.

A second form of Photoshop Help is available as a PDF file. Again, pressing the F1 key or choosing Photoshop Online Help on the Help menu opens the Adobe Community Help page on the Web. Then, you can click the Help PDF link to open a searchable help documentation, called Using Adobe Photoshop CS6, in book format. You can save this help file on your storage device, or continue to use it on the Web. If you prefer to view documentation in print form, you can print the Photoshop Help PDF file.

Photoshop Help displays two main panes. The left pane displays a search system. The right pane displays help information on the selected topic. Using Adobe Photoshop CS6 displays a chapter navigation system on the left, and pages from Photoshop Help documentation on the right.

## Using Help

The quickest way to navigate the Photoshop help system is by clicking topic links on the Help pages. You also can search for specific words and phrases by using the **Search box** in the upper-left corner of the Adobe Community Help Web page. Here you can type words, such as *layer mask, hue,* or *file formats,* or you can type phrases, such as *preview a Web graphic,* or *drawing with the Pen Tool.* Adobe Community Help responds by displaying search results with a list of topics you can click.

Here are some tips regarding the words or phrases you enter to initiate a search:

1. Check the spelling of the word or phrase.
2. Keep your search specific, with fewer than seven words, to return the most accurate results.
3. If you search using a specific phrase, such as *shape tool,* put quotation marks around the phrase — the search returns only those topics containing all words in the phrase.
4. If a search term does not yield the desired results, try using a synonym, such as Web instead of Internet.

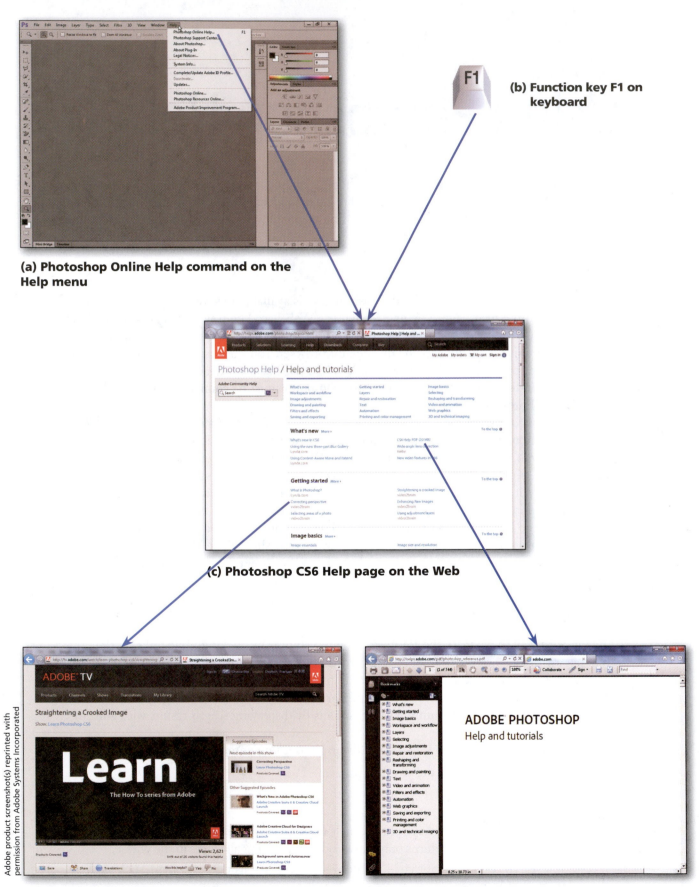

**(a) Photoshop Online Help command on the Help menu**

**(b) Function key F1 on keyboard**

**(c) Photoshop CS6 Help page on the Web**

**(d) Sample video page**

**(e) Help in PDF format**

**Figure D–1**

## To Access Photoshop Online Help

The following step shows how to open Photoshop Online Help.

- With Photoshop running on your system, press the F1 key to display the Photoshop Help window.

- When the Adobe Community Help window is displayed, double-click the title bar to maximize the window, if necessary (Figure D–2).

**Figure D–2**

## To Use the Topics List

The Topics List is similar to a table of contents in a book. Because Adobe updates the topics on a regular basis, your Topics List will look different. The following steps use the topics list to look up information about what is new in CS6.

- Click the topic, What's new in CS6 to display its contents (Figure D–3).

**Figure D–3**

**2**

- Click the link, Retouching and transforming, to display information about the new retouching tools (Figure D–4).

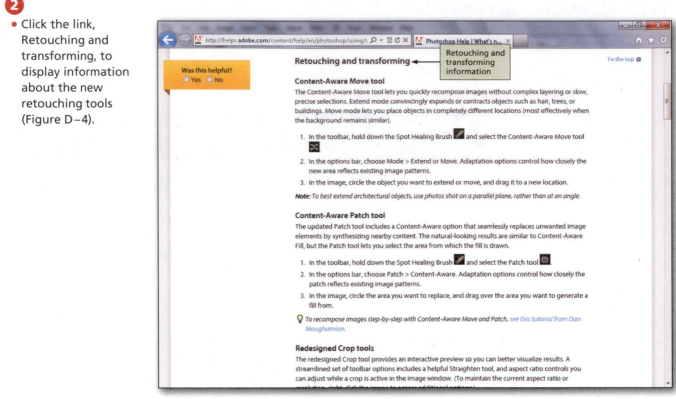

**Figure D–4**

## To Use the Adobe Community Help Search Box

The following steps use the Search box to obtain useful information by entering the keywords, ruler origin.

**1**

- Click the Search box.

- Type `ruler origin` and then press the ENTER key to display the search results (Figure D–5).

**Figure D–5**

**2**

- When the list of Help topics is displayed, click Adobe Photoshop* Rulers, the grid, and guides, or a similar topic in your list.

- Scroll as necessary to display the Change a ruler's zero origin topic (Figure D–6).

**Figure D–6**

On the right, Photoshop Help displays information about the topic, instructions, and a graphic. A light bulb icon indicates a Photoshop tip.

If none of the topics presents the information you want, you can refine the search by entering another word or phrase in the Search box.

## To View a Video on Adobe TV

Using Photoshop Help while connected to the Web, you can view online videos and tutorials, as done in the following steps.

**1**
- Scroll as necessary to display the Search box at the top of the page.
- In the Search box, type adobe tv type styles, and then press the ENTER key to perform the search (Figure D–7).

Figure D–7

**2**
- Click the link named Type Styles in Photoshop CS6 to open the page and start the video (Figure D–8).

Figure D–8

**3**

- When the video is finished playing, click the Close button on the title bar of the browser window to quit Help (Figure D–9).

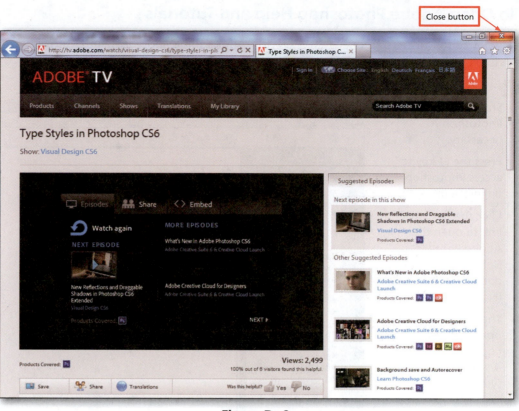

Figure D–9

# Using Help PDF Documentation

The PDF file, Adobe Photoshop Help and Tutorials, is a complete set of documentation for using Photoshop CS6. The PDF file is organized into chapter topics with a table of contents like a regular book. You can access Adobe Photoshop Help and Tutorials by clicking the link on the Photoshop Online Help page.

## To Open Adobe Photoshop Help and Tutorials

The following step opens the PDF file, Adobe Photoshop Help and Tutorials, from the Photoshop Online Help page. You will use Adobe Acrobat to view the documentation.

**1**

- Start Photoshop if necessary.

- Press the F1 key to access Photoshop online Help.

- Click the Help PDF link to open the Adobe Photoshop Help and Tutorials documentation. (Figure D–10).

**Q&A**

The file would not open because I do not have Adobe Acrobat on my system.

See your instructor for ways to access the file.

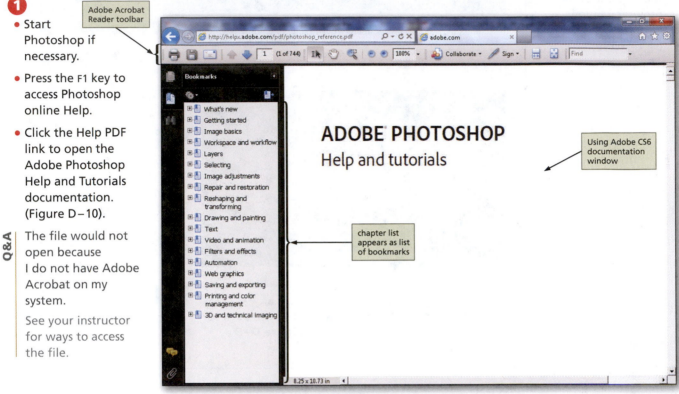

**Figure D–10**

## To Navigate the Documentation by Chapter Topic

The following steps use the left pane of the documentation window to find information related to color.

**1**

- With the Adobe Photoshop Help and Tutorials documentation file still displayed, click the plus sign next to the words, Image Basics, and then click About color, to display the topic (Figure D–11).

**Figure D–11**

**2**
- Click the words, Understanding color, to display the information on the right side of the window.
- Click the Collpase button to hide the Search pane (Figure D–12).

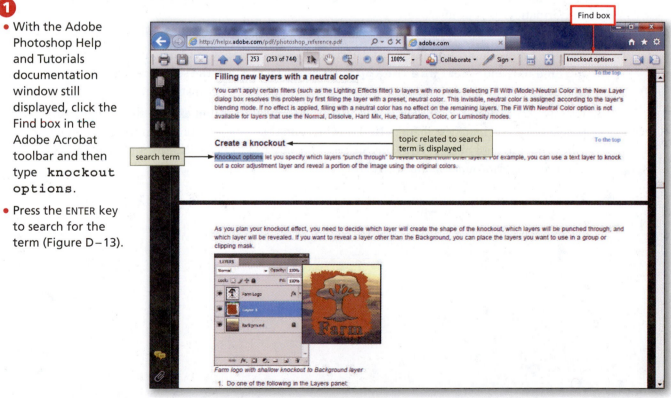

**Figure D–12**

## To Use the Find Box

The following step searches the documentation for information about the topic, knockout, using the Adobe Acrobat Find box.

**1**
- With the Adobe Photoshop Help and Tutorials documentation window still displayed, click the Find box in the Adobe Acrobat toolbar and then type `knockout options`.
- Press the ENTER key to search for the term (Figure D–13).

**Figure D–13**

## Use Help

### 1: Using Adobe Help on the Web

*Instructions:* Perform the following tasks using Adobe Community Help.

1. On the Photoshop Online Help page, type `pencil tool` in the Search box to obtain help on using the Pencil tool, and then press the ENTER key.

2. When the topics are displayed, click the topic, Adobe Photoshop* Drawing with the Pen tools.

3. One at a time, click two additional links and print the information. Hand in the printouts to your instructor. Use the Back to previous page and Forward to next page buttons to return to the original page.

4. Use the Search box to search for information on linking layers. Click the Adobe Photoshop* Selecting, grouping, and linking layers topic in the search results. Read and print the information. One at a time, click the links on the page and print the information for any new page that is displayed.

5. Use the Search box to search for information on tutorials. Navigate to a tutorial of your choice and follow the directions. Write three paragraphs describing your experience, including how easy or difficult it was to follow the tutorial and what you learned. Turn in the paragraphs to your instructor.

6. Close Photoshop Online Help.

## Use Help

### 2: Using Adobe Photoshop CS6 Documentation

*Instructions:* Use the Adobe Photoshop CS6 documentation to understand the topics better and answer the questions listed below. Answer the questions on your own paper, or hand in the printed Help information to your instructor.

1. Open the PDF file, Adobe Photoshop Help and Tutorials from the Photoshop Online Help page.

2. Use the Adobe Photoshop Help and Tutorials documentation to find help on snapping. Use the Find box, and enter `use snapping` as the term. Click the search result entitled, Use snapping, and then print the page. Hand in the printouts to your instructor.

3. Use the Adobe Photoshop Help and Tutorials documentation and expand the bookmarks, if necessary. Navigate to Chapter 10: Drawing, and then click the plus sign to expand the topic. Click the plus sign next to Drawing Shapes. One at a time, click each link and print the page. Hand in the printouts to your instructor.

## Appendix E

# Using Adobe Bridge CS6

This appendix shows you how to use Adobe Bridge CS6. Bridge is a file exploration tool similar to Windows Explorer, but with added functionality related to images. Bridge replaces previous file browsing techniques, and now is the control center for the Adobe Creative Suite. Bridge is used to organize, browse, and locate the assets you need to create content for print, the Web, and mobile devices with drag-and-drop functionality.

## Adobe Bridge

You can access Bridge from Photoshop or from the Windows 7 Start menu. Bridge can run independently from Photoshop as a stand-alone program.

### To Start Bridge Using Windows

The following steps start Bridge from the Windows 7 Start menu.

**1**

• Click the Start button on the Windows 7 taskbar to display the Start menu.

• Type **Bridge CS6** as the search text in the 'Search programs and files' text box, and watch the search results appear on the Start menu (Figure E–1).

**Figure E–1**

**2**

- Click Adobe Bridge CS6 in the search results on the Start menu to start Bridge.

- When the Bridge window is displayed, double-click its title bar to maximize the window, if necessary.

- Click Computer on the Favorites panel, if necessary (Figure E–2).

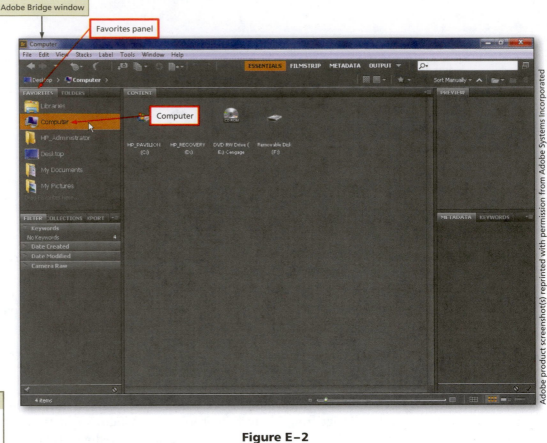

**Other Ways**

1. In Photoshop, click File on menu bar, click Browse in Bridge

2. Press ATL+CTRL+O

**Figure E–2**

## To Reset the Workspace

To make your installation of Bridge match the figures in this book, you will reset the workspace to its default settings in the following step.

**1**

- Click Window on the menu bar, and then point to Workspace to display the Workspace submenu (Figure E–3).

- Click Reset Workspace on the Workspace submenu.

**Figure E–3**

**Other Ways**

1. Press CTRL+F1

# The Bridge Window

The parts of the Bridge window are displayed in Figure E–4. The window is divided into panels and includes a menu bar, a toolbar, and a status bar.

**Figure E–4**

# The Panels

Several panels are displayed in the Bridge workspace in default view. To select a panel, click its tab. You can change the location of the panels by dragging their tabs. You can enlarge or reduce the size of the panels by dragging their borders. Some panels include buttons and menus to help you organize displayed information.

**Favorites Panel**   The Favorites panel allows quick access to common locations and folders, as well as access to other Adobe applications. You can click a location to display its contents in the Content panel.

**Folders Panel**   The Folders panel shows the folder hierarchy in a display similar to that of Windows Explorer. You can click the plus sign to expand folders and the minus sign to collapse them.

**Content Panel**   The Content panel is displayed in a large pane in the center of the Bridge window. The content panel includes a view of each file and folder, its name, the creation date, and other information about each item. The Content panel is used to select files and open folders. To select a file, click it. To open a folder, double-click it. You can change how the Content panel is displayed on the Bridge status bar.

**Preview Panel**   The Preview panel displays a preview of the selected file that is usually larger than the thumbnail displayed in the Content panel. If the panel is resized, the preview also is resized.

**Filter Panel**   The Filter panel is displayed in the lower-left region of the Bridge window. The Filter panel includes many categories of criteria used to filter or control which files are displayed in the Content panel. By default, three categories are displayed when you first start Bridge: Keywords, Date Created, and Date Modified. As you click files, the criteria categories change to include metadata that is generated dynamically depending on the file type. For example, if you click an image in the Content panel, the Filter panel includes criteria such as camera data. If you click an audio file, the criteria include artist, album genre, and so on.

**Collections Panel**   The Collections panel is displayed in the lower-left region of the Bridge window. **Collections** are a way to group photos in one place for easy viewing, even if the images are located in different folders or on different hard drives. The Collections panel allows you to create and display previously created collections, by identifying files or by saving previous searches.

**Export Panel**   The Export panel is displayed in the lower-left region of the Bridge window. The panel helps with saving and uploading to photo-sharing Web sites, including Facebook, Flickr, and Photoshop.com.

**Metadata Panel**   The Metadata panel contains metadata information for the selected file. Recall that metadata is information about the file including properties, camera data, creation and modification data, and other pieces of information. If multiple files are selected, shared data is listed such as keywords, date created, and exposure settings.

**Keywords Panel**   The Keywords panel allows you to assign keywords using categories designed by Bridge, or you can create new ones. The keywords help you organize and search your images.

## Toolbars and Buttons

Bridge displays several toolbars and sets of buttons to help you work more efficiently (Figure E–5).

**Figure E–5**

**Menu Bar**   The menu bar is displayed at the top of the Bridge window and contains commands specific to Bridge.

**Application Bar**   Below the menu bar is the Application bar, which includes the navigation buttons, file retrieval and output buttons, buttons for switching workspaces, and other buttons to search for files.

**Path Bar**   The Path bar displays the path for the current file. To the right of the Path bar are shortcut buttons to help you work with your files. Browse, filter, and sort buttons change the display in the Content panel. The 'Create a new folder' button inserts a new folder in the current location. The rotate buttons are active when an image file is selected in the Content panel. The Delete item button deletes the selected item.

**Status Bar**   At the bottom of the Bridge window, the status bar displays information and contains buttons (Figure E–6). On the left side of the status bar is information regarding the number of items in the current location and how many files are selected, if any. On the right side of the status bar, the Thumbnail slider sets the size of the thumbnails. To the right of the slider are four buttons used to change the display of the Content panel, including the 'Click to lock thumbnail grid' button, the 'View content as thumbnails' button, the 'View content as details' button, and the 'View content as list' button.

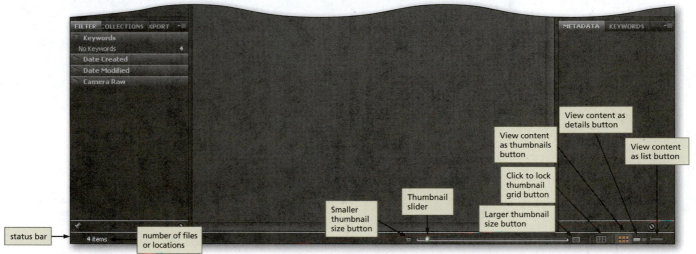

**Figure E–6**

# Bridge Navigation and File Viewing

The advantages of using Bridge to navigate through the files and folders on your computer system include an interface that looks the same in all folders, the ability to see the images quickly, and the ease with which you can open the files in Photoshop or other image editing software. Besides the four kinds of displays represented by the Workspace switcher buttons on the right side of the status bar, Bridge offers several other configurations or layouts of the workspace accessible on the Workspace submenu on the Window menu (Figure E–3 on page APP 44).

## To Navigate and View Files Using Bridge

The following step navigates to the Data Files for Students in order to view files. Visit www.cengage.com/ct/studentdownload for detailed instructions or contact your instructor for information about accessing the required files. You then will use the Workspace switcher buttons to view the Content panel in different styles.

**1**

- In the Content panel, double-click the drive associated with the Data Files for Students.

- When the folders and files are displayed, double-click the Photoshop folder, and then double-click the Chapter 01 folder to display the files (Figure E–7).

**Experiment**

- One at a time, click each of the workspace buttons on the options bar and note how the Content panel changes.

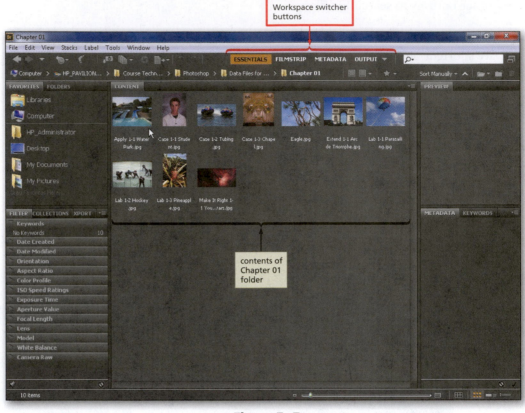

Figure E–7

| Other Ways | |
|---|---|
| 1. To view Filmstrip workspace, press CTRL+F2 | 4. To view Keywords workspace, press CTRL+F5 |
| 2. To view Metadata workspace, press CTRL+F3 | 5. To view Preview workspace, press CTRL+F6 |
| 3. To view Output workspace, press CTRL+F4 | |

**BTW**

**Duplicating Files**
Bridge also offers a Duplicate command on the Edit menu (Figure E–8) that makes a copy in the same folder. Bridge renames the second file with the word, Copy, appended to the file name.

## Managing Files

If you want to move a file to a folder that currently is displayed in the Content panel, you can drag and drop the file. The right-drag option is not available. If you want to copy a file, you can choose Copy on the Edit menu, navigate to the new folder and then choose Paste on the Edit menu. At anytime, you can press the DELETE key to delete a file or folder, or right-click and then click Delete on the context menu. To rename a photo in Bridge, right-click the file and then click Rename. Type the new name.

## To Copy a File

The following steps copy a file from the Data Files for Students to a USB flash drive using Bridge.

**1**

- With the Chapter 01 folder contents still displayed in the Content panel, click the Case 1-2 Tubing thumbnail to select it.

- Click Edit on the menu bar to display the Edit menu (Figure E–8).

**Experiment**

- Choose a picture and then use one of the rotate commands on the Edit menu to rotate the image. Press CTRL+Z to cancel the rotation. When you are done, click Edit on the menu bar.

**Figure E–8**

**2**

- Click Copy on the Edit menu.

- In the Favorites panel, click Computer.

- When the Computer locations are displayed in the Content panel, double-click Removable Disk (F:) or the drive associated with your USB flash drive.

- Click Edit on the menu bar, and then click Paste to display the copy in its new location (Figure E–9).

**Figure E–9**

**Other Ways**

1. To copy, press CTRL+C
2. To paste, press CTRL+V

# Metadata

A popular use for Bridge allows you to assign metadata to files. Metadata, such as information about the file, author, resolution, color space, and copyright, is used for searching and categorizing photos. You can use metadata to streamline your workflow and organize your files.

Metadata is divided into categories, depending on the type of software you are using and the selected files. The category File Properties includes things like file type, creation date, dimensions, and color mode. IPTC Core stands for International Press Telecommunications Council, which is data used to identify transmitted text and images, such as data describing the image or the location of a photo. Camera Data (Exif) refers to the Exchangeable Image File Format, a standard for storing interchange information in image files, especially those using JPEG compression. Most digital cameras now use the Exif format. The standardization of IPTC and Exif encourages interoperability between imaging devices. Other categories may include Audio, Video, Fonts, Camera Raw, and Version Cue, among others. You can see a list of all the metadata categories and their definitions by using Bridge Help.

## To Assign and View Metadata

The Metadata Focus workspace makes it easier to assign or enter metadata for photos. In the Metadata panel, you can click the pencil icon to select fields of metadata, or you can move through the fields by pressing the TAB key. The following steps enter description and location information for the selected file.

**1**

- Click the Case 1-2 Tubing thumbnail to select it.

- In the Metadata panel, move the mouse pointer to a location just right of the field names. When the mouse pointer changes to a double-headed arrow, drag to the right to display more of the words.

- Drag the left border of the Metadata panel to widen the panel itself.

- In the Metadata panel, scroll down to the IPTC Core area.

- Click the arrow next to the heading, IPTC Core to expand the area if necessary (Figure E–10).

**Figure E–10**

**2**

- Scroll down to the Description field and then click the pencil icon to the right of the Description field. Type **Tubing Adventure** as the description.

- Scroll as needed and then click the pencil icon to the right of the Sublocation field. Type **Raccoon Lake** as the location.

- Press the TAB key, Type **Rockville** as the city.

- Press the TAB key. Type **Missouri** as the state (Figure E–11).

**Figure E–11**

**3**

- Click the Apply button at the bottom of the Metadata panel to assign the metadata to the photo.

- Click File on the menu bar and then click File Info to display the Case 1-2 Tubing.jpg dialog box, and verify the information in the Description field (Figure E–12).

- Click the OK button to close the dialog box.

🔍 **Experiment**

- Click each of the thumbnail buttons on the Bridge status bar to see how they change the display.

**Figure E–12**

## To Enter a New Keyword

The Keywords panel lets you create and apply Bridge **keywords** to files. Keywords can be organized into categories called **sets.** Using keywords and sets, you identify and search for files based on their content. To assign keywords, you click the box to the left of the keyword in the Keywords panel, as shown in the following steps.

- With the Case 1-2 Tubing image still selected, click the Keywords tab to display the Keywords panel.

- Right-click the word, Places, to display the context menu (Figure E–13).

**Figure E–13**

- Click New Sub Keyword on the context menu.

- When the new field is displayed in the Keywords panel, type **Missouri** and then press the ENTER key to create the new item in Places.

- Select the photo again in the Content panel, if necessary.

- Click the check box to the left of Missouri to assign a Missouri keyword to the picture (Figure E–14).

**Figure E–14**

## To Rate a Photo

A rating system from zero stars to five stars is available in Bridge to rate your images and photos. A rating system helps you organize and flag your favorite or best files. Many photographers transfer their digital photos from a camera into Bridge and then look back through them, rating and grouping the photos. You can rate a photo using the Label menu or using shortcut keys. Once the photo is rated, stars are displayed below or above the file name depending on the workspace view. To change a rating, click Label on the menu bar and then either increase or decrease the rating. To remove all stars, click Label on the menu bar and then click No Rating. In some views, you can change a rating by clicking stars or dots that display below the thumbnail. You can remove the rating by clicking left of the stars.

The following step adds a rating to a photo file in Bridge.

**1**

- With the Case 1-2 Tubing image still selected in the Content panel, press CTRL+3 to assign a three star rating (Figure E–15).

**Q&A**

How do you remove the stars if you change your mind?

Click to the left of the stars in the Content panel, or press CTRL+0 (zero) to remove the stars.

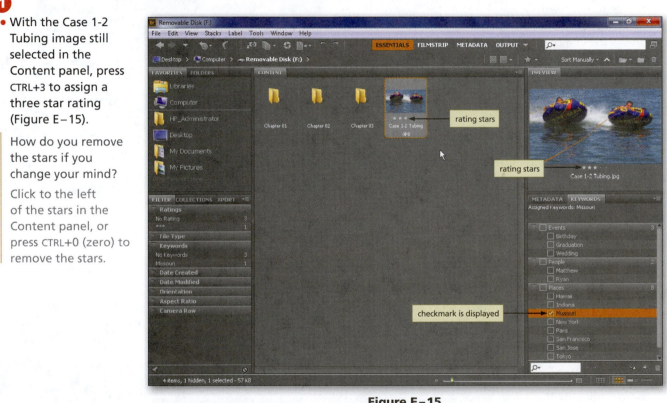

**Figure E–15**

**Other Ways**

1. On Label menu, select desired rating

## To Label a Photo with Color Coding

Another way to group photos in Bridge is to use a color coding system. Bridge provides five colors with which users can label or group their photos. Each color has a category keyword that can be used to group photos. Keywords such as Approved, Second, or Review are used in photojournalism to indicate the status of the photo for future usage. Some companies use the colors for sorting and selecting only. The steps on the next page add a green color indicating approval to the Case 1-2 Tubing image using the menu system. Shortcut keys also are available for labeling photos with color coding. You can edit the words associated with the various colors. To do so, press CTRL+K to enter Preferences and then click Labels in the left navigation pane.

**1**

- With the Case 1-2 Tubing image still selected in the Content panel, click Label on the menu bar to display the Label menu (Figure E–16).

**Q&A**

Can I change the colors associated with each label status?

No. Beginning with the Select command on the Label menu and going down, the colors are red, yellow, green, blue, and purple, respectively.

**Figure E–16**

**2**

- Click Approved to choose a label status.

- If Bridge displays a dialog box, click its OK button to apply the color (Figure E–17).

**Q&A**

Where will I see the word, Approved, that I chose from the Label menu?

In the Essentials workspace, you only see the green color around the rating. If you click the Metadata workspace switcher button, the status itself is displayed.

**Figure E–17**

**Other Ways**

1. For green color coding, press CTRL+8

## Searching Bridge

Searching is a powerful tool in Bridge, especially as the number of stored image files increases on your computer system. It is a good idea to enter keywords, or metadata, for every image file you store, to make searching more efficient. Without Bridge and the search tool, you would have to view all files as filmstrips in Windows, and then look at them a screen at a time until you found what you wanted.

## Using the Find Command

In Bridge, you can enter the kind of data or field that you want to search, parameters for that field, and the text you are looking for using the Find command. For example, you could search for all files with a rating of three stars or better, for files less than 1 megabyte in size, files with Missouri as their location, or files that begin with the letter, m.

**BTW**

**Saving Ratings**
Color coding and ratings are portable to other computers only when photos have embedded extensible markup platform (XMP) storage space. Otherwise, the colors and ratings are stored in your system's cached memory.

### To Use the Find Command

The Find dialog box displays many boxes and buttons to help you search effectively. In the following steps, you will look for all files with metadata that includes the word, lake.

**1**
- Click Edit on the menu bar, and then click Find to display the Find dialog box (Figure E–18).

**Q&A**
How do I search in other locations?

Click the Look in box arrow and choose a preset location, or click the Browse command in the list to navigate to the desired location.

**Figure E–18**

**2**

- If necessary, click the first Criteria box arrow, scroll down as necessary, and then click All Metadata to search all of the metadata fields.

- Press the TAB key twice, and then type **lake** in the Enter Text box to enter the criteria (Figure E–19).

**Experiment**

- Click the second Criteria box arrow to view the choices for delimiting the criteria. When you are finished, click contains.

Figure E–19

**3**

- Click the Find button to display all files that have the word, lake, in any part of their metadata (Figure E–20).

- Click the Cancel button in the Search title bar.

**Q&A**

Can I search for types of images?

Yes, click the first Criteria box arrow, and then click Document Type. The third Criteria box then lists types of images from which you can choose.

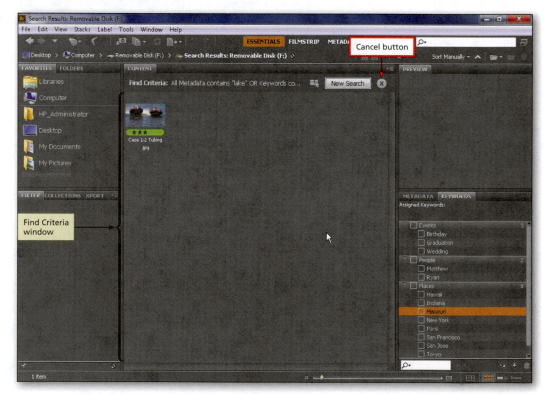

Figure E–20

**Other Ways**

1. Press CTRL+F, enter search criteria, click Find button

The plus sign to the right of the search boxes in the Find dialog box allows you to search multiple fields. You can add additional criteria by clicking the plus sign. For example, if you needed to find photos that were created last winter from your vacation in the Rockies, you could search for the date in the first line of boxes, and then enter a description in the second line of criteria boxes to narrow your search even further in the second line of boxes (Figure E–21). When clicked, the Match box arrow allows you to match any or all criteria.

**Figure E–21**

Bridge offers you a way to save common searches as a **collection** for use later. For example, if you were working for a grocery wholesaler who stores many files for artwork in advertising, searching for pictures related to dairy products would be a common search. Looking through folders of images for pictures of milk or cheese would be very time consuming. To create a stored search collection, click the New Smart Collection button and enter your criteria. Bridge then allows you to name the search. To display stored collections, click Collections in the Favorites panel. Then to perform the search again, double-click the collection. With metadata and collection searches, Bridge saves a lot of time.

## To Quit Bridge

The final step quits Bridge.

**1**  Click the Close button on the Bridge title bar.

# Using Bridge

## 1: Assigning Metadata

*Instructions:*   You would like to assign metadata to some of the photos you worked on in previous chapters in this book.

1. Start Bridge on your system. When the Bridge window is displayed, click Computer on the Favorites panel. In the Content panel, navigate to your storage location and open a folder that contains a photo or image file.

2. Click to select a file in the folder. In the Metadata panel, scroll down and click the pencil icon next to the word, Description. In the description box, enter a short description of the image. Scroll as necessary to click the Description Writer box. Enter your name. Enter Metadata for two other fields such as your e-mail address or location.

3. With the first photo still selected, click the Keywords tab. When the Adobe Bridge dialog box appears, click Apply to apply the changes you just made in the Metadata panel. On the Keywords tab, click to place a check mark next to any keywords that apply to the photo.

4. Scroll to the bottom of the keywords list. Right-click the Other Keywords category and then click New Keyword on the context menu. (*Hint:* if you do not have the Other Keywords category, click the Keywords panel menu button, and then click New Keyword.) When the new keyword box appears at the top of the panel, type a new keyword relating to the selected.

5. Repeat Steps 2 through 4 for each photo in the Content panel of the Bridge window.

# Using Bridge

## 2: Rating and Categorizing Photos

*Instructions:*   You would like to rate and categorize some of the photos you have created.

1. Start Bridge. Navigate to the location of a Photoshop file you created in a previous chapter.

2. Select the file. Assign a rating to the file on a scale from 1 to 5. On the Label menu, click the number of stars that corresponds to your rating. Repeat the process for other photos as directed by your instructor.

3. Click the file again to select it. Click Label on the menu bar. Choose a label setting, such as Approved. Repeat the process for the previous file you rated, choosing a different label setting.

4. Choose your favorite photo in the folder and right-click the file in the Content panel. Click Add to Favorites on the context menu.

5. Consult with at least three other members of your class to compare your ratings.

## Appendix F

# Changing Screen Resolution and Editing Preferences

This appendix explains how to change the screen resolution in Windows 7 to the resolution used in this book. It also describes how to customize the Photoshop window by setting preferences and resetting user changes.

## Screen Resolution

**Screen resolution** indicates the number of pixels (dots) that the computer uses to display the graphics, text, and background you see on the screen. The screen resolution usually is stated as the product of two numbers, such as $1024 \times 768$. That resolution results in a display of 1,024 distinct pixels on each of 768 lines, or about 786,432 pixels on the screen or monitor. The figures in this book were created using a screen resolution of $1024 \times 768$.

### To Change Screen Resolution

The following steps change your screen's resolution to $1024 \times 768$ pixels. Your computer already might be set to $1024 \times 768$ or some other resolution.

**1**

- If necessary, minimize all programs so that the Windows 7 desktop is displayed.

- Right-click the Windows 7 desktop to display the desktop shortcut menu (Figure F–1).

**Figure F–1**

**2**

• Click Screen resolution on the shortcut menu to open the Screen Resolution window. Maximize the window if necessary (Figure F–2).

Screen Resolution window

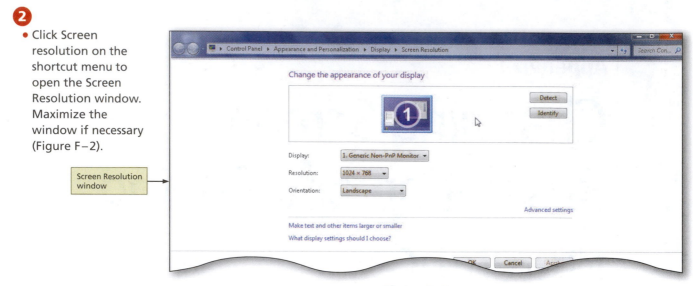

**Figure F–2**

**3**

• Click the Resolution button to display the list of available resolutions (Figure F–3).

Resolution button (your initial settings might differ)

depending on your monitor and the installed video adapter, your available screen resolutions will vary

slider

**Figure F–3**

**4**

• Drag the slider in the Resolution list so that the screen resolution changes to 1024 × 768, if necessary (Figure F–4).

screen resolution set to 1024 × 768

OK button

**Figure F–4**

**5**

- Click outside of the list to close the list.

- Click the OK button to change the screen resolution (Figure F–5).

**6**

- If Windows displays the Display Settings dialog box, click the Keep changes button to accept the changes.

**Figure F–5**

# Editing Photoshop Preferences

In Chapter 1, you learned how to start Photoshop and reset the default workspace, select the default tool, and reset all tools to their default settings. Photoshop has other preferences and settings you can edit to customize the workspace and maximize your efficiency.

## Editing General Preferences

**General preferences** include how Photoshop displays and stores your work. For example, you can change how many states are saved in the History panel, change the number of files shown on the Open Recent menu, or reset the display and cursors.

### To Edit General Preferences

In the steps on the next page, you will navigate through several Preferences dialog boxes to reset values and change preferences. You can access this set of dialog boxes by pressing CTRL+K or by clicking Preferences on the Edit menu.

**BTW**

**Screen Resolutions**
When you increase the screen resolution, Windows displays more information on the screen, but the information decreases in size. The reverse also is true; as you decrease the screen resolution, Windows displays less information on the screen, but the information increases in size.

- Start Photoshop CS6 for your system.

- Press CTRL+K to display the Preferences dialog box.

- Make sure the check boxes in the Options area are selected as shown in Figure F–6.

- Click the Reset All Warning Dialogs button, so your dialog boxes will match the ones in this book.

- When Photoshop displays a Preferences dialog box, click the OK button.

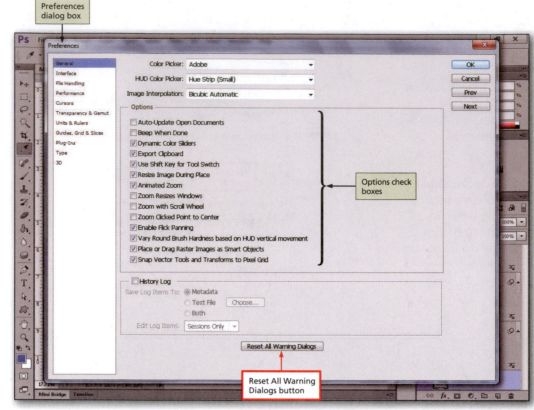

**Figure F–6**

- Click File Handling in the list of Preferences.

- Click the File Extension box arrow and then click Use Lower Case, if necessary, so Photoshop will use lowercase letters when saving.

- Make sure your check boxes are selected as shown in Figure F–7.

- Click the Maximize PSD and PSB File Compatibility box arrow and then click Ask, if necessary, so that Photoshop asks about saving files in PSD format.

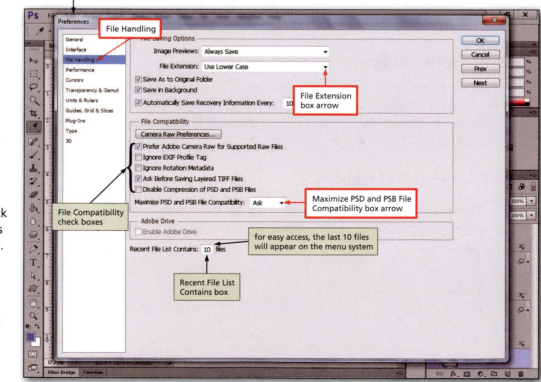

**Figure F–7**

- Type 10 in the Recent File List Contains box, if necessary, to specify that Photoshop will display the last 10 files.

**3**

- Click Performance in the list of Preferences.

- If necessary, type 2 0 in the History States box, so Photoshop will allow you to back up through the last 20 steps of any editing session (Figure F–8).

**Figure F–8**

**4**

- Click Cursors in the list of Preferences.

- If necessary, select Normal Brush Tip in the Painting Cursors area and Standard in the Other Cursors area, to reset those options back to their default values (Figure F–9).

**5**

- When you are finished, click the OK button to close the Preferences dialog box.

**Figure F–9**

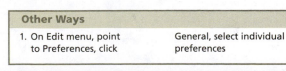

| Other Ways | |
|---|---|
| 1. On Edit menu, point to Preferences, click | General, select individual preferences |

BTW

**Changing Preferences**

If there is one particular setting you wish to change, you can open that specific Preferences dialog box from the menu. For example, if you want to change the color of a ruler guide, you can point to Preferences on the Edit menu and then click Guides, Grid & Slices on the Preferences submenu to go directly to those settings and make your edits.

BTW

**Resetting Preferences**

To restore all preferences to their default settings, you can press and hold ALT+CTRL+SHIFT as you start Photoshop, which causes the system to prompt that you are about to delete the current settings.

The Preferences dialog boxes contain a variety of settings that can be changed to suit individual needs and styles. The Reset All Warning Dialogs button in Figure F–6 on page APP 62 especially is useful to display the dialog boxes if someone has turned them off by clicking the Don't show again check box.

In Figure F–9, Normal Brush Tip causes the mouse pointer outline to correspond to approximately 50 percent of the area that the tool will affect. This option shows the pixels that would be most visibly affected. It is easier to work with Normal Brush Tip than Full Size Brush Tip, especially when using larger brushes. A Standard painting cursor displays mouse pointers as tool icons; a Precise painting cursor displays the mouse pointer as a crosshair.

# Menu Command Preferences

Photoshop allows users to customize both the application menus and the panel menus in several ways. You can hide commands that you seldom use. You can set colors on the menu structure to highlight or organize your favorite commands. Or, you can let Photoshop organize your menus with color based on functionality. If another user has made changes to the menu structure, you can reset the menus back to their default states.

## Hiding and Showing Menu Commands

If there are menu commands that you seldom use, you can hide them to access other commands more quickly. A hidden command is a menu command that does not appear currently on a menu. If menu commands have been hidden, a Show All Menu Items command will be displayed at the bottom of the menu list. When you click the Show All Menu Items command or press and hold the CTRL key as you click the menu name, Photoshop displays all menu commands, including hidden ones.

### To Hide and Show Menu Commands

The following steps hide a menu command and then redisplay it.

**1**

• Click Edit on the Application bar, and then click Menus to display the Keyboard Shortcuts and Menus dialog box (Figure F–10).

**Figure F–10**

**2**

- If necessary, click the Set box arrow and then click Photoshop Defaults.

- Click the right-pointing arrow next to the word File to display the File commands (Figure F–11).

**Figure F–11**

**3**

- In the Visibility column, click the Visibility button next to the Open Recent command so it no longer displays the eye icon (Figure F–12).

**Figure F–12**

**4**

• Click the OK button to apply the settings.

• Click File on the Application bar to display the File menu (Figure F–13).

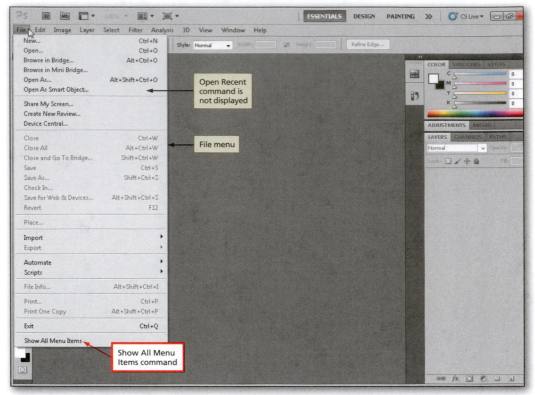

**Figure F–13**

**5**

• On the File menu, click Show All Menu Items to redisplay the command that you hid in Step 3 (Figure F–14).

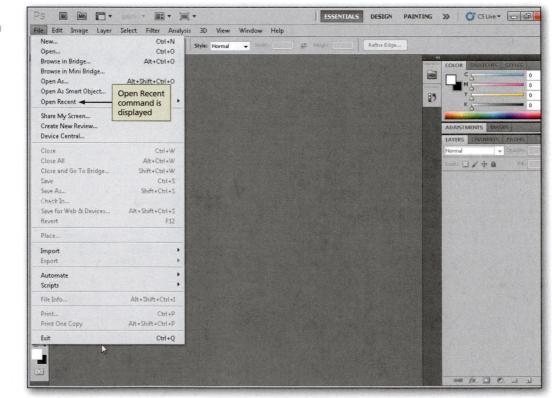

**Figure F–14**

**6**
- Click Edit on the Application bar and then click Menus to display the Keyboard Shortcuts and Menus dialog box again.

- If the arrow next to the word, File, is pointing to the right, click it to display the File list.

- Click the Visibility button next to the Open Recent command so it again is displayed (Figure F–15).

**Figure F–15**

| Other Ways |
|---|
| 1. On Window menu, point to Workspace, click Keyboard Shortcuts & Menus 2. Press ALT+SHIFT+CTRL+M |

## To Add Color to Menu Commands

You can add color to menu commands to help you find them easily or to organize them into groups based on personal preferences. The following steps change the color of the Open and Open As commands.

**1**
- With the Keyboard Shortcuts and Menus dialog box still displayed, click the word, None, in the row associated with the Open command to display a list of colors (Figure F–16).

**Figure F–16**

**2**

- Click Red in the list to select a red color for the Open command.

- Click the word, None, in the row associated with the Open As command, and then click Red in the list to select a red color for the Open As command (Figure F–17).

**Q&A**

What other menus are available?

If you click the Menu For box arrow, you can choose Application Menus or Panel Menus.

**Figure F–17**

**3**

- Click the OK button to close the Keyboard Shortcuts and Menus dialog box.

- Click File on the Application bar to display the new color settings (Figure F–18).

**Figure F–18**

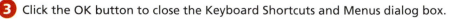

**BTW**

**Stored Menu Sets**
The Set box arrow (Figure F–17) lists three sets of stored commands: Photoshop Defaults, New in CS6, and Photoshop Defaults (modified). Photoshop will display related commands with color. For example, if you choose New in CS6, the menu commands that are new will appear in blue.

## To Reset the Menus

The following steps reset the menus, removing red from the Open commands.

**1** Click Edit on the menu bar and then click Menus to display the Keyboard Shortcuts and Menus dialog box.

**2** Click the Set box arrow and then click Photoshop Defaults in the list. When Photoshop asks if you want to save your changes before switching sets, click the No button.

**3** Click the OK button to close the Keyboard Shortcuts and Menus dialog box.

## Resetting the Panels, Keyboard Shortcuts, and Menus

A **tool preset** is a way to store settings from the options bar. Besides the default settings for each tool, Photoshop contains tool presets for many of the tools that automatically change the options bar. In a lab situation, if you notice that some tools are not working they way they are supposed to, or some presets are missing, it might be because another user changed the settings. The following steps reload all of the default tool presets.

### To Reset Tool Presets

**1**

• On the options bar, click the current tool's Preset picker and then click the menu button to display the Tool Preset menu (Figure F–19).

**2**

• Click Reset Tool Presets to reset the tool's preset list.

• If Photoshop displays a dialog box, click the OK button to reload all the default tool presets.

**Figure F–19**

**Other Ways**

1. From any panel menu, click Reset Tool Presets, click OK

## Resetting Panel Components

Many panels, including the Brushes, Swatches, and Styles panels, display preset samples with preset shapes, colors, and sizes. A few options bars, including the Gradient and Shape options bars, as well as the Contours box in the Layer Style dialog box, also display similar components — all of which may need to be reset at some time.

You can reset these presets using the Preset Manager (Figure F–19), or each panel menu.

### To Reset Panel Presets

The steps on the next page reset all panels that use presets.

**1**

- On the options bar, click the current tool's Preset picker and then click the menu button to display the Tool Preset menu.

- Click Preset Manager to display the Preset Manager dialog box.

- Click the Preset Type box arrow to display the list of panels that contain presets (Figure F–20).

- Click Brushes to select the Brush presets.

**Figure F–20**

**2**

- Click the Preset Manager menu button to display the list of commands and preset libraries (Figure F–21).

- Click Reset Brushes to reset the Brush presets. When Photoshop displays a confirmation dialog box, click the OK button.

**3**

- Repeat Steps 1 and 2 for each of the other panels that appear on the Preset Type box arrow list.

- When you are finished resetting all panels, click the Done button to close the dialog box.

**Figure F–21**

**Other Ways**

1. On each panel menu, click Reset command, click OK button

# Changing Preferences

## 1: Changing the color and style of guides, grids, and slices

*Instructions:* You would like to use some different colors and styles for grids and guides because the current colors are very similar to the colors in your image, making them hard to see. You decide to change the color and style preferences on your system as described in the following steps.

1. Start Photoshop CS6.

2. On the Edit menu, point to Preferences, and then click Guides, Grid & Slices.

3. When the Preferences dialog box is displayed, change the Color and Style settings as shown in Figure F–22.

4. Click the OK button.

**Figure F–22**

5. Open any image file you have saved on your system and drag a guide from the horizontal ruler. Note the Light Red colored line.

6. On the View menu, point to Show, and then click Grid. Note the grid with dashed gray lines.

7. To clear the guides, on the View menu, click Clear Guides.

8. To hide the grid, on the View menu, point to Show and then click Grid.

9. To reset the colors and styles, either change the guide color back to Cyan and the grid style back to Lines, or quit Photoshop and then restart Photoshop while pressing ALT+CTRL+SHIFT. If Photoshop asks if you wish to delete the previous settings, click the Yes button.

10. Quit Photoshop.

## Resetting Styles

*Instructions:*   Someone has loaded many styles into the style box, making it difficult to find the common styles you prefer. You decide to reset the styles using the following steps.

1. Start Photoshop CS6.

2. On the Edit menu, point to Presets, and then click Preset Manager to display the Preset Manager dialog box.

3. Click the Preset Type box arrow to display the Preset list, and then click Styles in the list (Figure F–23).

4. Click the Preset Manager menu button to display a list of commands about the Styles Presets. Click Reset Styles in the list.

5. When Photoshop asks if you want to replace the styles with the default set, click the OK button.

6. Click the Done button to close the Preset Manager dialog box.

7. Quit Photoshop.

**Figure F–23**

## Searching the Web

*Instructions:*   You want to learn more about optimizing Photoshop settings and your computer system's memory by setting preferences for file size, history states, and cached views. Perform a Web search by using the Google search engine at google.com (or any major search engine) to display and print three Web pages that pertain to optimizing Photoshop CS6. On each printout, highlight something new that you learned by reading the Web page.

# Appendix G

# For Mac Users

## For the Mac User of this Book

For most tasks, little difference exists between using Photoshop CS6 with the Windows 7 operating system and using it with the Mac OS X Lion 10.7 operating system. With some tasks, however, you will see some differences, or you might need to complete the tasks using different steps. This appendix demonstrates how to start an application, open a file, create a folder and save a file, close a file, display the application menu, and quit an application, using Photoshop CS6 and the Mac operating system.

## Keyboard Differences

One difference between a Mac and a PC is in the use of modifier keys. **Modifier keys** are special keys used to modify the normal action of a key when the two are pressed in combination. Examples of modifier keys include the SHIFT, CTRL, and ALT keys on a PC and the SHIFT, CMD, and OPT keys on a Mac (Figure G–1). The CMD key sometimes is referred to as the APPLE key.

**(a) PC keyboard**

**(b) Mac keyboard**

**Figure G–1**

Table G–1 explains the keystroke equivalencies. For instance, if PC instructions tell you to press CTRL+T to perform a task, Mac users would press CMD+T. In addition, many Mac menus display shortcut notations, using symbols to represent the modifier key.

| Table G–1 PC vs. Mac Keystroke Equivalencies | | |
| --- | --- | --- |
| **PC** | **Mac** | **Mac Symbol** |
| CTRL key | CMD key | ⌘ |
| ALT key | OPT key | ⌥ |
| SHIFT key | SHIFT key | ⇧ |

## To Start an Application

The following steps, which assume Mac OS X Lion 10.7 is running, start an application based on a typical installation. You might need to ask your instructor how to start Photoshop for your computer.

**1**

- Click the Spotlight button on the Mac desktop to display the Spotlight box.

- Type Photoshop CS6, as the search text in the Spotlight text box and watch the search results appear (Figure G–2).

Figure G–2

**2**

- Click Adobe Photoshop CS6 in the list to start the application.

- If the window is not maximized, click the green Zoom button on the application title bar to maximize the window (Figure G–3).

Figure G–3

**Q&A** Does the PC version of Photoshop have a title bar?

No. On the PC platform, Photoshop has an Application bar that combines the menu and clip controls. The clip control functions — minimize, maximize, and close — are inherited from the operating system, and are placed where the system user would expect to find them.

Adobe product screenshot(s) reprinted with permission from Adobe Systems Incorporated

**Other Ways**

1. Click Finder icon in Dock, navigate to applications, locate Adobe Photoshop CS6, double-click icon

2. Click Photoshop icon on dock

# Customize the Workspace on a Mac

In general, customizing the Photoshop workspace on a Mac is the same as customizing it on a PC. Chapter 1 covers selecting the Essentials workspace, selecting the default tool, and resetting the option bar. When using the Mac OS X operating system, the Preferences submenu is located on the Photoshop menu, rather than the Edit menu. Figure G–4 displays the Preferences submenu, which you use to reset the interface color.

**Figure G–4**

## To Open a File

The following steps open a file from the Data Files for Students. To complete this assignment, you will be required to use the Data Files for Students. Visit www.cengage.com/ct/studentdownload for detailed instructions or contact your instructor for information about accessing the required files.

**1**
- Start your application, if necessary, and reset the preferences.

- Click File on the title bar to display the File menu (Figure G–5).

**Q&A**
What does it mean when Adobe includes multiple symbols in the shortcut key notation?

Multiple symbols mean that you must hold down several keys. For example, a notation of ⌥ ⌘ O on the menu would mean to press and hold the option and command keys while you press the o key. Written instructions might say press OPT+CMD+O.

**Figure G–5**

**2**

- Click Open on the File menu to display the Open dialog box.

- Click the Where button to display a list of the available storage locations on your system (Figure G–6).

🔎 **Experiment**

- Click a location on the Favorites panel on the left side of the Open dialog box and watch the Where button change. Click the Where button.

**Figure G–6**

**3**

- Click the drive associated with the location of the Data Files for Students.

- Navigate to the Photoshop folder, and then the Data Files for Students folder (Figure G–7).

**Q&A**

What is the default location shown in the Open dialog box?

By default, the Open dialog box shows the first 10 items in the folder or volume last used during an open or save process. You can use the Icon view, List view, Column view, or Cover Flow view buttons to change the way the contents are presented. Cover Flow view allows you to see the contents of a file as a thumbnail.

**Figure G–7**

**4**

- Double-click the Chapter 01 folder.
- Click the file, Eagle.jpg, to select it (Figure G–8).

**5**

- Click the Open button to open the selected file and display the open file in the Photoshop workspace.

**Figure G–8**

**Other Ways**

1. Press CMD+O, select file, click Open button

## To Create a Folder and Save a File

After editing a file, you should save it. The following steps create a folder on a USB flash drive and save a file.

**1**

- Start Photoshop and open a file, if necessary.

- With a USB flash drive connected to one of the computer's USB ports, click File on the title bar to display the File menu and then click Save As to display the Save As dialog box.

- Type the name of your file, such as Eagle Edited, in the Save As box to change the file name. Do not press the RETURN key after typing the file name.

- Click the Where button to display the list of available drives (Figure G–9).

**Figure G–9**

**2**

- Click Removable Disk (F:), or the name of your USB flash drive, in the list of devices to select that drive as the new save location.

- Click the New Folder button to create a new folder on the selected storage device.

- When the new folder appears, type a new folder name such as `Appendix G`, to change the name of the folder, and then press the RETURN key (Figure G–10).

**Figure G–10**

**3**

- If necessary, click the new folder to open it.

- If necessary, click the Format button to display the list of available file formats. Choose the format appropriate for your application and purpose, in this case, the JPEG format (Figure G–11).

**4**

- Click the Save button to save the document on the selected drive with the new file name.

**Figure G–11**

**Other Ways**

1. Press SHIFT+CMD+S, choose settings, click Save button

## To Close a File

The following steps close an open file.

**1**

- Start Photoshop and open a file, if necessary.

- Click File on the title bar to display the File menu (Figure G–12).

**Q&A** Is the File menu different on a Mac?

The File menu is essentially the same. The commands might be grouped in a slightly different manner. The File menu does not contain the Exit command as it does on a PC. You will learn in the next steps that the Quit command is on the Photoshop menu.

**2**

- Click the Close command on the File menu to close the current open file without quitting the application.

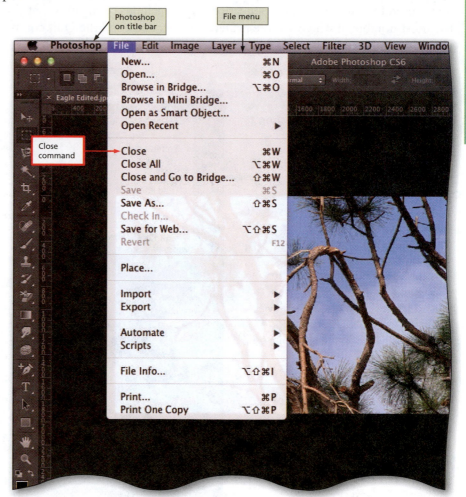

**Figure G–12**

| Other Ways |
| --- |
| 1. Press CMD+W |

## To Display the Application Menu and Quit the Application

Using the Mac operating system, Photoshop CS6 includes a Photoshop menu to the left of the typical menu used in Windows. This application menu includes commands that you find in different locations on a PC, the most notable of which are the preferences, services, and the Quit command for each application. The following steps open the Photoshop menu to quit the application.

**1**

- Start Photoshop, if necessary.

- On the title bar, click Photoshop to open the Photoshop menu (Figure G–13).

**Q&A**  What does the Services command do?

Mac OS X includes a Services submenu in many applications for tasks such as looking up a word in the dictionary, rotating an image, sending an e-mail, or compressing a video. Any Service installed on your Mac that manipulates files related to your application will be displayed on the Services submenu.

**2**

- Click Quit Photoshop to quit the application.

**Q&A**  Can I click the red Close button to quit the application?

The red button closes the application window, but the application will continue to run until you quit the application.

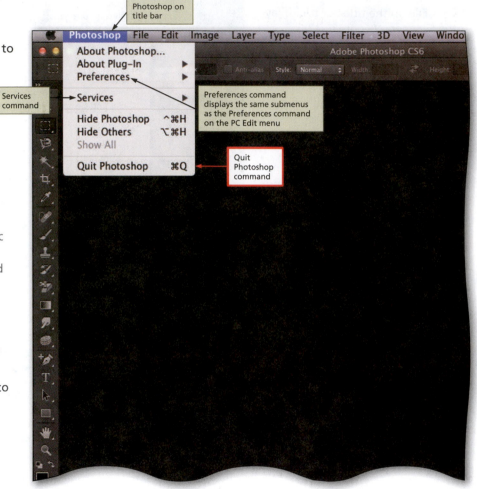

**Figure G–13**

**Other Ways**

1. Press CMD+Q
2. On Dock, click and hold mouse button, on context menu, click Quit

# Quick Reference Summary

## Adobe Photoshop CS6 Quick Reference Summary

| Task | Page Number | Mouse | Menu | Context Menu | Keyboard Shortcut |
|------|-------------|-------|------|--------------|-------------------|
| **Adjustment Layer** | PS 182 | Clip to Layer button on Adjustments panel | Layer \| New Adjustment Layer | | CTRL+L |
| **Background Eraser Tool** | PS 171 | Background Eraser Tool button on Tools panel | | | SHIFT+E |
| **Border, Create** | PS 36 | | Select \| Select All; Edit \| Stroke | | |
| **Border, Modify** | PS 37 | | Select \| Modify \| Border | | |
| **Brightness/Contrast, Adjust** | PS 186 | Brightness/Contrast icon on Adjustments panel or Create new fill or adjustment layer button on Layers panel; Brightness/Contrast | Layer \| New Adjustment Layer \| Brightness/Contrast | | |
| **Clone Stamp Tool** | PS 192 | Clone Stamp Tool button on Tools panel | Window \| Clone Source | | S |
| **Close** | PS 42 | Close button on document window tab | File \| Close | | CTRL+W |
| **Commit Edits (text)** | PS 49 | Commit any current edits button on options bar | | | |
| **Commit Change (transformation)** | PS 160 | Commit transform (Enter) button on options bar | | | ENTER |
| **Colors, Reset Default** | PS 51 | Default Foreground/Background Colors button on Tools panel | | | D |
| **Colors, Switch Between Background and Foreground** | PS 40 | Switch Between Background and Foreground Colors button on Tools panel | | | X |
| **Copy File in Bridge** | APP 49 | | Edit \| Copy; navigate to copy location; Edit \| Paste | Copy; Paste | CTRL+C to copy CTRL+V to paste |
| **Document Windows, Arrange** | PS 150, 151 | | Window \| Arrange | | |
| **Download Speed, Choose** | PS 54 | Select download speed button (Save for Web dialog box) | File \| Save for Web | | ALT+SHIFT+CTRL+S |
| **Elliptical Marquee Tool** | PS 76, 105 | Elliptical Marquee Tool button on Tools panel | | | SHIFT+M |
| **Eraser Tools** | PS 163, 167 | Eraser Tool button on Tools panel | | | E |
| **Essentials Workspace, Select** | PS 6 | Essentials button on Application bar | Window \| Workspace \| Essentials | | |
| **Find File in Bridge** | APP 55 | | Edit \| Find | | CTRL+F |
| **Fit on Screen** | PS 110, 184 | Fit screen button on Zoom Tool options bar | View \| Fit on Screen | | CTRL+0 (zero) |
| **Grid, Hide or Show** | PS 96 | | View \| Show \| Grid | | CTRL+ APOSTROPHE (') |

## Adobe Photoshop CS6 Quick Reference Summary *(continued)*

| Task | Page Number | Mouse | Menu | Context Menu | Keyboard Shortcut |
|---|---|---|---|---|---|
| Guides, Create | PS 97 | Drag from ruler | View \| New Guide | | |
| Guides, Hide or Show | PS 97 | | View \| Show \| Guides | | CTRL+SEMICOLON (;) |
| Hand Tool | PS 28 | Hand Tool button on Tools panel | | | H |
| Help | PS 58, Appendix D | | Help \| Photoshop Help | | F1 |
| History, Step Backward | PS 86 | Click state on History panel | History panel menu \| Step Backward | | CTRL+ALT+Z |
| History, Step Forward | PS 87 | Click state on History panel | History panel menu \| Step Forward | | CTRL+SHIFT+Z |
| Hue/Saturation, Adjust | PS 184 | Hue/Saturation icon on Adjustment panel or Create new fill or adjustment layer button on Layers panel; Hue/Saturation | Layer \| New Adjustment Layer \| Hue/Saturation | | CTRL+U |
| Image, Crop | PS 33 | Crop Tool button on Tools panel | Image \| Crop | | C |
| Image, Flatten | PS 195 | | Layer \| Flatten Image or Layers panel menu \| Flatten Image | Flatten Image | |
| Image, Resize | PS 45 | | Image \| Image Size | | ALT+CTRL+I |
| Keyboard Shortcuts, Create | PS 114 | | Edit \| Keyboard Shortcuts | | ALT+SHIFT+CTRL+K |
| Keyboard Shortcuts, Reset Default | PS 118 | Set Photoshop Defaults in Keyboard Shortcuts and Menus dialog box | Edit \| Keyboard Shortcuts \| Photoshop Defaults | | |
| Lasso Tool | PS 100 | Lasso Tool button on Tools panel | | | L |
| Layer, Assign a Color | PS 146 | | Layers panel menu | Indicates layer visibility button \| color | |
| Layer, Create | PS 151 | | Layer \| New \| Layer or Layers panel menu \| New Layer | | SHIFT+CTRL+N |
| Layer, Display Current | PS 164 | ALT+click layer visibility icon on Layers panel | | | |
| Layer, Hide | PS 147 | Indicates layer visibility icon on Layers panel | Layer \| Hide Layers | Indicates layer visibility button \| Hide this layer | |
| Layer, Rename | PS 145 | Double-click layer name \| enter new name | Layers panel menu \| Layer Properties \| enter new name | Layer Properties \| enter new name | |
| Layer, Show | PS 147 | Indicates layer visibility icon on Layers panel | Layer \| Show Layers | | |
| Layer, Show Only Current | PS 164 | ALT+click layer visibility icon on Layers panel | | | |
| Layers, Rearrange | PS 174 | Drag layer on Layers panel | | | CTRL+[ or CTRL+] |
| Layer Mask, Create | PS 176 | Add layer mask button on Layers panel | | | |
| Layer, Move | PS 152 | Select Move Tool, drag layer in document window | | | |
| Layers Panel Options, Change | PS 142 | | Layers panel menu \| Panel Options | | |
| Layer Style, Add | PS 189 | Add a layer style button on Layers panel | Layer \| Layer Style | | |
| Layer Via Cut, Create | PS 143 | | Layer \| New \| Layer via Cut | Layer Via Cut | SHIFT+CTRL+J |
| Levels, Adjust | PS 182 | Levels icon on Adjustments panel or Create new fill or adjustment layer button on Layers panel; Levels | Image \| Adjustments \| Levels | | CTRL+L |

## Adobe Photoshop CS6 Quick Reference Summary *(continued)*

| Task | Page Number | Mouse | Menu | Context Menu | Keyboard Shortcut |
|---|---|---|---|---|---|
| **Magic Eraser Tool** | PS 164 | Magic Eraser Tool button on Tools panel | | | SHIFT+E |
| **Magic Wand Tool** | PS 102 | Magic Wand Tool button on Tools panel | | | SHIFT+W |
| **Magnetic Lasso Tool** | PS 99 | Magnetic Lasso Tool button on Tools panel | | | SHIFT+L |
| **Magnification, Change** | PS 29 | Enter number in Magnification box on status bar | | | |
| **Masking Error, Correct** | PS 178 | | Layer \| Layer Mask \| Reveal All | Disable Mask | |
| **Menus, Hide or Show** | APP 7 | | Edit \| Menus | | ALT+SHIFT+ CTRL+M |
| **Metadata, Add** | APP 50 | Description field on Metadata panel, enter description | | | |
| **Move Tool** | PS 80 | Move Tool button on Tools panel | | | V |
| **Navigate Files using Bridge** | APP 48 | Double-click file location, click workspace buttons | | | |
| **Opacity, Change** | PS 180 | Drag Opacity scrubby slider on Layers panel | | | |
| **Open** | PS 11 | | File \| Open | Document tab \| Open Document | CTRL+O |
| **Open Recent** | PS 43 | | File \| Open Recent | | |
| **Panel, Collapse** | PS 18, 27 | Collapse to Icons button on panel | | Panel tab \| Collapse to Icons | |
| **Panel, Open** | PS 26 | Panel button on vertical docking of panels | Window \| panel name | | |
| **Paste** | PS 102 | | Edit \| Paste | Paste | CTRL+V |
| **Pattern Stamp Tool** | PS 190 | Pattern Stamp Tool button on Tools panel | | | SHIFT+S |
| **Perspective, Change** | PS 169 | | | Perspective | |
| **Preview, Web** | PS 55 | Preview button (Save for Web & Devices dialog box) | File \| Save for Web & Devices | | ALT+CTRL+ SHIFT+S |
| **Polygonal Lasso Tool** | PS 93 | Polygonal Lasso Tool button on Tools panel | | | SHIFT+L |
| **Preferences, Edit** | APP 62 | | Edit \| Preferences \| General | | CTRL+K |
| **Print** | PS 52 | | File \| Print | | CTRL+P |
| **Print One Copy** | PS 52 | | File \| Print One Copy | | ALT+SHIFT+CTRL+P |
| **Quick Selection Tool** | PS 83 | Quick Selection Tool button on Tools panel | | | W |
| **Quit Photoshop** | PS 60 | Close button | File \| Exit | | CTRL+Q |
| **Rate File in Bridge** | APP 53 | | | | CTRL+1 through CTRL+5 |
| **Rectangular Marquee Tool** | PS 79 | Rectangular Marquee Tool button on Tools panel | | | M |
| **Refine Edge** | PS 89 | Refine Edge button on options bar | Select \| Refine Edge | Refine Edge | ALT+CTRL+R |
| **Reselect** | PS 108 | | Select \| Reselect | | |
| **Reset All Tools** | PS 9 | | | Reset All Tools | |
| **Rule of Thirds Overlay, Position** | PS 33 | Drag overlay | | | |
| **Rulers, Show or Hide** | PS 30 | View Extras button on Application bar | View \| Rulers | | CTRL+R |
| **Save** | PS 20 | | File \| Save | | CTRL+S |
| **Save for Web** | PS 56 | | File \| Save for Web & Devices | | ALT+SHIFT+ CTRL+S |

**Adobe Photoshop CS6 Quick Reference Summary** (continued)

| Task | Page Number | Mouse | Menu | Context Menu | Keyboard Shortcut |
|---|---|---|---|---|---|
| Save in PDF Format | PS 112 | | File \| Save As; Format box arrow \| Photoshop PDF (*.PDF; *.PDP) | | |
| Save with New Name | PS 51 | | File \| Save As \| enter new name | | SHIFT+CTRL+S |
| Screen Mode, Change | PS 30 | Screen Mode button on Applications bar | View \| Screen Mode \| select mode | | F |
| Select All | PS 36 | | Select \| All | | CTRL+A |
| Selection, Add To | PS 76–77 | Add to selection button on options bar | | | SHIFT+drag |
| Selection, Deselect | PS 91 | | Select \| Deselect | | CTRL+D |
| Selection, Distort | PS 157, 169 | Enter rotation percentage on options bar | Edit \| Transform \| Distort | Free Transform mode \| Distort | |
| Selection, Duplicate | PS 82 | | Edit \| Copy \| Edit Paste | | CTRL+ALT+drag |
| Selection, Flip Horizontal | PS 88, 157 | | Edit \| Transform \| Flip Horizontal | Free Transform mode \| Flip Horizontal | |
| Selection, Flip Vertical | PS 88, 157 | | Edit \| Transform \| Flip Vertical | Free Transform mode \| Flip Vertical | |
| Selection, Free Transform | PS 156 | | Edit \| Free Transform | Free Transform | CTRL+T |
| Selection, Grow | PS 94 | | Select \| Grow | | |
| Selection, Intersect with | PS 77, 102 | Intersect with selection button on options bar | | | |
| Selection, Rotate | PS 156 | Enter degree rotation on options bar | Edit \| Transform \| Rotate | Free Transform mode \| Rotate | |
| Selection, Rotate 180° | PS 156 | Enter degree rotation on options bar | Edit \| Transform \| Rotate 180° | Free Transform mode \| Rotate 180° | |
| Selection, Rotate 90° CCW | PS 156 | Enter degree rotation on options bar | Edit \| Transform \| Rotate 90° CCW | Free Transform mode \| Rotate 90° CCW | |
| Selection, Rotate 90° CW | PS 156 | Enter degree rotation on options bar | Edit \| Transform \| Rotate 90° CW | Free Transform mode \| Rotate 90° CW | |
| Selection, Scale | PS 156 | SHIFT+drag corner sizing handle | Edit \| Transform \| Scale | Free Transform mode \| Scale | |
| Selection, Skew | PS 157 | | Edit \| Transform \| Skew | Free Transform mode \| Skew | |
| Selection, Snap | PS 98 | Drag selection near object or guide | | | |
| Selection, Subtract From | PS 102 | Subtract from selection button on options bar | | | ALT+drag |
| Selection, Transform Perspective | PS 157, 169 | | Edit \| Transform \| Perspective | Free Transform mode \| Perspective | |
| Selection, Warp | PS 157 | Warp button on Transform options bar | Edit \| Transform \| Warp | Free Transform mode \| Warp | |
| Single Column Marquee Tool | PS 76 | Single Column Marquee Tool button on Tools panel | | | |
| Single Row Marquee Tool | PS 76 | Single Row Marquee Tool button on Tools panel | | | |
| Smart Object, Layer | PS 153 | | Layer \| Smart Objects \| Convert to Smart Object or Layers panel menu \| Convert to Smart Object | Convert to Smart Object | |

**Photoshop Quick Reference**

## Adobe Photoshop CS6 Quick Reference Summary *(continued)*

| Task | Page Number | Mouse | Menu | Context Menu | Keyboard Shortcut |
|------|-------------|-------|------|--------------|-------------------|
| **Smooth, Modify** | PS 88, 89 | | Select \| Modify \| Smooth | | |
| **Snapping, Turn On** | PS 96, 98 | | View \| Snap | | SHIFT+CTRL+ SEMICOLON (;) |
| **Transform Controls, Display** | PS 158, 159 | Show Transform Controls checkbox on options bar | Edit \| Free Transform | | CTRL+T |
| **Undo** | PS 34 | Click previous state in History panel | Edit \| Undo | | CTRL+Z |
| **Windows, Consolidate** | PS 151 | Arrange Documents button on Application bar; Consolidate All button | Window \| Arrange \| Consolidate All to Tabs | Document tab \| Consolidate All to Here | |
| **Zoom In** | PS 24 | Zoom In button on Navigator panel | View \| Zoom In | Zoom In | CTRL+PLUS SIGN (+) |
| **Zoom Out** | PS 24 | Zoom Out button on Navigator panel | View \| Zoom Out | Zoom Out | CTRL+MINUS SIGN (−) |
| **Zoom Tool** | PS 24 | Zoom Tool button on Tools panel | | | Z |
| **Zoomify** | PS 53 | | File \| Export \| Zoomify | | |